PUBLIC POLICY
TOWARD MERGERS

PUBLIC POLICY

GOODYEAR PUBLISHING COMPANY, INC.
Pacific Palisades, Calif.

Antitrust Policy Seminar, Univ. of Calif. at Los Angeles 1968.

TOWARD MERGERS

Edited by

J. Fred Weston

and

Sam Peltzman

University of California at Los Angeles

PUBLIC POLICY TOWARD MERGERS
edited by
J. FRED WESTON
SAM PELTZMAN

Library of Congress Catalog Card Number:
75-77542

Current printing (last digit):
10 9 8 7 6 5 4 3 2 1

Printed in the United States of America

preface

The structure and performance of the United States economy are of great importance for the well-being of the nation. Public policy toward mergers can potentially have considerable impact upon the structure and performance of the United States economy. This was the basic reason for our seminar, which consisted of invited papers and seminar discussion based on the previously circulated papers.

University seminars of the type represented by our two-day meeting perform a unique function in advancing basic theory and in increasing understanding of important public policy issues. The time for discussion is more extended than is possible at the periodic meetings of the professional economic associations. The interaction of ideas is more direct and continuous than is possible through the pages of the professional journals. Since the participants are the leading experts on the subject, the level of analysis and discussion can be more penetrating than is possible at business association or public conference meetings. Finally, the atmosphere differs from congressional hearings in being less adversary and advocative in spirit and in the complete freedom of participants to raise questions and explore topics.

To stimulate analysis and to provide maximum time for discussion during the seminar, an effort was made to circulate papers in advance. We were largely successful in achieving this objective. To encourage the free expression of ideas, we assured the participants that our summaries of the seminar discussions would not associate ideas with individuals. Our aim was to develop concepts and insights without relating them to sources that would either exalt or denigrate the ideas because of authorship—to let the arguments be evaluated on their inherent qualities.

One central focus of the seminar papers and the discussion was to analyze public policy positions toward mergers on the basis of the implicit economic theories or empirical evidence upon which they were based. In the process, an inventory of empirically supported theories was developed. But the empirical support for other public policy positions was either nonexistent or inconclusive. Consequently, the pages that follow also provide an agenda for further research on vital public policy issues.

In our summaries of the discussion, our format has been influenced by the nature of the materials. In some instances, the discussion developed what we considered to be a fully rounded treatment of the subject; therefore, we added little to the summarizations of such discussions. On other topics, the seminar participants explored some aspects at great length, with the consequence that discussion of other aspects was neglected. Our summaries of these discussions added points developed by one or both of the editors. The participants in the seminar discussions are therefore not to be held responsible, individually or collectively, for the views expressed in the summaries of the discussions. For all materials not associated with the individual presentations, we accept full responsibility although not necessarily full agreement.

We were fortunate to have participating in the seminar a number of economists connected with government bodies. The usual disclaimer is applicable both to their prepared presentations and their comments during the seminar. The views they expressed were their personal positions and do not necessarily reflect the views of the government agencies with which they are connected.

Our appreciation is expressed to Dean Neil H. Jacoby and

George A. Steiner for guidance in developing the concept and format of the seminar. We are grateful for the assistance of a number of graduate students at UCLA in the preparations and conduct of the seminar, as well as in the preparations of the papers and discussions for publication. These include Lee Hoskins, Solomon Jones, Barry Gertz, Virginia Elwood, and Pauline Grossman.

A grant from the General Electric Company to the Division of Research of the UCLA Graduate School of Business Administration for the study of government-business relations provided the necessary financial support to make the conference possible.

Los Angeles, California   J. FRED WESTON
July 1968   SAM PELTZMAN

participants

ANTITRUST POLICY SEMINAR
March 13, 14, 1968
University of California at Los Angeles

co-chairmen

SAM PELTZMAN
Economics Department
University of California at Los Angeles

J. FRED WESTON
Graduate School of Business Administration
University of California at Los Angeles

contributors

WALTER ADAMS
Department of Economics
Michigan State University

H. IGOR ANSOFF
Graduate School of Industrial
Administration
Carnegie-Mellon Institute

PHILLIP AREEDA
School of Law
Harvard University

JOHN M. BLAIR
Chief Economist
Subcommittee on Antitrust and
Monopoly of the Committee on the
Judiciary, United States Senate

ROBERT H. BORK
School of Law
Yale University

YALE BROZEN
Graduate School of Business
University of Chicago

NORMAN R. COLLINS
Graduate School of Business
University of California at Berkeley

ANN HOROWITZ
IRA HOROWITZ
Graduate School of Business
Indiana University

WILLARD F. MUELLER
Bureau of Economics
Federal Trade Commission

ix

SAUL NELSON
Senior Staff Economist
Council of Economic Advisers to
the President

LEE E. PRESTON
Graduate School of Business
University of California at Berkeley

JOHN H. RUBEL
Vice President
Litton Industries, Inc.

discussants

EARLE BIRDZELL
Assistant General Counsel
General Electric Company

BETTY BOCK
National Industrial Conference Board

THEODORE CRAVER
Litton Industries, Inc.

JAMES M. FERGUSON
College of Business Administration
University of Rochester

J. BARRY GERTZ
Economics Department
University of California at Los Angeles

LEE HOSKINS
Economics Department
University of California at Los Angeles

NEIL H. JACOBY
Graduate School of
Business Administration
University of California at Los Angeles

W. J. LIEBELER
School of Law
University of California at Los Angeles

IRVING LIPKOWITZ
Director, Economic Affairs
Reynolds Metals Corporation

ROBERT LENTZ
Vice President and General Counsel
Litton Industries, Inc.

C. B. MCLAUGHLIN
Corporate Counsel for Antitrust
International Business Machines

JORA MINASIAN
Graduate School of Commerce
University of Southern California

JOHN C. NARVER
Bureau of Economics
Federal Trade Commission

ALFRED NICOLS
Graduate School of
Business Administration
University of California at Los Angeles

DONALD J. WATSON
General Electric Company

DOUGLAS C. WHITE
Morrison, Foerster, Holloway
Clinton and Clark

ROBERT M. WILLIAMS
Graduate School of
Business Administration
University of California at Los Angeles

contents

I
INTRODUCTION

II
STRUCTURE, PERFORMANCE, AND BEHAVIOR

III

IMPLICATIONS OF PROFITABILITY STUDIES

IV

ASPECTS OF VERTICAL INTEGRATION
THEORY AND POLICY

V

THE RECENT TREND TOWARD
CONGLOMERATE MERGERS

VI

BASIC ISSUES OF ANTITRUST POLICY

PUBLIC POLICY
TOWARD MERGERS

part

I

INTRODUCTION

1

issues in public policy toward mergers

by J. FRED WESTON AND SAM PELTZMAN

THE RECENT MERGER MOVEMENT

Much concern continues to be expressed toward merger trends. In its 1967 report, issued in March 1968, the Federal Trade Commission pointed to developments in the totals and directions of merger activity. It stated, "Merger activity in 1967 experienced the sharpest increase in modern industrial history...."[1] The Commission was particularly concerned with the increase in the number of "large" mergers—those involving the acquisitions of firms with assets of $10 million or more. The Commission noted 155 large mergers in manufacturing and mining during 1967. The aggregate assets of such large company acquisitions totaled $8 billion, a nearly 100 percent increase over the $4.1 billion recorded for 1966.[2] The report also noted that the rate of large mergers was continuing at a high level in

[1] Federal Trade Commission, news release, "Merger Activity Set New Record Last Year," FTC Reports (March 18, 1968), p. 1.
[2] *Ibid.*

3

1968. During the first two months of 1968, 19 large mergers with aggregate assets of $1.3 billion were completed and 20 others involving a total of $2.3 billion of assets were pending.[3]

The total number of mergers which occurred in 1967 appears to have approximated 3000. The number in 1966 was about 2400, representing an increase during 1967 of about 25 percent in merger activity.

Some paradoxes may be observed within these global figures. A number of large mergers appeared to have gone unchallenged. Of greatest size was the $6 billion Penn-Central merger. In addition, unlitigated mergers included the merger of Pure Oil into Union Oil, and of Sunshine Biscuits into American Tobacco. In both cases the resulting company had sales in 1966 of $1.4 billion. The Atlantic Richfield merger also produced a company with revenues in excess of $1 billion.

On the other hand, the regional grocery company, Von's, of Los Angeles, which after its acquisition of Shopping Bag would have had revenues of $172 million, was required to dispose of at least 35 of the Shopping Bag stores acquired. The 1958 acquisition by Pabst Brewing Company of Blatz Brewing Company was declared illegal in mid-1966, a year during which Pabst Brewing had total revenues of $282 million. The holdings of the plumbing manufacturing company, Grinnel Corporation, in a number of burglary and fire protection service companies were declared illegal. The total revenues of Grinnel were $300 million.

Not only are the numbers and dollar magnitudes of mergers involved of major significance but effects on individual companies clearly have a great impact on the nature of the future development of the United States economy. Some mergers are approved, some are prevented. It is therefore important to know whether the effects of mergers on individual firms are desirable or undesirable. Even more important, it is necessary to know what the effects on the economy as a whole are. Do the mergers contribute to favorable desirable performance or do they have undesirable consequences?

ISSUES POSED BY LARGE FIRMS AND CONCENTRATION

The economic issues involved are of great importance. There is hardly a facet of the operations of an economic system not affected

[3]*Ibid.*

by issues that arise in connection with the development of public policy toward mergers. It has been argued that the behavior of large firms in following a practice of rigid prices that did not decline in response to the depressed condition of the 1930's aggravated the recession and increased unemployment. At the same time in recent years it has also been argued that the policy of administered prices leads to inflation and excess profits to large firms that control their markets.

Some argue further that the existence of highly concentrated industries is associated with higher than normal profits. These in turn reflect protected markets and inefficiency. Thus, it is argued that resources and factors of production are not distributed in the most efficient fashion. It is also argued that income distribution is not as fair and equitable as it would otherwise be if industries were generally less concentrated.

The view has also been expressed that concentration and monopoly are associated with lack of innovation and progress. Thus, it is sometimes said that if the United States is to keep pace in the international growth race, it is handicapped by the existence of large firms in highly concentrated industries. Yet, a quickening of trends toward mergers and the development of large firms in countries outside the United States is observed.

One of the causes of the persistence of concentration and high profits is said to be barriers to entry in a number of industries. This in turn is said to reduce the opportunity to small firms to become established in these industries and to reduce the opportunity for venture capital and entrepreneurial individuals to have an impact in the competitive processes in the United States economy.

Finally, charges have been made in recent years that the very quality of life in the United States has been impaired by the unsocial behavior of the large firms. The complaint has been made that American business has not been sufficiently aware of the externalities of its operations. The operations of business firms and the performance of their products have polluted the air and waterways and disfigured our highways with billboard signs. But the responsibilities of business in this connection have not been spelled out, nor has it been made clear how a changed structure of industries would have produced significantly different results.

Nevertheless, the concern with large size of firms, concentrated industries, and the increased pace of merger activity has led to a stiffening of public policies toward mergers. Thus, the antitrust agencies and the Supreme Court appear to have developed a relatively inflexible structural approach to the evaluation of mergers. The comment has been made with wide agreement that one element of certainty introduced in connection with public policies toward mergers is that in taking cases to the Supreme Court the government always wins. Thus it is said that a tremendous amount of power has been placed in the hands of the antitrust agencies both in the selection of cases brought to litigation and in the enforcement principles they decide to follow.

Upon Dr. Donald F. Turner's retirement as its head, the Justice Department's Antitrust Division, on May 30, 1967, published a set of guidelines indicating the types of mergers that would be challenged. Three broad types of mergers may be distinguished. *Horizontal* mergers are mergers between two or more firms in the same industry. *Vertical* mergers represent combinations between firms in which supplier or buyer relationships may exist. The third broad type of merger has been called *conglomerate* mergers. The Federal Trade Commission has differentiated three types of conglomerate mergers: market extension mergers involve firms whose market areas do not overlap completely; product extension mergers involve product additions with sufficient differences to involve new managerial problems; and conglomerate mergers which are not classed as market extension or product extension mergers are thrown into a general or "other" category. A set of guidelines was formulated for each of these three broad types of mergers.

With regard to horizontal mergers, if the four largest companies control 75 percent or more of a market, one of the top four may not acquire another firm if the share of the market involved in the acquired firm ranges from 4 percent (if the acquiring firm has a 4 percent market share), down to 1 percent (if the acquiring firm has a 15 percent market share). If the four large companies control less than 75 percent of the market, none of the top four may acquire another firm if the acquired firm holds from 5 percent of the market (if the acquiring firm controls 5 percent) to 1 percent (if the acquiring firm holds 25 percent of the market). Mergers that violate these standards will definitely be challenged. If the acquiring firm in a concentrated industry holds as much as 5 to 10 percent of the market, it is uncertain whether *any* horizontal acquisitions would be permitted.

Standards were also set forth for vertical mergers. If a supplier has at least 10 percent of its market and the customer takes at least 6 percent of the total market, a merger between the two would be subject to challenge. If it can clearly be demonstrated that entry barriers into the customer's market would not thereby be increased, such vertical mergers *may be* approved. On the other hand, if a supplier has about 20 percent of its market, if its product is essential to a customer's business and the customer has 10 percent of its own market, such a vertical merger would be challenged.

Although most of the success of the antitrust agencies in prosecuting cases before the Supreme Court had involved horizontal and vertical mergers, guidelines have been developed for conglomerate mergers as well. A conglomerate merger will be challenged if a company with 25 percent of the market acquires a company with potential to enter that market. Similarly the merger would be challenged if one of the four largest companies in the market or one of the top eight controlling 75 percent or more of the market acquires a company with potential to enter that market. A conglomerate merger is also likely to be challenged if it appears that reciprocal buying arrangements might be facilitated by such a merger.

Although some are disturbed by the apparent increased vigor of action by the antitrust agencies, others are concerned that the antitrust agencies have not acted with sufficient vigor. Critics cite the small percentages of mergers challenged. During 1967 the Justice Department filed only 10 merger cases and the Federal Trade Commission, 11. Thus, less than 1 percent of the some 3000 reported mergers in 1967 were challenged by the antitrust enforcement agencies. Also, it is said that the Federal Trade Commission during 1967 reviewed some 1350 mergers and acquisitions but only 56 appeared to warrant "in-depth analysis."

On the other hand, it now appears that the antitrust authorities would be successful in efforts to stop any horizontal merger if the participants are of substantial size. The antitrust agencies have turned increasing attention to vertical mergers and are beginning to develop a record of success in efforts to prohibit mergers of this second type. Only a few actual successful prosecutions of conglomerate mergers have thus far taken place. The Clorox case is a notable example (see page 41, Chapter 3). But considerable emphasis is placed on conglomerate mergers in the last report of the Federal Trade Commission and in public statements by officials in the antitrust agencies. It appears, therefore, that increased attention and increased efforts will be directed toward the third class of mergers as well.

Considerable concern has been expressed by both businessmen and some academic economists with regard to efforts by the antitrust authorities to prohibit vertical mergers and conglomerate mergers. As some of the discussion in subsequent chapters of this monograph indicate, the motive for vertical mergers appears to be primarily increasing efficiency of operations. For conglomerate mergers, the emphasis is on securing the benefits of synergy or carry-over between firms in related activities. The August 1968 issue of *Fortune* expressed it as an objective which seeks "to apply management capabilities in a broader number of lines of business activity."

As a consequence of the successful efforts of the antitrust agencies to prohibit horizontal and vertical mergers and of the increased threats to conglomerate mergers as indicated by the guidelines described above, the legal counsel of many firms increasingly stop incipient mergers at a very early stage. Concern has been expressed that thousands of potential mergers, many of which would have resulted in improved efficiency and performance of individual firms, were never developed very far because of the fear of antitrust attitudes. Furthermore, a number of mergers that received approval by the antitrust agencies carried conditions affecting future mergers. Approval by the antitrust agency increasingly carried either a prohibition against future acquisitions by the acquiring firm in a particular market or markets, or the requirement that prior approval be obtained from the Department of Justice or the Federal Trade Commission. The latter trend raises an issue of public policy because attempts to establish the general power of prior approval for either the Department of Justice or the Federal Trade Commission have failed when such bills were introduced into Congress. Yet on an individual *ad hoc* basis, the antitrust agencies are increasingly achieving what has been turned down as a general policy by the legislative branch to achieve the equivalent result over a widening sector of industry on the basis of administrative decisions.

To determine the consequences of these trends and to evaluate the issues involved requires careful examination of the theories, principles, and policies involved. Has the vigor of activity of the antitrust agencies been insufficient or excessive? Have both the direct and indirect effects of merger prohibitions had desirable or undesirable consequences for the performance of the economy?

It was the aim of this Seminar on Public Policy Toward Mergers to attempt to review antitrust policy in a fundamental way. Conflicting philosophies and theories were subjected to the test of our empirical knowledge to date. Incomplete empirical study of some issues was supplemented by the direct experience of participants, who included representatives of government enforcement agencies, businessmen, lawyers associated with business corporations, and academic scholars with research interests and activities in the area of antitrust policy. The issues are clearly significant. The public policy alternatives are of great importance. The papers that follow and the seminar discussions of the papers as summarized herein sought to achieve progress in assessing the alternative theories and policies.

Four important areas in connection with public policy toward mergers were covered in these papers. Part II covers the issues involved in the alternative standards of structure, performance, and behavior. Part III of the monograph analyzes profitability studies and the relation between industry structure and profitability. Part IV deals with aspects of vertical integration theory and practice. Part V seeks to provide some basis for understanding the implications of the heightened recent trends in the United States toward conglomerate mergers.

Each of the parts presents first the papers that provided a basis for the seminar discussions. At the end of each of the sections, the editors have attempted to summarize the salient points of the discussion that developed. We have purposely avoided associating ideas with individuals in order to facilitate a free exchange of opinion and exploratory discussion of the fundamental issues involved.

part
II

STRUCTURE, PERFORMANCE, AND BEHAVIOR

2

the case for structural tests

by WALTER ADAMS

Almost two decades ago, in a landmark article, Edward S. Mason argued that a sound antimonopoly policy should aim at promoting not only workably competitive industrial structures but also effective business performance. The market structure and performance tests, he observed, "must be used to complement rather than exclude each other."[1]

In advocating a greater attention to performance considerations, Mason tentatively offered the following criteria for measuring business performance:

1. Progressiveness: are the firms in the industry actively and effectively engaged in product and process innovation?

2. Cost-price relationships: are reductions in cost, whether due to falling wages or material prices, technical improvements, discovery of new sources

[1]Mason, "The Current Status of the Monopoly Problem in the United States," *Harvard Law Review*, 62, 8 (June 1949), 1280.

of supply, passed on promptly to buyers in the form of price reductions?

3. Capacity-output relationships: is investment excessive in relation to output?

4. The level of profits: are profits continually and substantially higher than in other industries exhibiting similar trends in sales, costs, innovations, etc.?

5. Selling expenditures: is competitive effort chiefly indicated by selling expenditures rather than by service and product improvements and price reductions?[2]

In suggesting an increased reliance on a performance standard, Mason was careful to point out that "although it is probably possible to arrive at informed judgments, it is extremely difficult to devise tests that can be administered by a court of law." Indeed, he recognized quite explicitly that of the possible applications of a performance standard—on the legislative level, the adjudicatory level, or the case selection level—it was probably most relevant in case selection. Mason was primarily concerned with combating the tendency of the enforcement agencies to ask "what cases can be won?" rather than "what difference does it make?" His suggestions were cautious, tentative, and exploratory.

Some three years later, S. Chesterfield Oppenheim published his famous guideposts for a revision of antitrust policy, based on the twin concepts of "workable competition" and the "rule of reason." Central to the suggested reformulation of the antitrust laws was the adoption of the following criteria for judging performance in the public interest:

(1) Alternatives available to customers or sellers; (2) Volume of production or services; (3) Quality of the services or goods; (4) Number of people benefited; (5) Incentives to entrepreneurs; (6) Efficiency and economy in manufacturing or distribution; (7) The welfare of employees; (8) The tendency to progress in technical development; (9) Prices to customers; (10) Conditions favorable to the public interest in defending the country from aggression; (11) The tendency to conserve the country's natural resources; (12) Benefits to the public

[2]*Ibid.*, 1281–1282.

interest assuming the relief requested by the government in the proceedings.[3]

One cannot help but note, in passing, the contrast between this vague articulation of performance standards and the precise, carefully circumscribed, and tentative language of the earlier Mason proposal.

It is significant that the Attorney General's National Committee to Study the Antitrust Laws, which was created in response to Oppenheim's suggestion and of which he became co-chairman, did not choose to endorse the adoption of a performance standard in the adjudication of the antitrust laws. The stony silence with which the Committee treated "performance" in its final report is perhaps the most remarkable aspect of its conclusions and recommendations.

In this paper, I propose to explore some of the reasons for rejecting performance as a workable antitrust criterion. The concrete examples cited in support of each major proposition are for illustrative purposes only, and not intended as definitive, conclusive empirical evidence.

In the absence of effective competition, there are no scientific yardsticks by which to measure an industry's performance. There are no operationally reliable criteria for determining whether an industry has done "well," or whether it could have done "better" in the light of the opportunities available to it. One can make impressionistic judgments concerning product quality, design, variety, and improvement, for example, but how are we to know that the industry's performance on that score reflects "the best attainable balance between buyer satisfaction and the cost of production"? How are we to establish whether the observed rate of technological progress is as rapid as it could have been? In a market structure characterized by monopoly or tight-knit oligopoly, the necessary yardsticks are either unavailable or difficult to implement operationally.

[3]S. Chesterfield Oppenheim, "Federal Antitrust Legislation: Guideposts to a Revised National Antitrust Policy," *Michigan Law Review,* 50 (1952), 1188 [Quoting Blackwell Smith, "Effective Competition: Hypothesis for Modernizing the Antitrust Laws," 26 *New York University Law Review,* 405 (1951)]. See also riposte by Walter Adams, "The 'Rule of Reason': Workable Competition or Workable Monopoly?" *Yale Law Journal,* 63, 3 (1954), 348–370.

The automobile industry is a case in point. Despite its high degree of concentration, Mason argued that "it is possible from the record of the last two or three decades to determine that the performance of the automobile industry is relatively good." But how valid is that (admittedly impressionistic) judgment in the light of the following considerations:

1. Is the "mauve and cerise, air-conditioned, power-steered, and power-braked automobile" a good product? Is the complex and luxurious amalgam of super-engines, tailfins, quadruple headlights, and cornucopia of chrome a product which satisfies consumer wants, or a product which consumers are taught to accept by the industry's massive selling effort?

2. Does the estimated $5 billion spent by the industry on annual model changes constitute a "sound" contribution to welfare maximization?

3. Should the industry's "stylistic orgy" be replaced by a greater concern for safety, such as "the installation of superior braking systems, safer tires, fuel tanks that do not rupture and incinerate passengers in otherwise survivable accidents—collapsible steering columns, safer instrument panels, steering assemblies, seat structures and frame strengths"? Is 0.02 percent of its gross receipts enough for General Motors to spend on safety research and development? Should the industry have adopted a systematic and more effective program for recalling defective makes and models *before* being forced to do so by governmental pressure? What percentage of the more than 50,000 deaths and 4 million injuries attributable annually to automobile accidents would be avoidable if the industry were to follow a different product-safety policy?[4]

4. Has the industry performed "creditably" in trying to prevent and/or reduce air pollution, 60 percent of which has been attributed to the internal combustion engine? Would Los Angeles, for example, be a more livable city if the industry had been more aggressive in its efforts to eliminate this environmental hazard?[5]

[4]*Federal Role in Traffic Safety*, Hearings before the Subcommittee on Executive Reorganization, Senate Committee on Government Operations (1966), Part 3, pp. 1263 ff.

[5]*The Automobile and Air Pollution: A Program for Progress*, U.S. Department of Commerce (October 1967), Part I, p. 10.

5. Did the industry lag because of its failure so far to introduce a feasible electric automobile?[6]

6. Does an advertising outlay of $100 per car (in 1957) represent an "acceptable" level of selling costs?

7. Should the industry have introduced a "compact" car long before it was compelled to do so by the Volkswagen invasion of the late 1950's—i.e., before its domestic markets began to be eroded by import competition?

8. Is the dramatic deterioration of the industry's export position during the 1950's, and the concomitant transfer of its export efforts to its overseas plants, an element of good performance?

9. Is General Motors' target-rate-of-return pricing, which has yielded the industry (including American Motors) an average net profit of 17 percent on investment between 1954 and 1966, consistent with good performance?

10. Finally, how are we to evaluate the harassment and intimidation to which the industry subjects such critics as Ralph Nader who dare to challenge the adequacy of its performance?[7]

Obviously, as Mason points out, it is extremely difficult to devise meaningful performance tests, especially tests that could be administered by a court of law: "no one familiar with the statistical and other material pertaining to the business performance of firms and industries would deny the extreme difficulty of constructing from this material a watertight case for or against particular firms in particular industries."[8]

Application of the performance standard, in a court of law or before an administrative tribunal, affords unusual opportunities for dilatory tactics and stratagems of confusion. It opens a Pandora's box of procedural obstructionism which is conducive neither to the scientific use of economic evidence nor to the expeditious determination of the issues in the light of such evidence. Given the inexactness of economic knowledge, even the more "objective" components

---

[6]*Ibid.*, Part II, pp. 83 ff.
[7]*Federal Role in Traffic Safety, op. cit.*, Part 4, pp. 1379 ff.
[8]Mason, *op. cit.*, p. 1282.

of performance—such as profit levels—can be the subject of seemingly endless and inconclusive wrangling.

Indicative of the problem is the 1968 controversy over the proper interpretation of drug industry profits before the Senate Small Business Committee.[9] The facts were available, and there was no dispute over their measurement: (1) Between 1959 and 1965, the drug industry had an average rate of return of 17.5 percent, ranking fourth among 59 industries. (2) The median rate of return for all 59 industries was 10 percent. Only four of the 29 drug companies evaluated earned less than that during the period in question; of these, three were companies whose operations were only marginally involved in the development and production of ethical drugs. (3) Only 12 of the companies earned less than 10 percent in any one year during the period. Only two ever showed a loss—in both cases for but a single year. (4) Between 1950 and 1955 the eight largest drug companies showed a profit performance about equal to or slightly above that of the eight largest firms in 22 major manufacturing industries; but, starting in 1956, the leading drug companies ranked either first or second among all large manufacturing industries, sometimes exceeding the average profit rate by substantial margins. (5) In a comparison of *all* drug companies with *all* manufacturing firms for the period between 1956 and 1967, their profit performance ranked first in all years except two (when they ranked second). Again, they exceeded the average by rather comfortable margins.

While no one challenged the accuracy of these data, the Nelson Committee witnessed a lively (and heated) dispute over their interpretation. Representing the Pharmaceutical Manufacturers Association, Gordon R. Conrad and Irving H. Plotkin of Arthur D. Little, working in consultation with Professors Jesse W. Markham and P. J. Cootner, argued that the high level of drug profits was due primarily to the uniquely high risks incurred by large drug manufacturers. By econometric techniques, they attempted to show that the level of drug profits was positively correlated with the degree of risk assumed. They tried to quantify the risk factor by measuring the dispersion of individual companies' rates of return about their industry's average rate of return in a given year, and

[9]*Competitive Problems in the Drug Industry*, Hearings before the Subcommittee on Monopoly, Senate Small Business Committee (Dec.-Jan., 1967–68), Part 5, pp. 1618–89, 1807–61.

then computing a simple average of these values for the 1950–66 period. By this measure—which assumes that the greater the *variation* of company profit rates around the industry average, the *riskier* the industry—they found that the drug firms in their sample had an average profit of 17.5 percent over the period, with a standard deviation of 8.6 percent around this average. Put differently, this meant that roughly two-thirds of the companies in the industry fell in the range between 8.9 and 26.1 percent. By contrast, the Conrad-Plotkin-Markham-Cootner group found that the average rate of return for aluminum companies was 7.8 percent, with a standard deviation of 1.3 percent. This meant that two-thirds of the time aluminum company profits fell in the range between 6.5 and 9.1 percent. On the basis of such comparisons, the PMA economists concluded that the drug industry was a high-risk industry, and aluminum a low-risk industry.

Willard Mueller, representing the Federal Trade Commission, disputed both the accuracy and propriety of the Conrad-Plotkin-Markham-Cootner risk measure. Its chief conceptual shortcoming, he said, was that it tells us nothing about the probability of losses. Indeed, using this measure, an industry might be defined as risky even though most firms earn excessively high profits, whereas an industry might be put in the low-risk category even though most firms earn little or no profits. Given the two-to-one chance that profits in the drug industry will fall in the 8.9–26.1 range, and that profits in aluminum will fall in the 6.5–9.1 range, how can it be argued that drugs are a risky investment but aluminum is not? After all, there is only one chance in six that drug companies will earn a profit below 9 percent (the high in the aluminum range), whereas there are four chances in six that they will earn between 9 and 26 percent, and one chance in six that they will earn over 26 percent.

Moreover, comparing the Big Eight in the drug industry with their counterparts in 21 other major manufacturing industries, Mueller found that between 1954 and 1966 the range of profit rates for the latter was from 5 to 15 percent. If this range is considered a "norm," the eight largest drug manufacturers were in this "normal" range 25 percent of the time, and none ever fell below it; 75 percent of the time they earned profits exceeding 15 percent; and fully 17 percent of the time they earned profits of more than 25 percent.

Finally, citing the Fisher-Hall study done for the RAND Corporation, Mueller concluded that risk accounts for a very small portion of the high profits of drug companies. On the contrary, he advanced the hypothesis that such profits are due primarily to the entry barriers created by patents, high advertising outlays, and other promotional efforts. He pointed out that intra-industry profit variance measures the height of an industry's entry barriers, and not—as Conrad-Plotkin-Markham-Cootner contended—the industry's investment risks.

Whether Mueller was right or wrong may be debatable, but Plotkin was certainly wide of the mark when he tried to assure Senator Nelson that "If economics has made any progress in the last 20 years, it is our ability to take things out of the field of judgment, out of the field of authority and whose textbook you read, and into objective, verifiable, repeatable experiments."[10]

The performance standard, because it focuses only on market results rather than market structure, contains no mechanism for assuring that performance will systematically and predictably be "good." Unlike the structure standard, it only permits good results; it does not compel them. It is devoid of any built-in, inherent safeguards to insure that the "good" results of today will not be the "bad" results of tomorrow. It provides no reward-and-punishment system to discipline delinquent firms or industries. In the absence of exogenous competitive pressures, or direct government interference to control particular performance variables, it lacks the necessary compulsions which militate toward the reform of market conduct with a view to achieving market results that are in the public interest.

An outstanding example, of course, is the steel industry, to which I have devoted not inconsiderable attention elsewhere.[11] In this industry, after World War II, the oligopoly "planning" which Galbraith so glowingly extolled in *The New Industrial State* resulted in truly shabby performance. There was an almost unbroken climb

---

10*Ibid.*, p. 1652.

11Walter Adams and Joel B. Dirlam, "Steel Imports and Vertical Oligopoly Power," *American Economic Review*, 54 (Sept. 1964), 626–656; also Adams and Dirlam, "Big Steel, Invention, and Innovation," *Quarterly Journal of Economics*, 80 (May 1966), 167–189.

in steel prices, in good times and bad, in the face of rising or falling demand, increasing or declining unit costs. Prices rose even when only 50 percent of the industry's capacity was utilized. Price policy was based on a break-even point to be reached at 30 percent utilization of capacity. The typical operating rate seemed to decline steadily from the 82.2 percent of capacity worked in 1957. Domestic markets were eroded by substitute materials and burgeoning imports. Steel's export-import balance deteriorated in both absolute and relative terms: whereas the industry once exported about five times as much as it imported, the ratio today is almost exactly reversed, and steel exports are confined almost exclusively to AID-financed sales guaranteed by "Buy American" provisos.

Most remarkable was the technological somnolence of the giants in this highly concentrated industry. Spending only 0.7 percent of their sales revenue on research and development, the dominant firms in this industry consistently (and almost perversely) lagged behind their smaller domestic rivals as well as their smaller foreign competitors. Thus, the basic oxygen furnace—considered the "only major breakthrough at the ingot level since before the turn of the century" was invented in 1950 by a miniscule Austrian *firm* which was less than one-third the size of a single *plant* of the United States Steel Corporation. The innovation was introduced in the United States in 1954 by McLouth Steel, which at the time had about 1 percent of domestic steel capacity—followed some 10 years later by the steel giants: United States Steel in December 1963, Bethlehem in 1964, and Republic in 1965. Despite the fact that this revolutionary invention involved an average operating cost saving of $5 per ton and an investment cost saving of $20 per ton of installed capacity, the steel giants during the 1950's, according to *Business Week*, "bought 40 million tons of the wrong capacity—the open-hearth furnace," which was obsolete almost the moment it was put in place.

It is significant that only after they were subjected to actual and threatened competition from domestic and foreign steelmakers in the 1960's, did the steel giants decide to accommodate themselves to the oxygen revolution. Thus, it was the cold wind of competition, and not the catatonia induced by industrial concentration, which proved conducive to innovation and technological progress, i.e., improved performance. In this industry, at least, better performance had to await the appearance of structural changes in the market which *compelled* the reforms in market conduct thus belatedly and grudgingly adopted.

Antitrust regulation is basically a "prohibitory" mechanism designed to preserve competitive market structures which militate toward competitive market conduct and indirectly compel "good" industrial performance. Its prohibitory approach is designed to avoid precisely the type of direct interference with business decisions and the pervasive controls over market conduct which application of a performance standard would necessitate. Indeed, a performance standard can be applied intelligently only within an explicit regulatory framework, where an industry is subjected to the comprehensive and continuing surveillance of an administrative board or "independent" regulatory commission. And this, I submit, would be neither wise nor prudent—in the light of our disastrous experience with this form of economic statecraft.

As I have shown elsewhere, regulation by independent regulatory commissions has not turned out to be the new, flexible, creative control instrument envisaged by the New Deal philosophers of the administrative process.[12] On the contrary, regulation has been static, negative, and protective. Even in the absence of venality and corruption, regulation has come to suffer from deep-seated institutional infirmities which militate against the competitive entrepreneur and dynamic innovator. The cost and delay of proceedings; the harassment by powerful protestants; the slavish adherence to technicalities; the pharisaical devotion to a case-by-case approach; the sacrifice of substance for form; the use of differential, inconsistent, and often discriminatory standards; the adoption of restrictive and protective policies; the undue identification with established interests; the petulant defense of the status quo; the sensitivity to organized pressures; the pervasive distrust of large numbers—these have become the hallmark of the regulatory process. Lacking boldness of vision, and beset by an anticompetitive bias, a bureaucratic rigidity, and an annoyance with the forces of change, the commissions have generally been hostile to the newcomer, the challenger, the innovator.

Experience has shown that what starts as regulation almost in-

12Walter Adams, "The Role of Competition in the Regulated Industries," *American Economic Review*, 48 (May 1958), 527–543.

variably winds up as protection. The power to license becomes the power to exclude; the regulation of rates, a system of price supports; the surveillance of mergers, an instrument of concentration; and the supervision of business practices, a pretext for harassing the weak, unorganized, and politically underprivileged. Typically, the commissions have used their power to dispense and protect privilege—to shield their regulatees from competition rather than to protect the public from exploitation. Indeed, in those areas where performance can be said to approximate what might be called "good," such performance has been achieved as a result of "institutional" competition (e.g., the yardstick provided by TVA) or by the marginal competition of unregulated interlopers—the truckers carrying agricultural commodities, the nonscheduled airlines, private operators without common-carrier status, FM radio and UHF television, etc. It is this form of very limited yardstick competition that has modified the conservative, unexperimental, unprogressive, and restrictionist conduct of regulated firms, whose performance languished under the protective umbrella of public regulation.

This experience is hardly worthy of emulation and proliferation under the guise of promoting better performance in the public interest.

The performance standard, if used to replace the structure standard or allowed to supersede it in importance, is subject to serious erosion by giant firms in a concentrated industry. Economic power, after all, is more than a decorative status symbol. It is there to be used when needed—benignly if possible, antisocially if necessary. Thus, a powerful oligopoly will attempt to shield itself from the Schumpeterian gales of creative destruction, and use all its economic and political power to do so. Willy-nilly, it will build storm shelters against those gales, either by private action or by manipulation of the state. Where necessary, and by whatever means, it will try to shield its questionable performance from public criticism or against reform by public authority. And, in the absence of the structural constraints and discipline of a competitive market structure, its efforts may well succeed.

Again the steel industry provides a dramatic illustration. It could luxuriate in its persistently poor performance as long as it commanded a large, protected market, undisturbed by competition-minded rivals or outside interlopers. A high degree of concentration, seemingly immune from antitrust attack, seemed to sanction its monopolistic price policy and technological catatonia. But, starting in 1959, accelerating imports convinced the industry that free international trade may be an effective antimonopoly policy, and that barriers were needed to insulate itself from this subversive force. Instead of meeting import competition in the market place, the industry proceeded to use its political power to preserve the *status quo ante*. Successively, it filed "peril point" proceedings before the Tariff Commission, followed by antidumping action under a 1921 statute, followed by demands to Congress for "temporary" tariff protection, and followed finally by a request for legislatively fixed import quotas. In pursuing what Barron's calls the "protection racket," the industry seemed intent on neutralizing the one exogenous force that could compel it to reform its laggard ways—competition. Roger Blough, congenitally unable to resist the ludicrous, opined that

> ... obviously there are many things in life that should and must be protected. For example, millions of our people—and a number of government agencies—are laudably striving to protect certain vanishing forms of wildlife that are threatened with extinction; and one may reasonably wonder, I suppose, how far down the road to oblivion some of our major industries must go before they are deemed to merit similar concern.

To this, the President of the American Iron and Steel Institutes added the ominous warning that "a first-class power with global responsibilities cannot afford to rely for any important part of its needs on overseas sources of steel thousands of miles away, lying in the shadow of Communist China and the Soviet Union." Finally, the United Steel Workers of America, upon whom Galbraith once relied as a source of countervailing power, not to be outdone in their concern for the public interest and national security, lent their voice and not inconsiderable political influence to the fight for a quota law to limit steel imports.[13]

What is at stake, of course, is the steel industry's right to preserve its administered price structure, to remain the catalyst of seller's inflation, to impose periodic price squeezes on independent

---

[13]Walter Adams, "The Military-Industrial Complex and the New Industrial State," *American Economic Review* (May 1968), 663–64.

fabricators, to price itself out of world export markets, to encourage the growth of substitute materials, and to persist in its technological lethargy. Given the concentrated economic power of the industry, its concomitant political power, and its "vertical integration" with the power of the United Steelworkers, this effort to perpetuate the industry's discretion over "performance"—its right to determine what performance the public must accept as "adequate," "reasonable," or "good"—may well be legitimized by congressional sanction.

General Motors affords a different illustration of how concentrated power can be employed, in the "private sector," to insulate entrenched positions—not from outside competition, or potential competition, but mere verbal criticisms of "performance." When Ralph Nader's *Unsafe at Any Speed* was published, and after he appeared before a congressional committee investigating traffic safety, General Motors hired a private detective agency to investigate Nader's "background"—his professional clients, his education, his friends, his sex habits, his alleged anti-Semitism, etc. Only after exposure by the press did General Motors revoke its orders to the detective agency; only then did a contrite General Motors president apologize to the committee for a decision made by his subordinates without his knowledge. Apparently no challenge, large or small, in the market place or the forum of public opinion, is too insignificant to escape the ubiquitous attention of the octopus. The task of attaining and maintaining power brooks no interference.[14]

Such examples can no doubt be multiplied, even though some are buried without spectacular (temporary) publicity. They underscore the fact that economic concentration is not a neutral phenomenon. Indeed, where it is free from the structural checks and balances of competition, economic power tends to be self-perpetuating—almost irrespective of "good" or "bad" performance.

The foregoing propositions aside, we may note, in conclusion, that no affirmative showing has yet been made of the need for a performance standard (except in the selection of antitrust cases). No one has yet demonstrated, validly or convincingly, that reliance on the structure standard has resulted in *bad* performance, and that far-reaching modification of current antitrust criteria is necessary to assure *good* performance. No one has yet proved that such policy goals as efficiency and progress are incompatible with the preserva-

[14]*Federal Role in Traffic Safety, op. cit.*, Part 4, pp. 1379 ff.

tion of effectively competitive market structures. I suspect that the failure to make such a case is best explained by the lack of evidence to support it.

In the last 20 years enough empirical data have become available to dispel the naive belief, so fashionable in our age of innocence, that firms are big because they are efficient; that firms are big because they are progressive; that firms are big because they are good; that firms are big because consumers have made them big. By now, we should have learned that industrial concentration in some sectors of the economy is not the result of natural law, or the outgrowth of inexorable technological imperatives, but rather the product of unwise, man-made, discriminatory, privilege-creating action of Big Government—the result of governmentally sanctioned privilege, protection, and subsidy.[15]

If this be so, a comprehensive antimonopoly policy, going beyond mere enforcement of the antitrust laws, could result in substantially more competitive industries and markets—and without demonstrable damage to "performance." Thus, the withdrawal of tariff protection from concentrated industries; the refusal to grant patents on publicly financed research and development; a greater reliance on advertised-bid, competitive defense procurement; the termination of government sanction for private cartels (as in petroleum and transportation); the circumscription of the patent, agency, and franchise privileges; the toleration, if not encouragement, of more competition in the regulated industries; the removal of government protection from product-differentiation devices (as in drugs) which serve few other functions than to raise entry barriers— these are only illustrative of the measures which would liberate the natural forces of competition from the heavy hand of a protectionist state. Their implementation, I believe, would not only promote a more competitive industrial structure in many industries, but do so without detracting from good performance.

[15]Walter Adams and Horace M. Gray, *Monopoly in America: The Government as Promoter* (New York: The Macmillan Company, 1955), p. 221.

3

structure-performance assumptions in recent merger cases

A merger changes, in however minor or temporary a way, the structure or composition of some market. Such structural changes can impede the achievement of economic efficiency or progress or other social objectives. Mergers are therefore subject to social scrutiny under many special statutes and, more generally, under the Sherman Act, Section 1, and the Clayton Act, Section 7. This chapter deals with the Supreme Court's implementation of these statutes and especially the judges' premises relating market structure to economic performance. The topic has its difficulties, for the justices seldom elaborate or even state the relevant economic premises. And worse, they sometimes seem indifferent to economic analysis. It is easy to criticize their opinions, and we should, for honest criticism is an important check on the Court's power and an important aid to its future work. But analysis and criticism should be grounded in sympathetic appreciation of the judges' concerns in carrying out the responsibilities dumped upon them by the political organs,

27

which seem capable of speaking only rarely and only in empty generalities.

This brief paper will therefore commiserate as it criticizes. I begin with two problems of vertical mergers, continue with horizontal mergers, and conclude with two conglomerate cases.[1]

VERTICAL ACQUISITIONS

Possible Competitive Clogs

A shoe manufacturer's acquisition of a retail chain "forecloses" competing manufacturers from the opportunity of winning the patronage of the acquired retailer. Antitrust courts regularly characterize such a vertical merger as a "clog" on competition. Large foreclosures are said to be worse than small ones, but the nature and significance of the clog is seldom explained.

Three fears are apparent. First, denying certain outlets to rival manufacturers may so weaken them that they will cease to be viable competitors. Second, if vertical integration comes to characterize the industry, new entry may become impossible at either the manufacturing or distribution level alone. Without independent suppliers or distributors, a new entrant might have to enter at both levels simultaneously. Thus the new entrant would face higher capital costs, the necessity of acquiring more diverse skills, and greater risk generally. Extensive vertical integration in an industry —whether by exclusive dealing contracts, mergers, or internal growth —could increase entry barriers and thus permit existing producers greater latitude for noncompetitive pricing. Third, suppose that oligopolistic sellers face numerous buyers, of which one is particularly important. The patronage of the largest buyer might be so

---

[1]The following cases will be discussed: *Brown Shoe Co.* v. *United States*, 370 U.S. 294 (1962); *United States* v. *Philadelphia National Bank*, 374 U.S. 321 1963); *United States* v. *Aluminum Co. of America (Rome Cable)*, 377 U.S. 271 (1964); *United States* v. *Continental Can Co.*, 378 U.S. 441 (1964); *United States* v. *Von's Grocery Co.*, 384 U.S. 270 (1966); *Federal Trade Commission* v. *Procter & Gamble Co. (Clorox)*, 386 U.S. 568 (1967).

The remaining recent merger decisions were these: *United States* v. *El Paso Natural Gas Co.*, 376 U.S. 651 (1964); *United States* v. *First National Bank and Trust Co. of Lexington*, 376 U.S. 665 (1964); *United States* v. *Penn-Olin Chemical Co.*, 378 U.S. 158 (1964); *Federal Trade Commission* v. *Consolidated Foods Corp.*, 380 U.S. 592 (1965); *United States* v. *Pabst Brewing Co.*, 384 U.S. 546 (1966).

important that even the oligopolistic sellers would shade prices to win its business, and such price shading may contribute to more fluid pricing generally. One supplier's merger with that large buyer would eliminate its possibly salutary effect on price rivalry among suppliers.

Foreclosure's Significance

The first of these dangers is the one emphasized by the courts when they speak of "foreclosure of competing sellers (or buyers)" as if the economic and social significance were self-evident. In *Brown Shoe*, for example, the Supreme Court spoke of the vertical "clog" only in terms of competing shoe manufacturers' diminished opportunities to sell to the Kinney retail chain acquired by manufacturer Brown. Although Kinney accounted for only 1+ percent of shoe sales, it was true that the opportunities of independent manufacturers were affected not only by Brown's acquisition of Kinney but also by the past vertical integration, through merger or otherwise, of other "major" shoe manufacturers. One of the justices alluded to this fact, but the "aggregate foreclosure" was not specified.

Whether the viability of rivals is in fact threatened depends, of course, not only on the present market share of the foreclosed outlets but on the availability of adequate outlets to rivals. A rival shoe manufacturer could not in any event sell to all retailers. And even if a desired outlet were foreclosed, another manufacturer might easily find alternatives among the nation's 70,000 to 100,000 retail shoe outlets. Moreover, entry into retail shoe distribution seems relatively easy—not only in opening a shoe store but, even easier, in adding shoes within existing retail clothing or department stores. The *Brown Shoe* Court, however, failed to consider these issues. Does this failure reflect faulty economic premises or other concerns?

Concentration as a Cumulative Process

To rest on the preceding criticism would ignore the specter that haunts the courts: each of a series of mergers in an industry may seem individually harmless but the aggregation might transform a more or less competitive industry into one that is not "workably competitive." This fear of cumulative harm clearly distresses the judges. Perhaps they will take pains to avoid, if not to expiate, the supposed sins of earlier judges whose insistence upon clear proof of harm permitted gigantic "merger movements" which helped make our economy as concentrated as it is.

This fear of cumulative harm explains the Court's emphasis upon "trends," which shift the focus away from the rather modest merger actually being litigated. In *Brown Shoe*, the Court spoke repeatedly of vertical integration trends and concentration trends and even seemed to equate the two. But although the major manufacturers had been acquiring ownership or control of retail outlets, there was little evidence of greater concentration at retail[2] and concentration at the manufacturing level had declined.[3] Does this suggest that the Court was mistaken? Or that it was unconcerned with actual concentration effects or even with the adequacy of alternative outlets for nonintegrated buyers and sellers?[4] Should we conclude that *Brown Shoe* and similar vertical decisions were unconcerned with economic performance?

Coping with Uncertainty

If I may supply a few propositions possibly implicit in what the *Brown Shoe* Court actually said, perhaps it came to this: (1) Vertical mergers can be quite harmless when the market share foreclosed is trivial. (2) At the opposite extreme, the competitive dangers are assumed significant when the market share foreclosed is overwhelming. (3) In all other cases, some anticompetitive harm is possible, and the law should take the precaution of avoiding such possible

[2]The Court pointed out that the percentage of national retail shoe-store sales by shoe chains of 11 outlets or more increased between 1948 and 1954 from 20.9 percent to 25.5 percent. "Shoe stores" are defined as outlets receiving more than half their receipts from shoe sales. The definition thus excludes clothing chains and department stores, which are often more important distributors than so-called shoe stores. To speak of shoe sales generally, it appears that the percentage of total national retail shoe sales by chains of eleven outlets or more remained roughly constant at 19.5 percent between 1948 and 1954.

[3]Although the number of manufacturers had declined from 1077 in 1947 to 872 in 1958, the market share of the largest four, eight, and fifteen had declined.

[4]The second and third fears stated earlier can be independent of any change in concentration at either the manufacturing or distribution level, but *Brown Shoe* did not raise those issues.

harm where this can be done without sacrificing "worthy" social and economic values. (4) In the *Brown* case itself, the merger was not believed to produce "any countervailing competitive, economic, or social advantages."

The second proposition is subject to the reservations earlier suggested, and the fourth proposition may carry the implicit judgment that mergers are presumptively undesirable and have little social and economic value. That issue needs examination. It is not enough to assert that businessmen should be able to do what they please in the absence of clear proof of social harm. Those who believe that the law should not interfere with mergers except on convincing demonstration of substantial anticompetitive effects or tendencies must show what the economy and society lose by a rule that is less hospitable to mergers. We commentators have not focused very acutely on that question.

VERTICAL EXTENSIONS OF MARKET POWER

There may be another set of judicial assumptions concerning vertical mergers involving a tight oligopoly at the primary level. Consider the *Rome Cable* case. Alcoa, the leading producer of aluminum ingot, also fabricated aluminum cable used as electrical conductor and insulated some of that cable itself. Its market shares were 32.5 percent for bare aluminum conductor and 11.6 percent for insulated aluminum conductor. It acquired Rome Cable, an insulator, which had shares of 0.3 percent and 4.7 percent respectively, for bare and insulated aluminum conductor. The Court discussed the merger in horizontal terms, although Rome's 0.3 percent seemed to add little to Alcoa's share of bare aluminum conductor. And the validity of an insulated aluminum conductor market seems questionable.[5] Although aluminum and copper conductor are not fully interchangeable for ultimate buyers, the insulating job can be performed interchangeably by copper insulators who use the same machines, same technology, and similar distribution channels. Thus the numerous copper insulators are of significance in judging concentration in insulated aluminum conductor. If one

[5] I shall not discuss the Court's aggregation of bare and insulated aluminum conductor into a single hybrid "market."

regarded insulated conductor (both copper and aluminum), therefore, as the appropriate market, the Alcoa and Rome shares would be 0.3 percent and 1.3 percent respectively. The Supreme Court majority gave no attention to production interchangeability among insulators.

And perhaps there was good reason to de-emphasize copper insulators' ability to handle and sell aluminum conductor: they might not have access to competitive aluminum ingot, for there are few producers of primary aluminum and most of them have integrated, usually through merger, into bare and/or insulated aluminum conductor. The details are not apparent from the Court's opinion, for it did not focus expressly on the facts or significance of vertical integration. But the Court did point out that there were only four nonintegrated aluminum conductor producers with market shares of more than 1 percent. The Court's opinion is remarkably elliptical, but I wonder whether the result would have been different had Rome been acquired by a conductor fabricator and insulator with Alcoa's share in those lines but without involvement in primary aluminum.

It is thus possible—I would not go further—that *Rome Cable* reflects an unarticulated assumption about the behavior of vertically integrated firms and about the economic results that can be expected when a very few primary producers operate at a subsequent level of fabrication and also sell to independent fabricators. I have outlined this matter elsewhere and will not repeat it here.[6]

HORIZONTAL MERGERS

The Supreme Court's treatment of classic horizontal mergers[7] reflects four phenomena: (1) the partial triumph of economics, (2) curious notions of the "concentration" that is relevant to economic analysis, (3) the fear of cumulative harm from mergers that are individually inoffensive, and (4) deep scepticism about the social value of mergers.

[6]See Phillip Areeda, *Antitrust Analysis* (Boston: Little, Brown and Co., 1967) , pp. 521–525.

[7]Horizontal mergers can present many of the issues discussed in pages 39–44. And some of the mergers discussed later might be classified as "horizontal." The classifications are of little relevance, and it is convenient to focus attention on the classic case of two present competitors merging.

Oligopoly Theory Reaches the Courts

Although there is much noneconomic or even anti-economic reasoning in the opinions, most of the justices assert the proposition that competition is likely to be greater or more vital in markets of many sellers none of whom possesses significant market power. That standard and contemporary formulation seems much too simple. A large number of small grocers selling to immobile housewives will be less competitive than a much smaller number of supermarkets operating at lower unit costs and selling to housewives shopping over a wider geographical range by private automobile. And even a very few firms earning substantial profits might possibly be "more competitive" in every significant social sense if and when the oligopolists are more progressive than more numerous firms would be, and oligopoly prices might even be lower. Apart from their legal significance, these qualifications do mean that economists are not generally agreed upon the standard formulation. Nevertheless, the general textbook proposition which the Court probably means to invoke is: when other things are equal, the likelihood of price competition becomes smaller as the firms become fewer.

But of course this textbook proposition tells us nothing about the threshold of significance or whether or when other things are equal.

Markets

Significance cannot be assessed apart from meaningful markets. Perhaps large market shares for the merging parties would, other things equal, imply a threat to competition. This is the meaning of the *Philadelphia Bank* statement that substantial anticompetitive effects or tendencies may be presumed (in the absence of clear proof to the contrary) from a merger resulting in a significant increase in concentration and resulting in a firm with an undue share of the market. The validity of such a presumption depends upon the reasonableness of the market definition with which it is used. It seems whimsical to place significance in the simple magnitudes of the bare-plus-insulated-aluminum-conductor "market" asserted in *Rome Cable* or in the cans-and-bottles-but-not-competing-containers "market" of *Continental Can*.

Even *Philadelphia Bank* itself rests on the conviction that commercial banking is a separate market and that local loans and services are a separable market likely to be adversely affected by the merger whether or not the merged bank could add to competition for large loans. Granted that commercial banks offer a unique combination of services, the Court did not much consider whether each individual bank service might face substantial competition from other institutions such as insurance companies, savings banks, savings and loan associations, credit unions, and investment advisory and management services. Demand deposits are held by no one else, but is competition in offering and pricing checking accounts so important? Perhaps it is, but are these matters simply to be assumed?

Assessing Significance; Trends

To find a significant and meaningful market is only to begin the inquiry. The quantitative and qualitative appraisal remains. And it is not intelligibly assessed through the nostalgic populism of *Von's Grocery*, where the Court repeatedly emphasized the declining number of single-store owners. In 1950 there were 5365 and in 1963 only 3590. This "steady erosion" of small independent businesses was said to offend the Clayton Act's objective of keeping a large number of smaller competitors in business. This is economic and legal nonsense. If the number of single-store owners is the meaningful measure of competition, why worry about this market with 3590 competitors remaining? If the number of single-store owners is not a sensible measure of competition, why fuss over steady and perhaps technologically inevitable growth of supermarkets at the expense of small traditional grocery stores? Indeed, that numerical decline may well have been accompanied by lower distribution costs and more mobile buyers and thus by greater competition and greater variety at lower prices for consumers.

To reject the easy numerology of *Von's* is not necessarily to quarrel with the result. Even granting what the Court did not mention—that entry is relatively easy in this business and especially in exploding Los Angeles, that the share of the several top firms has declined, and that there is substantial exit and entry into the category of the leading 20 firms—the fact remains that the challenged merger produced a firm with some 7 percent of Los Angeles area grocery sales.

We must allow for the crudities of market definition and the fact that many of the merged stores had not been in direct competition with each other. Nevertheless, would we be troubled if, say, a dozen 7-percent firms dominated Los Angeles grocery sales?

There again is the troubling specter. If we now approve the merger before us, said the *Brown Shoe* Court, we might have to approve similar mergers in the future. That is not actually true: if a market should become more concentrated in the future, a future merger would have to be judged in its own context. Yet, the claim of equity is hard to resist when only the last of the large New York City bank mergers was challenged, whereas its competitors' mergers in the same decade were untouched. Even so, is there any great likelihood that the Los Angeles grocery business will take this path?

To aid the prediction and also to appraise the possible consequences, we might ask whether the economy would be seriously harmed if the Los Angeles grocery business were dominated by a dozen 7-percent firms. That number of firms is sufficiently small to permit parallel pricing to mutual advantage—collective though not collusive oligopoly pricing. Even so, relatively easy entry and aggressive behavior by the smaller firms might severely limit the monopoly gains available to our hypothetical oligopolists.

The *Von's* Court did not attempt to assess the economic consequences either of the challenged merger or even of the more concentrated market that might conceivably lie ahead.[8] But, putting ourselves in the Court's place, let us ask ourselves this question: if we permit the *Von's* merger, will we prevent the next similar merger in the Los Angeles grocery trade? The one after that? Are we sure enough that entry is easy and will remain easy enough to assure more or less competitive results from an oligopolistic structure? Might area-wide advertising become too expensive for all but the largest chains? Might suburban newspapers be inadequate as a substitute? Might such devices as trading stamps to which a shopper becomes addicted induce him to deal with the one chain that most satisfies him rather than shift patronage frequently? Might automobiles become so expensive to operate or streets so con-

---

[8]Neither did *Philadelphia National Bank* nor *Lexington Bank*. In the bank cases entry was restricted by law and one might expect less competitive pricing of at least some bank services with shrinkage in the already limited number of significant banks serving an area.

gested that housewives would confine their patronage to the nearest large store where the next-nearest large store is a fellow oligopolist?

In short, if we feared that major structural changes might be under way, are we sure enough of easy entry (etc.) to tolerate the change? To answer that question, how precisely need one predict a particular merger's impact upon economic performance? The answer should depend upon two further questions: How much can we learn by trying to make such a prediction?—a question I shall not discuss here. And, what does society lose by forbidding a merger that an omniscient oracle would declare harmless?

The Social Loss of Undue Prohibition

This issue has seldom been squarely posed by actual defendants, who have mainly sought to disprove competitive harm rather than to prove social benefit. Supreme Court opinions do not note highly plausible claims to social benefits in any case other than *Philadelphia Bank*, in which defendants urged the importance of increasing competition for large loans within the capacity of the merged institution but beyond the lending power of either predecessor bank. How effectively that argument was developed in principle or proved in fact, I do not know. In *Von's* one of the merging chains was allegedly directed by an aged chief who doubted that his subordinates could carry on. But perhaps such self-serving statements may not warrant great weight in the absence of credible suggestions that the requisite skills are in short supply.

Apart from litigants' claims, what can be said of mergers' affirmative social benefit? Of course, the market for capital assets, broadly defined, involves trading in whole businesses as well as in individual pieces of plant and equipment. Mergers are often the means by which less efficient managements transfer resources and economic operations into hands that will use or serve them more successfully. More specifically, we can do little more here than list the commonplace benefits that might possibly result from mergers: (1) economies of scale in research, production, or distribution, (2) efficient combinations of complementary resources, including entrepreneurial talents, (3) greater risk-bearing innovative capacity, (4) facilitating exit at minimum loss or maximum gain, (5) facilitating entry by firms outside the industry or expansion by existing competitors, and many other possibilities including the rather private advantages involving federal taxes.

I do not mean to suggest that any of these benefits justifies any particular merger. Certainly many challenged mergers could not make any plausible claim to greater efficiency. And many of the merging parties are already large enough to reap whatever economies of scale appear in the scanty data that are available. Whatever efficiencies might seem plausible, moreover, might well elude successful proof in actual cases. But can the Court be so sure that mergers generally are without redeeming virtues?

The Supreme Court seems to avoid that issue. It has allowed a few small points but generally has confused the issue by ill-considered dicta or otherwise evaded it by passing the buck to Congress. The Court spoke generally in *Brown Shoe* as if it might have reached a different conclusion had defendants shown some "countervailing competitive, economic, or social advantages" flowing from the merger. There and elsewhere, however, the Court has expressly recognized legitimacy only for the merger of two "small" firms in an industry dominated by large firms or for the acquisition of a "failing company." Indeed, several majority opinions have gone further. In *Brown Shoe*, the Court assumed that the vertical merger would result in more efficient distribution and used that assumed fact as grounds for condemning the merger. In *Procter & Gamble*, the Court said that "possible economies cannot be used as a defense to illegality. Congress was aware that some mergers which lessen competition may also result in economies but it struck the balance in favor of protecting competition." That statement deserves analysis.

Now it is true that Clayton Act, Section 7, says nothing of economic efficiency. It is true also that the legislative histories underlying the original enactment and the 1950 amendment say little of efficiency. It should be expected, however, that the legislative history of an antimerger statute will rehearse the dangers of mergers, the values of small business, and the distrust of business giants. To condemn sin, however, is to give little guidance on whether particular conduct is or is not sinful. And if a proponent of amended Section 7 had been asked whether he was condemning all mergers, would he not have said, "Of course not; only those which tend substantially to lessen competition"?

The point is that the Clayton Act, Section 7, does not purport to condemn mergers absolutely. It invokes concepts of competition and monopoly. And one of the reasons we value competition is for its results, including efficiency in the use of resources. Of course there are other values in competition: the Jeffersonian notion of dispersed resources. Even the great Judge Hand said in the *Alcoa* monopoly decision that "throughout the history of these statutes it has been constantly assumed that one of their purposes was to perpetuate and preserve, for its own sake and in spite of possible cost, an organization of industry in small units which can effectively compete with each other." But what is the utility of preserving inefficient and high-cost producers who "compete with each other" only within the framework permitted by excessive costs? And those who would rely on the authority of Judge Hand should remember that the quoted statement was offered in answer to the proposition that acknowledged monopolies should be tolerated if they do not charge excessive prices.

The problem is very clear. The justices fear that acceptance of efficiencies as a legal defense would invite ever-increasing concentration. If we were faced with an attempt by General Motors to absorb its automobile rivals on a claim of increased efficiency, we might very well say "efficiency be damned." Perhaps the courts assume that monopoly or increasingly gigantic size are an inevitable tendency of modern industrial life. But neither historical concentration trends nor efficiency studies, as crude as they are, suggest that large-firm economies threaten to confront us with the prospect of ever increasing concentration. One reason may be that economies of scale are a function of a firm's absolute size, which can grow as the economy grows even though its market share remains stable. Both principle and data seem to suggest that firms with relatively small shares of large markets may be large enough in absolute size to achieve most possible economies. Of course, in some markets, this may not be true. And small shares of national capacity may imply significant levels of concentration in narrower geographic or product submarkets. Even so, the fear that hospitality to economic efficiency would justify superconcentration seems ill-founded.

In any event, the statute gives us little guidance. The Court must try to make what sense of it they can. It is their decision to make. Neither the courts nor the commentators can escape the fact that they, not Congress, are deciding. And it should be especially clear that the Clayton Act, Section 7, does not reject the possibility of redeeming social virtue in cases in which the anticompetitive effect or potential of the merger is not so clear. The existence of a significant interest in favor of a merger should, at the very least, make us hesitant to condemn a merger without some reasonably satisfying indication that competition is or may be substantially lessened in some significant market.

In any particular case, one might believe that offsetting social benefits cannot be assessed with any assurance and ought therefore to be rejected, at least where market shares are sufficiently large in magnitude to create a strong danger of excessive market concentration. Observe, however, that the intellectual process just described differs greatly from the refusal to give any claim to redeeming virtue on the ground that Congress has already made that choice. Congress did not make that choice but passed the buck to the courts.

CONTINENTAL CAN

Definition of Market

Somewhere between horizontal and conglomerate mergers lie the curious decision and assumptions of *Continental Can,* which condemned a merger of the country's second largest can producer with the nation's third largest producer of glass containers. Cans and bottles are in general confrontation with each other in the effort to obtain the patronage of producers of particular end-use products such as beer or soft drinks. The Court did not focus on this fact.[9] Instead, the Court focused on the "general confrontation" between cans and bottles and created a market consisting of bottles and

---

[9] I am not sure why, but four reasons suggest themselves. First, perhaps the Court was unconcerned with identifying the precise market impact of the merger but was ready to proceed on more gross consideration. Secondly, to look to end-uses in which can-bottle competition was significant and exclusive of other containers might find that both merging companies had not in fact been significant in such particular end-uses. Third, producer shares in any particular end-use might be highly unstable and subject to considerable erosion. Fourth, isolating particular end-uses does not necessarily identify the locus of price determination. If, for example, a certain type of can or bottle or other container were used for a dozen end-uses and if that type of container generally carried a uniform price regardless of each end-use, no single end-use would reflect the operative price determining forces.

cans and ignoring different sizes, ignoring the returnable feature of some bottles, and ignoring plastic, paper, and other containers that were also in general confrontation with cans and bottles. In this custom-made market, the two firms possessed some 22 percent and 3 percent, whereupon the Court invoked the presumptions in *Philadelphia Bank* which condemned mergers resulting in a "significant" increase in concentration and a firm controlling an "undue" percentage of the market. To draw any performance inferences from the structure of the Court's gerrymandered market would seem very difficult indeed.

Relevant Competition

The Court seemed to fear that the merger would reduce competition between cans and bottles. But of course, the main competition of glass is glass, and concentration with respect to intra-product competition has not changed. And, importantly, inter-product competition will remain so long as the fate of significant producers lies in one product or another. For example, even though *Continental* obtained a third of the market defined by the Court, it is hard to see a significant diminution in the incentive for independent glass firms to win the patronage of can users. And even if all can and bottle firms made both containers, the likelihood of interdependent noncompetitive results is not obviously great. Recognized interdependence will exercise a stronger restraint on price competition among oligopolists than on rivalry in analogous product variation. Can-bottle rivalry would probably continue even if all firms made both containers. Furthermore, competing plastic and paper containers will continue to exert significant inter-product competition. What then is the competitive harm?

The Court seemed to fear diminished innovation, but that seems unlikely for the reason just stated. Perhaps there is significance in wide-line coverage. A customer content with Continental Cans may, other things equal, buy his jars from Continental as well. Conceivably, other jar makers might be unable to lure the customer away from the merged firm, even though, without the merger, all jar manufacturers would be on an equal footing. But perhaps it is equally conceivable that the attempt to "blast" a customer away from a wide-line company will mean more intensive price competition. Still, it may remain possible that the wide-line company will gain good will amounting to a priority on the business, at least when prices and other circumstances are equal. A clog on competition is not implausible, but plausibility is not significance. Nevertheless, is there any social loss in prohibiting the acquisition? If not, could we define even-handed criteria for determining when to intervene—assuming that all mergers are not to be condemned presumptively?[10]

CLOROX

To explore the structure-performance assumptions of the *Procter & Gamble (Clorox)* decision is to expose a multitude of plausible economic premises. It will be recalled that Procter, a large producer of detergents and related products, acquired Clorox, which accounted for nearly 50 percent of national bleach sales. Clorox was the sole producer selling nationwide. Six firms accounted for about 80 percent of industry sales; the remainder was divided among a large number of very small firms.

Promotional Economies

The Court noted that national advertising media customarily grant quantity discounts to large advertisers such as Procter. Procter's bleach rivals are presumably too small to obtain similar discounts. Furthermore, Procter's involvement with many related products means that it could feature several products in its promotional mailings to consumers and thus achieve a lower cost-per-product than a single-product firm would incur from similar printings and mailings. And the sponsorship of a single network program would enable Procter to give each of its products network exposure at a fraction of the cost-per-product that a single-product firm would incur. It is true that advertising seems to be important in soaps, detergents, and bleach—as reflected in Clorox's ability in some areas to obtain a premium price for a chemically identical product (although, it was said, some competitive bleaches did not maintain

---

[10]The government suggested in *Can* that inter-industry mergers be forbidden when there is substantial competition between those industries, when one or both industries are highly concentrated, and when each of the merging firms is dominant in its own industry.

consistent strength). The Court did not discuss whether smaller firms might have effective alternative means of exposure. Nor do we learn whether any promotional savings by the large firm were significant in relation to the over-all production or marketing costs of bleach. Nevertheless the Court used the stated advertising advantages as an element of proof toward its next two conclusions.

Relative Strength

The Court believed that Procter's gigantic size was relevant to the psychological response of other bleach producers. To the extent that Procter was thought by them to be large, affluent, and powerful, "its prowess as a competitor gains an added and even sinister dimension." There was the danger, the Court thought, that Procter would be the price leader. But one may ask whether the many local producers of bleach would be led. And anyone looking for a price leader already had one in the dominant but independent Clorox.

Secondly, the Court suggested that Procter's advertising resources and advantages could be concentrated tactically on particular local bleach markets. Bleach competitors might willingly battle an independent Clorox but fear that they could never prevail against Procter in a fight to the finish.

Third was the danger that Procter would use its vast resources to "underprice" bleach in order to drive out its competitors. This assertion by the Court seems fanciful. Although entry into nationally branded and promoted bleach was difficult, entry at the local level appeared rather easy, as reflected in a large number of local bleach producers. The question is whether a predatory firm could ever recover the costs of driving out rivals through uneconomical pricing. A predatory firm might succeed in driving out its rival, but any effort thereafter to extract a monopoly price could well induce re-entry. Given the fact that many competing bleaches are sold under the private labels of large retail chains who have nothing to fear from Clorox or from Procter, local private label producers could probably enter or re-enter the bleach business whenever it is profitable to do so.

Entry Barriers

The Court asserted that Procter's acquisition of Clorox would increase the barriers to entry into liquid bleach production. That conclusion seems to rest on the two preceding arguments: it would be more difficult for a new entrant to fight Procter, with its resources and advertising advantages, than to fight Clorox.

We might wonder, however, whether other large companies with assets or advertising economies comparable to Procter would be affected by Procter's presence, although perhaps it might cost more to fight Procter than an independent Clorox. We might also wonder whether many potential entrants would not find an independent Clorox sufficiently formidable that the substitution of Procter would create no additional operative barrier. Finally, we could ask whether there would be any effect at all on the likelihood of entry by local multitudes content merely to sell unadvertised bleach for less than Clorox.

Potential Competition

The Court believed that Procter was a potential entrant into the liquid bleach business. It is, of course, possible that Procter would have entered independently. The Federal Trade Commission found that

> Procter was a progressive and experienced manufacturer of many products in the same product line as liquid bleach; it had in the past frequently extended its product line . . . ; it . . . was powerful enough to challenge, with some hope of success, Clorox's entrenched position in the bleach market; and it had actually pondered the possibility of entry into the liquid bleach market on its own.[11]

The Court further emphasized the absence of any obstacle to entry in the form of patents, trade secrets, or raw material or equipment difficulties.

The Commission and the Court declared, in effect, that liquid bleach was Procter's manifest destiny. The Court believed that "Procter was the most likely entrant." But the Court stated nothing about other possible entrants. Indeed, given the absence of technological barriers to entry and the existence of many other firms with effective advertising and with experience in exploiting the same merchandising channels used for bleach, one might suppose that there was a substantial universe of potential entrants. How far should we look? Perhaps we shouldn't linger too long in identify-

---

[11]*FTC* v. *Procter & Gamble, op. cit.*

ing potential entrants (or measuring entry barriers) when possible entry is a paramount factor in the market being examined. Was *Clorox* such a case?

The Court said: "It is clear that the existence of Procter at the edge of the market exerted considerable influence on the market" because existing firms consider actual and potential competitors and there was no barrier to Procter's entry. Again, however, one may wonder whether the possibility of Procter's independent entry had any effect at all on the behavior of the existing producers. Clorox's power may have been restrained not by fear of potential entry but by actual competition from many small bleach producers making unadvertised brands for the private labels of large retailers. But none of this appears in the Court's opinion. I sense in many recent decisions that the courts are too ready to declare the acquiring company a potential competitor, the universe of potential competitors a small one, and potential entry significant in the immediate market.

MARKET STRUCTURE AND ECONOMIC PERFORMANCE

Critics of the Supreme Court might be tempted to ask whether that tribunal knows or cares about the relationship of market structure to economic performance. There is, to be sure, the occasional language of oligopoly theory and even talk of entry barriers. A good portion of the time, however, the disinterested reader senses that the economic formulations are the modern dialectical garb for the populist sentiments that sometimes surface directly. Still, any one merger's impact on competition will usually be indeterminate and perhaps it is inevitable that the exact point of interference by the law is arbitrary. And in determining the point of such interference the courts are given little precise guidance by Congress, by precedent, by economic science, or by critics like ourselves.

4

concentration, competition, and mergers in brewing

by ANN AND IRA HOROWITZ

Within the past two decades there has been a growing sense of uneasiness about the trend of concentration in the brewing industry. The largest brewer in the United States, Anheuser-Busch, held 13.1 percent of the national market in 1966. Although this is scarcely monopolistic control, the *trend* in concentration, which has seen the 25-firm concentration ratio rise from 39.2 percent in 1944 to 90.4 percent in 1966, is often taken as evidence of a pronounced and unhappy decline in competition.

There is no question about the tide of events in the brewing industry. Concentration, whether based on 5 firms, 25 firms, or anything between, has been increasing at a steady pace. Simultaneously, the number of brewers has been steadily declining, from 374 firms in 1944 to 129 firms in 1964. One cannot, however, necessarily equate *concentration* or the number of competitors with the *degree of competition* in an industry. It is competitive performance and not a concentration statistic that counts, and performance must be evaluated with regard to the extent to which an optimal degree of competition is being attained *in light of* the constraints under which the industry is forced to operate.

In particular, the economic facts of life in brewing have seriously curtailed, if not completely negated, the possibility of maintaining the number of viable competitors and intensifying competition among them. Any attempt to assess the trend of competition in brewing will therefore require both an appropriate surrogate with which to measure the degree of competition and an understanding of the economic conditions that have been instrumental in effecting this trend. With this in mind, we shall discuss competitive trends in brewing as well as the treatment accorded mergers of brewers by the government and the courts.

The major purpose of the paper, then, is to suggest that *detailed* economic analysis is essential both in explaining *why* concentration data and the like behave as they do and in evaluating the effects of mergers. With specific reference to brewing, it will be argued that demand and cost conditions have forced the demise of the majority of brewers disappearing from the industry and that a *necessary* concomitant of these disappearances has been an increase in concentration. Mergers have also contributed to the decline in the brewing population and to some extent, a comparatively minor extent, to the increase in concentration. But *competition among the survivors* has to all intents and purposes been maintained at historical levels, and these levels are rather high.

MERGER TRENDS IN THE BREWING INDUSTRY

Antitrust and Brewing Mergers

Although a significant number of mergers has taken place in the brewing industry since the end of World War II, only since the late 1950's has the government exhibited concern over brewing mergers. This concern was first manifested in a complaint filed by the Justice Department against Anheuser-Busch's 1958 acquisition of Regal, owned by American Brewing Company and marketing in Florida. In a consent decree in 1960, Anheuser-Busch was ordered to divest itself of Regal. Anheuser-Busch was also prohibited from acquiring interest in *any* Florida brewing facility and, for five years, from acquiring *any* interest in *any* brewing facility in the United States without court approval.

About the same time, 1959, the Justice Department filed a complaint against the 1958 merger of the Pabst and Blatz Brewing Companies. This case, which was considered by the Supreme Court in 1966, will be discussed below. In 1965, the government also charged that Schlitz's 1961 acquisition of Burgermeister and its 1964 acquisition of a 39 percent interest in Labatt, Ltd., of Canada was a violation of Section 7 of the Clayton Act.

During 1965, the Justice Department sought several injunctions against proposed mergers. The targets included the proposed acquisition of Theo. Hamm Brewing Company by Molson Ltd. (a Canadian brewer), the proposed acquisition of Duquesne Brewing Company by Pittsburgh Brewing, the since realized merger of Falstaff and Narragansett Brewing Companies, and the acquisition of Jacob Ruppert by Liebmann (Rheingold). The latter two injunctions were denied, but the Justice Department has indicated its intention to pursue these cases. The Hamm-Molson and Pittsburgh-Duquesne merger plans were dropped by the companies involved.

Some fairly sizable mergers have, however, apparently passed the government's scrutiny. The 1965 merger of Associated, with 1.5 percent of the 1964 market, and Drewrys, with 2.6 percent, is a prime example. The fact that the Justice Department did not take action against this merger assumes added significance when one recognizes that Drewrys had previously acquired Piel's in 1962. At the time, Drewrys had 2.2 percent of the market and Piel's, one of the major metropolitan New York brewers, had 1.6 percent.

Court Decisions in Litigated Cases

The government has, however, been successful in its prosecution of the two major cases that have reached the courts. Less than two years ago the Supreme Court reversed the earlier decision of the Wisconsin District Court, which had dismissed the government complaint alleging that the acquisition of Blatz by Pabst had the effect of substantially lessening competition in the production and sale of beer in the United States, the State of Wisconsin, and the three state area of Wisconsin, Illinois, and Michigan.

The District Court held that the government had failed to establish that either the State of Wisconsin or the three-state area is a relevant geographic market in which to measure the effect of the allegedly illegal acquisition. In particular, the lower court held that the government

> ... in order to satisfy its burden of proving the three-state area is a relevant geographic market, must demonstrate something beyond the fact that isolation of that area from the national market would result in percentages favorable to its position. It must first demonstrate that under the "commercial realities" of the beer industry, Illinois, Michigan, and Wisconsin is a relevant market area.[1]

Concluding that the entire United States was the only geographic area either proved or agreed by both parties to be a market, the lower court further held that in its opinion, "proof that Pabst had a 4.49 percent share of the market after the acquisition in 1959, which percentage had grown to 5.83 percent in 1961, is not sufficient to establish that the acquisition is inherently likely to lessen competition. . . ."[2]

The Supreme Court's reversal contains two points of interest. The Court held that (1) it is not necessary for the government to prove the section of the country where the anticompetitive effect exists, and (2) a merger resulting in a combined market share of 5 percent of industry sales represents a violation of Section 7 of the Clayton Act when a trend toward increasing concentration exists in the industry.

With respect to the first point, the Court emphasized that the Celler-Kefauver Amendment

> ... requires merely that the Government prove the merger may have a substantial anticompetitive effect somewhere in the United States—"in *any* section" of the United States. This phrase does not call for the delineation of a "section of the country" by metes and bounds. . . . Proof of the section of the country where the anticompetitive effect exists is entirely subsidiary to the crucial question in this and every Section 7 case which is whether a merger may substantially lessen competition anywhere in the United States.[3]

[1]233 F. Supp. 475 (1964), p. 488.
[2]*Ibid.*, p. 491.
[3]384 U.S. 549 (1966).

The Court further held that "the evidence as to the probable effect of the merger on competition in Wisconsin, in the three-state area, and in the entire country was amply sufficient to show a violation of Section 7 in each and all of these three areas."[4] Emphasis was placed on the facts that the tenth and eighteenth largest brewers in the nation combined to become the fifth largest, with 4.49 percent of the sales, and that in three years this was up to 5.83 percent in an industry marked by steadily increasing concentration. The Court held that "a trend toward concentration in an industry, whatever its causes, is a highly relevant factor in deciding how substantial the anticompetitive effect of a merger may be."[5]

It should be noted that the Court equated both concentration and the number of competitors with the degree of competition. As evidence of the increasing concentration, the opinion cites figures showing that the number of breweries fell from 714 in 1934 to 229 in 1961, the number of *different* competitors fell from 206 in 1957 to 162 in 1961, and the market shares of the leading 10 brewers rose from 45.06 percent in 1957 to 52.60 percent in 1961. Although concentration *may* be related to competition, the government did not present any evidence showing a decline in competitive performance, and the wording of the Court's opinion seemed to indicate that the Court did not recognize the need for such evidence. The fact that the number of large efficient producers has been steadily increasing was *not* noted. The existence of such a trend is exemplified by the fact that in 1947 only 14 firms sold over a million barrels whereas in 1966 this figure was up to 22. Furthermore, in citing the increased concentration ratios, the Court did not consider that the leading firms do not remain the same over the years: e.g., only 8 of the top 15 brewers in 1947 remained in the top 15 in 1961.

Several justices concurred with the opinion that this particular merger substantially lessened competition in well-defined sections of the country or in the country as a whole but offered dissenting opinions with respect to the Court's interpretation of the phrase "any section of the country." Justice Harlan, whom Justice Stewart joined, concurred on the ground "that the Government's evidence is sufficient to establish prima facie that Wisconsin and the tri-state area ... are both proper sections of the country in which to measure the probable effect of the acquisition of Blatz by Pabst

4*Ibid.*, 552.
5*Ibid.*, 553.

under Section 7," but stated that he is "wholly unable to subscribe to the Court's opinion which appears to emasculate the statutory phrase 'in any section of the country.' "[6] Justice Fortas did not join in the Court's opinion because he believes, "in Section 7 cases, it is the Government's duty as plaintiff to prove the 'market' or the 'section of the country' in which the claimed effect of the acquisition is manifest."[7]

The only other major brewing merger to come before the courts for trial is Schlitz's acquisition of Burgermeister and a 39 percent interest in Labatt, owner of General Brewing of California. Here, too, the district court's decision was based primarily on evidence regarding market shares, both nationally and in California. The district court ruled that the mergers did substantially lessen competition and ordered Schlitz to divest itself of both Burgermeister and its stock in Labatt.[8] Shortly after its Pabst-Blatz decision, the Supreme Court affirmed the judgment against Schlitz without opinion.[9]

Given the emphasis on market shares, it may well be that the courts (and the Justice Department) will look more kindly on the Falstaff-Narragansett merger since these firms do not market in the same areas. Falstaff has a heavy concentration of its sales in the Southwest, South, and parts of the Midwest. Narragansett is the largest brewer in New England, an area in which Falstaff has heretofore not been sold. If, in the Court's view, the separation of their markets does work in favor of the Falstaff and Narragansett merger, it will serve to point up the fallacy in the Court's current preoccupation with market shares. Such a preoccupation seems to involve an implicit neglect of the possibility that Falstaff would begin to market its own brand in New England. The availability of the Narragansett plant and distributing system probably provides Falstaff with an easier means of expanding the marketing territory of the Falstaff brand. It is likely, however, that since the expansion was accomplished by acquiring a potential competitor, the effect may well be a lessening of competition. Falstaff's past acquisitions have generally been followed by the introduction of the Falstaff brand in the marketing area of the acquired brand, and one is

[6] *Ibid.*, 555.
[7] *Ibid.*, 562.
[8] 253 F. Supp. 129 (1966).
[9] 1966 Trade Cases 71,916.

probably safe in assuming that expansion into the New England area was a major objective in acquiring Narragansett.

SOME RELEVANT ECONOMIC FACTS ABOUT THE BREWING INDUSTRY

The Demand for Beer

Using a simultaneous equation econometric model, we have previously analyzed some of the factors affecting the demand for beer. Because these are germane to any discussion of competitive trends, we highlight our major conclusions here.[10]

In particular, estimates were made of the cross-section relationship (that is, across states) between the per capita demand for beer and two independent variables, per capita income and state taxes on beer, for each year from 1949 to 1961. The choice of income as an independent variable is clear. Although price would also seem to be relevant, these data were not available. As a proxy, taxes were used in lieu of the price data in the hope that perhaps these could serve as an indication of interstate differences in retail price.

The analysis led to the inference that if differences in state beer taxes actually do reflect differences in retail prices, these results provide reason to believe that the demand for beer is insensitive to existing price differences or that demand is price inelastic. The other extremely interesting result is that there has been a historical positive relationship between income and demand for beer, contrary to the beliefs of those who hold beer is an "inferior" good.[11] This relationship, though remaining positive in each of the 13 years, has declined in strength quite sharply over time. In 1955 it was about half as strong as in 1949 and in 1956 only 40 percent as strong as in 1955. In fact, for each year from 1956 on, the regression coefficient has not been significantly different from zero. The implication is that in the late forties and early fifties beer consumption and income were quite closely related, at least as regards interstate differences in beer consumption and income, but that the strength of the relationship has been dissipated over time.

[10]For the gory details, see our article "Firms in a Declining Market: The Brewing Case," *Journal of Industrial Economics*, XIII, 2 (March 1965), 129–153.

[11]Inferior in the classical economic sense that the demand for it declines as income rises.

Although the evidence indicates that beer is not an inferior good, since income has been increasing over time the change from a significantly positive relationship to a nonsignificant relationship between income and the demand for beer might be *interpreted* as supporting the claim that beer is an inferior good. This possibility seems dubious, however, in light of the finding that the partial correlation coefficient between income and the cross-section relationship between income and demand is not significantly different from zero when a trend factor is removed. This indicates that the marginal propensity to consume beer is declining over time, rather than with increasing income.

In addition to the hypothesis that income and consumption are positively related but the strength of the relationship has been declining over time (as indicated by the steady decline in the cross-section coefficients between 1949 and 1961), consideration was also given to several alternative explanations of the fact that *per capita* beer consumption has declined over time while per capita income was increasing. Two such alternative explanations are: (1) that price increases had caused the relative stability of quantity demanded despite the increases in income; and (2) that population has increased while total beer consumption remained constant, thereby reducing per capita consumption not because of a change in tastes or in income but because the increase in population was concentrated in the nondrinking age groups.

Due to the dearth of price data, it is impossible to statistically test the first hypothesis; but the nonsignificant relationship found between taxes and demand indicates a relatively inelastic demand which would eliminate it as a possible explanation. Furthermore, the information that is available on price changes over the period indicates that changes were very infrequent and fairly small. This, in conjunction with the insensitivity of demand to taxes, indicates that the relative stability of per capita beer consumption over time is not a reflection of price increases.

The relationship between beer consumption and income as measured by the cross-section regression coefficient for each year analysed appears to have had a greater effect on per capita consumption than the percent of population in the drinking age groups. Both factors, however, have contributed to the decline in per capita consumption. With income and consumption closely related, consumption would rise as per capita income rises. Simultaneously, however, the influence of income on beer consumption declined and the percent of the population in the beer drinking age group fell. The result was a falling off of per capita consumption. The increasing total population has decreased the denominator of per capita consumption while over the same period the ability of increases in income to increase the numerator has lessened.

Supply Conditions for the Production and Sale of Beer

Our earlier study also shed light on minimum plant size and on comparative average costs for different-size firms. An analysis of beer production by state indicated that the average gain or loss in state production resulting from the arrival or departure of the 'last' firm to assume production in the state, or the 'first' firm to cease production, was close to 100,000 barrels in each of the previous 14 years. If it is presumed that the 'last' firm is the "marginal" firm, the results suggest that the minimum efficient size of a firm in the brewing industry is about 100,000 barrels of beer a year.

Further information on the nature of costs in the brewing industry was gleaned from the coefficient of correlation of the Gini coefficient and the concentration ratio over time. Ten coefficients of correlation were calculated by considering the leading 50 firms taken in successive groups with the addition of 5 firms at a time. That is, the coefficient of correlation between the Gini coefficient and the concentration ratio was calculated for the leading 5 firms, the leading 10 firms, the leading 15 firms and so forth up to the leading 50 firms. Assuming that the demand curves facing *individual* firms are to some degree elastic, if not perfectly so, within the relevant price range, the signs of these correlation coefficients provide some insight as to the nature of average costs.

The results indicated that: (1) the industry leaders have a slight cost advantage over the other firms comprising the top 5; (2) at least some of the smaller producers among the top 10 and top 15 firms operate in a range of average costs below that for the first 10 and 15 firms as a whole; (3) not all of the 16th through 20th firms operate with average cost advantages with respect to the top 20 firms as a whole; (4) the remaining firms operate with much higher average costs than the top 50 as a whole. Specifically, we concluded that the lowest average cost range is somewhere above 1 million barrels a year, probably closer to 1.5 million barrels, and at or below 3 million. Higher average costs arise at other levels, but firms with production levels in excess of 5 million barrels enjoy economies.

The Role of Advertising

The advertising data available at that time did not appear to support the view that there were economies resulting from advertising. In fact, the average advertising expenditures per barrel were greater for the top five firms than for any other group, implying that there are diseconomies of advertising expenditure beyond a certain point. This reinforces the argument that there must be other cost economies resulting beyond the 5-million-barrel mark.

Advertising data in 1960 and 1961 showed that Anheuser-Busch and Schlitz spent more than double the amount of any other firm in the industry. We felt that this probably reflected a good deal of interfirm rivalry between the two since their sales were not correspondingly greater than those of the other large brewers. More recent advertising figures indicate, however, that there may be some economies at higher production levels and/or the earlier figures were affected by unusually heavy advertising expenditures incurred in promoting a new brand (Busch Bavarian or Old Milwaukee). Thus, in 1966 when Anheuser-Busch had increased its sales to 13.6 million barrels its advertising costs per barrel were $.98, whereas Schlitz, with sales of 9.5 million barrels, had advertising costs of $1.82 per barrel. The Anheuser-Busch figure is substantially less than that for 1965, $1.41, but Schlitz's advertising costs were quite constant for the two years, equaling $1.80 in 1965. An indication of the heavy advertising costs incurred in promoting a new brand is given by Rheingold's experience with Gablinger's. Advertising for Gablinger's was in excess of $5 per barrel in 1966.

Definition of Brewing Market

Some comment should also be made on the question of what constitutes the brewing market. We shall discuss the issue of competition in brewing in terms of the *national* market. Moreover, we shall assume that beer, whether premium, super-premium, popular-price, or so-called price beer can be broadly construed as a single product. One can argue about whether a super-premium such as Michelob and a price beer such as Senator Club are *perfect* substitutes. Undoubtedly the cross-elasticity of demand between a premium beer such as Schlitz and a popular-price beer such as Falstaff is higher than that between the former two. By and large, however, and given the impracticability of separating brands because of the data difficulties, treating all beers as one product will, for the present analytical purposes, do little harm.

The question of market is a more serious one. It is certainly true that all beers do not sell in each and every state or section of the country. The fact that two brands are not in direct competition does not mean, however, that they may not be in indirect competition. First, even where a brand is not available in a state or city it can be a potential competitor whose potential presence on the scene acts as a deterrent to price increases. Second, even though Narragansett does not directly compete with Rainier, both must confront a number of common direct competitors, and the interdependence among brewers becomes quite complex. The ability of Miller to compete with Rainier in Washington is inhibited by the presence of Narragansett in Massachusetts and of Fall City in Kentucky and by Miller's need to divert limited resources in competing with them.

Third, the modern firm does not exist solely in the short term and cannot plan solely in terms of the short term. Firms change their marketing areas and consumer populations shift. The consumer who purchases Olympia beer today may not have the practical option of purchasing Schmidt beer today; but he may have the option tomorrow, either because he moves to a marketing area in which Schmidt is sold or because Schmidt extends its marketing area. Further, Pabst will want to fight for the Olympia customer *both* for his current patronage *and* because if he should move, Pabst will want to secure his business and not see it go to Schmidt.

CONCLUSIONS

The foregoing analysis provides a basis for some policy recommendations with respect to the role of mergers in the future evolution of the brewing industry. The brewing industry is characterized by substantial entry costs of investing in production and distribution facilities. Promotional outlay requirements are large, with uncertain results. Total industry demand has not been growing at a high rate, profits have been moderate, and competition is strong. We suggest that competitive forces will result in a continuing shake-out resulting in the survival of between 15 and 25 healthy firms in the brewing industry.

The nature of the brewing industry and the functions of mergers provide a basis for evaluation of alternative public policies. The number of firms in the industry is likely to decrease whether or not they are absorbed by merger. They lack either the size or management strength to meet the competitive pressures in the industry. At the one extreme, it would be inappropriate for government policy to suspend competition to preserve competitors. At the other extreme, no basis exists for prohibition of all mergers.

Mergers can perform three functions for acquiring firms. First, the merger may provide a brewery and distribution system in a new geographical region. Second, the merger can provide a product and brand name that the weaker firm is incapable of continuing in the face of competition. Third, mergers can enable weaker firms to increase their ability to challenge the leading firms in the industry.

Merger policy in the brewing industry can be used to strengthen further competition. Mergers between healthy competitors should be prohibited because the market power of the combined firm would be increased. But some firms will face demise because of their inability to compete effectively. Other firms will seek to obtain their plants, distribution systems, and brand acceptance. Public policy may appropriately influence such acquisitions in the direction of the firms in the second and third rank in the industry. Acquisitions of failing or floundering firms by firms in the second and third rank or mergers among these firms themselves may strengthen their competitive posture. Such mergers can strengthen the processes of competition in the brewing industry.

5

antitrust and economic efficiency

by SAUL NELSON

There can be no question of the contribution which our antitrust policies have made to our leading industrial position in the world. Nor, conversely, can there be much question that the lack of an equally effective philosophy and policy in other leading industrial nations has been at least in part responsible for their failure to match our economic achievements. In recent years, in fact, they have begun to pay us the tribute of imitation.

By and large, our efforts to maintain effective competition have paid off handsomely in yielding us an efficiently functioning economy. Certainly we must not relax in these efforts since no substitute palatable to a free society is in sight—dare I add, even in the New Industrial State.

STABILITY AND EFFICIENCY GOALS

The preservation of effective competition is peculiarly important today, when we are wrestling with a challenge no industrial nation has yet learned to meet successfully. I refer to the urgency of restoring and maintaining reasonable price stability without sacrificing our goal of maximum utilization of our human and material resources. We must find ways to shift the position of the Phillips Curve and somehow lessen the inflationary bias of a full-employment economy.

The Cabinet Committee on Price Stability which the President has just appointed has this problem high on its agenda. It is instructed, among other responsibilities, to "study intensively and make constructive recommendations concerning all aspects of government policy that affect prices in particular sectors." It is also asked to "recommend suitable legislation which would advance the objective of price stability in a free market economy." In the course of its work it will focus on structural problems which appear to impede the most efficient utilization of our economic resources.

Although the Committee will not be working directly in the antitrust field, it is clear that our success in meeting this challenge—of lessening the inflationary bias of high resource employment—will be largely conditioned by the degree to which we can keep our economy working at maximum efficiency. And in this effort antitrust obviously has an important role to play.

The promotion of economic efficiency through the hard discipline of vigorous competition is, of course, only one of the objectives of antitrust policies. Indeed, it was perhaps the least significant conscious motive in the minds of the legislators who voted for our first antitrust statutes and their successive enlargements. Yet, in broadest perspective, it is precisely in the promotion of economic efficiency that antitrust has made its most notable contribution. And, although it cannot be the sole test against which today's policies should be measured, it must surely be a principal test. In my own judgment, it should be *the* principal test.

I hasten to add that I am in no sense suggesting the substitution of a performance standard as such for our existing legal criteria. Dr. Adams' paper has clearly set forth the impracticality of such an approach. What I am saying is that the basic economic rationale of our antitrust policies and of the rules we have established must rest on their contribution to economic performance, and that this is the test which must be applied to the assessment of our laws regulating business structure and market behavior and to the administration of those laws. By and large they have met this test. It cannot be expected that generally applicable rules can be so framed as to always avoid prohibiting business conduct which would have no significant effect on performance. But we should appropriately question rules which actually impair economic efficiency and administrative decisions which affect performance adversely. Such rules and decisions do not meet our basic test. And, as Dr. Adams has pointed out, the performance criterion is surely relevant in selecting cases for intervention.

In raising these questions I must emphasize that I am speaking for myself and not as a representative of the Council of Economic Advisers. I emphasize this point because some of the questions I will raise are likely to touch rather sensitive issues of policy affecting other government agencies. I should also make it clear that, even for myself, I am raising questions rather than proposing conclusions.

A PROPOSED FRAME OF REFERENCE

First, let us see how far we can agree on our terms of reference. Antitrust has, of course, political and social as well as economic objectives. It seeks to protect the weak against the market power of the strong, and to preserve the institution of the small businessman as far as this is compatible with our current environment. Although steps to further these purposes generally parallel those appropriate to strictly economic goals as well, they cannot always do so. Where divergencies occur, they need to be carefully examined in the light of today's priorities, both short and long-run.

I assume we can agree, too, that antitrust policies and actions must at all times focus on objectives and that intervention in private business decisions should be limited to those instances in which these objectives are in fact, or threaten to be, imperiled. In terms of the strictly economic sphere, I suggest that the appropriate touchstone is the impact of any business practice or decision on the maintenance of effective competition, as this in turn affects the most efficient utilization of our economic resources. Standards of action must be sufficiently flexible to maintain this orientation.

The merger problem is a good example of what I have in mind. Our objections to concentrations of economic power lie in the fact or potential of their misuse especially, though not exclusively, as they may lessen the vigor of competition. And our objection to mergers derives from the same concern. Mergers conflict with our economic objectives to the extent, but only to the extent, that the increased concentration of power opens the door to the possible misuse of that power. And some mergers, at least, hold sufficient potential of improved economic performance to offset, partly or wholly, the dangers stemming from increased concentration or enhanced economic power. Others, though decreasing the number of firms in a market, may actually increase the vigor of competition among those remaining. Obviously, decisions as to whether or not to intervene must follow a careful assessment of all these factors— in other words, on a judgmental cost-benefit analysis. And statistical concentration ratios can be only one of the relevant criteria.

So far, I believe we can still remain in accord on principle. The questions arise largely concerning the weights to be accorded to the several elements of the equation, especially as regards the degree of risk to our objectives that may be tolerable in any specific situation. In those cases in which a merger does promise substantial operating efficiencies, are these thrown fully into the balance against the potential impairment of competitive vigor resulting from a reduction in the number of competitors in the market? This question would appear especially pertinent where the possible injury to competition is envisaged not in the context of the specific merger in question, but rather in the possibility that, although unobjectionable in itself, it may lead to other mergers whose effect would be serious. Does it necessarily follow that abstention in such a case would preclude intervention in others if a dangerous trend actually developed?

CRITERIA OF CASE SELECTION EMPLOYED BY ENFORCEMENT AGENCIES

I would be the last to imply that our antitrust policy has ignored these considerations, but it may be legitimate to ask whether they have all been accorded sufficient weight. The very interesting papers of Ann and Ira Horowitz and of Phillip Areeda are far from the first that have raised this question. But whereas they—

especially Areeda's paper—focus on the decisions of the Courts, I prefer to go back one step—to the decisions of the agencies that brought the actions. I make no pretense of assessing the merits of any of the specific cases referred to in these papers. But I do wonder whether, in deciding to initiate the proceedings, the responsible agency always gave as much weight to possible benefits as to potential risks, both measured in terms of impact on economic efficiency.

It is probably inevitable, in the bureaucratic process, that an official charged with the enforcement of a congressional mandate will tend to act rather than withhold action on doubtful or marginal cases except, perhaps, when he regards the risk of adverse court ruling too great. In doing so he may—perhaps unconsciously —liken his position to that of a prosecutor who will seek an indictment on probable cause, secure in the knowledge that the defendant will have his day in court.

But the situation is simply not analogous. It is just not possible for courts or juries to form reliable independent judgments on the highly complex economic issues involved in antitrust cases. More and more the courts tend to rely not only on the findings of fact of the enforcement agencies, but also on their interpretations of the philosophy of the law. And, of course, even findings of fact can rarely be pure findings of objective fact; they inevitably include inferences and conclusions drawn from the data at hand. As a result, though the cards are not entirely stacked against the respondent, he rarely enjoys a truly even break.

The great weight given by the courts to administrative findings of fact is perfectly illustrated by the March, 1968 Supreme Court ruling on the New England Electric case, which said: "The dissection and evaluation of an economic projection is a function Congress committed to the Commission, not the courts."

The situation differs, of course, between cases brought directly by the Justice Department and those which pass first through the quasi-judicial process of the Federal Trade Commission. Even in the latter, however, similar problems arise. Can hearing examiners and Commissioners really divorce themselves completely from reliance on staff findings and recommendations? And is there not an inescapable tendency to find against the respondents in marginal cases in order to obtain court rulings on difficult issues of policy?

As a practical matter, therefore, the fate of a planned or consummated merger depends very largely on the decision within the antitrust agency as to whether a case should or should not be brought. Inescapably, senior staff recommendations weigh heavily in these decisions, though obviously the Justice Department and the FTC are in somewhat different positions in this regard.

I would therefore restate my questions as follows: Do those who participate in the formulation of agency decisions and are thus largely responsible for the outcome really give due weight to all the potential consequences of a merger—favorable and neutral as well as unfavorable? Do they tend to start with the assumption that any merger which has a significant effect on the concentration ratio is presumptively bad, so that the entire burden of proving it harmless or beneficial falls on the respondents? The cases cited in the Horowitz and Areeda papers leave at least some room for doubt.

As I mentioned earlier, although it is impractical to formulate law in terms of a performance standard, performance should be a legitimate and indeed vital consideration in case selection.

CONGLOMERATE MERGERS

The increasing trend toward conglomerate mergers has become so broad that we turn our backs to it at our peril. Sheer bigness is a matter of real concern, and the diversification of a conglomerate's interests may permit it to compete in a selected area or areas with a very heavy hand to the discomfiture of more specialized concerns. There are times, also, when bigness is associated with sclerosis of the corporate arteries, though this is not peculiarly a conglomerate disease.

On the other hand, and keeping our focus on economic efficiency, there may be significant compensating gains. Thus, does the resulting diversification of risk permit the conglomerate to adopt bolder policies in research, innovation, and marketing? Is its greater ability to compete vigorously in selected fields an unmixed evil? Can the entry of a vigorous conglomerate shake up an industry that has grown too fat and complacent? Is a conglomerate in a better position to resist excessive union demands for increases in compensation far exceeding improvements in productivity? Our policies toward the conglomerate movement, and especially toward specific cases, must weigh all these factors in careful balance.

GOVERNMENT POLICIES WHICH PROTECT
COMPETITORS, NOT COMPETITION

I turn now to another problem area which bears directly on the price structure. Over the years, the distributive spread between primary and retail markets has steadily widened. Between 1947 and 1967, prices of consumer finished goods rose 24 percent at wholesale but 35 percent at retail. For foods the discrepancy was even wider—21 percent at wholesale and twice that—42 percent—at retail. This spread has increased despite notable improvements in the efficiency of the distributive process, especially in food retailing.

Yet this is an area in which antitrust legislation and policies at both the state and federal levels have been far from helpful. In good part this reflects a number of depression-born pieces of legislation—Resale Price Maintenance, Unfair Practices Acts, and the Robinson Patman Act. On the first two of these I expect we will be in general agreement, but probably not on the third. They were all enacted during periods of general business distress and reflected efforts on the part of many small businessmen to keep their heads above water in the face of aggressive new forms of competition. To use the familiar cliché, they were oriented more toward the protection of competitors than of competition.

There are few economists today who would support either resale price maintenance or cost-plus legislation. They were put over by concentrated and very effective campaigns, mainly sparked by retail druggists for the former and retail grocers for the latter. Although their effect has been weakened over the years, partly through adverse court decisions, they still exert an unhappy influence on the retail prices of many commodities in many areas. Let us hope that those that remain will gradually be relegated to the limbo of misbegotten legislation, and the sooner the better.

The Robinson Patman Act raises much more difficult issues. It should be remembered that here too the legislation resulted from highly effective lobbying by a trade group—in this case the wholesale grocers and food brokers who were striving to maintain their economic position in the face of the chain store challenge.

In principle, the Act has on its face the apparently laudable purpose of preventing sellers from discriminating in favor of purchasers with great market power. (However, at least one of its provisions, that dealing with brokerage, was specifically designed to protect a traditional channel of distribution whose services newer channels did not require.) Provisions were also included to permit price differentials related to costs or for the purpose of meeting competition, with the burden of proving such justification—necessarily I suppose—placed on those against whom the complaints might be filed. I need not detail other provisions of the Act, such as those relating to advertising allowances; the principle is essentially the same.

Now for my questions, some of which relate to the Act itself and some to its administration. They stem from the obvious proposition that the focus of the Act was on a concept of equity and not of economic efficiency, and that its provisions all relate not to preventing cost or price increases, but to restricting cost or price reductions. I wonder, therefore, to what extent the prohibitions of the Act, backed by treble damage penalties, may have tended to introduce or strengthen rigidities in our price system. In its absence, changes in market conditions could readily be reflected in concessions first to one buyer and then another, with some tendency of the entire price structure to ratchet down as markets weaken. With the Act, the seller must reduce his price all along the line or not at all; this obviously is a more difficult decision to make. Of course those who failed to get concessions in the first instance would be at a temporary disadvantage; the question is whether this might not be balanced by greater flexibility of the entire price structure.

Along the same lines, one might question whether it is really in the true interest of the economy as a whole to weaken the bargaining position of large buyers, especially in dealing with large sellers. Would prices be lower if Sears Roebuck and A&P and Kroger were free to make the best bargains they can with their suppliers, and might this not be beneficial to the community at large? Has the proliferation of private brands, stimulated partly by the restrictions of the Act, been a really desirable development? Again, let me emphasize that I merely raise these questions; I do not pretend to answer them.

However, the Act is on the books, its repeal in the foreseeable future is most unlikely, and we must live with it. This need not preclude us from raising some questions about its administration and interpretation, again bearing in mind the extent to which the views of the antitrust agencies tend to influence court decisions.

Has the Act been so administered as to minimize its interference with business price and marketing practices which do not clearly fall within its prohibitions? Or has it gradually been extended to doubtful or marginal cases, and has there been a tendency progressively to erode the flexibility which could be provided by a liberal interpretation of the provisions permitting discrimination reflecting cost differences or for the purpose of meeting competition?

The recent Supreme Court decision on the Utah Pie case (386 U.S. 689) strikes me as a good illustration of the lengths to which the Act has been extended. Although this case was not brought by the Commission, it is reasonable to assume that the court was influenced by previous Commission actions of a not dissimilar nature. As I read this case, damages were awarded by the jury to Utah Pie against Pet Milk and several other respondents because the latter, in meeting Utah Pie's prices for frozen pies, sold their products at levels lower than they charged in other markets. As a result of the increased competition, the entire price structure in the area declined, to the clear benefit of the consumers. Despite this competition, Utah Pie was able to retain the largest single share of the market and to continue to earn substantial profits.

The Court of Appeals reversed the verdict on the ground that there was no proven injury to competition, but the Supreme Court reversed the Court of Appeals and found in favor of Utah Pie. Part of the Supreme Court's decision rested on the proposition that the decline in prices resulting from the action of Pet and the other respondents could properly be construed as injury to competition! I find myself far more in accord with the dissenting opinion by Mr. Justice Stewart, who said, in part: "But lower prices are the hallmark of intensified competition." Nor do I find a shred of *economic* logic in a proposition which would limit the respondents' freedom to engage in effective price competition with the dominant seller in the Utah market by their willingness to cut prices correspondingly in all their other markets.

This may be an extreme illustration, but I think that it does raise a very legitimate question as to whether the trend of interpretations of the Act may not be hampering rather than preserving and strengthening competition. Have we been gradually moving toward the position that price discrimination is evil per se, even though it may actually invigorate competition in a market? Does the present trend of interpretation unduly restrict the free play of competition in local markets? Have we given any weight at all to the price benefits that might flow from marginally questionable acts of discrimination?

CONCLUSIONS

I have limited my analysis to mergers and price discrimination because these seem to me the areas of antitrust activity in which there may be most need for a very careful look at our economic objectives. I hasten to add—if that be necessary—that I fully share the concern of the antitrust agencies regarding the implications of the merger movement, and believe that their intervention has been justified in the great majority of cases. Similarly, the Robinson Patman Act is on the books and, regardless of any reservations as to its principles, the congressional mandate must be executed. In both instances, however, there may be room for giving greater weight to economic efficiency in the interpretation of the law and in the selection of cases.

Vigilant and vigorous antitrust enforcement is essential to the health of our economy. The preservation of effective competition must be a major reliance toward our objective of having our economy function at its full potential. But let us make sure that the actions we take under our antitrust laws are truly consistent with that objective, and that our decisions to intervene or abstain in particular cases are even-handed in our assessments of their impact on the effective functioning of our economy. It is the policies and decisions of our antitrust agencies rather than of our courts which will primarily influence the outcome.

6

structure, performance, and behavior

by J. FRED WESTON

The recent trend of Supreme Court decisions, as pointed out in Professor Areeda's paper, has been increasingly to apply the structural tests to mergers. Professor Areeda's paper raised some questions about this philosophy which were further explored in the discussion. The flavor of the discussion can be conveyed by beginning with a brief summary of the case for the application of structural standards set forth in Professor Adams' paper and restated in compact form during the discussion.

THE THEORETICAL CASE FOR THE APPLICATION OF STRUCTURAL STANDARDS

It is argued that a highly concentrated industry is likely to result in oligopolistic awareness of rivals, actions, and reactions. This produces spontaneous collusion among the small number of firms whose output and sales account for a high percentage of industry output. These dominant firms will discipline or coerce the remainder of the industry to administer and control prices. One form of administrative price control is price leadership. As a consequence of administered prices, output will be limited, prices will be high, overcapacity will result, and excess profits will be earned by the oligopolists. The result is similar to that in an industry characterized by monopoly.

The case for the structural standards is rooted in a foundation of economic theory. It is supported on both economic grounds and the economic liberal philosophy of political freedom achieved through the operation of relatively small economic units.

In a philosophic sense, if industries can be maintained in a competitive structure, then the market place will be the regulator of economic activity. In economic reasoning, a structurally competitive market will be conducive to competitive behavior, which, in turn, will achieve economically desirable performance.

Another advantage argued for the structural approach represents a divergence in the definition of the attitudes of "economic liberals." During the 1930's one branch of the liberal economic point of view argued that government regulation in the public interest was a desirable alternative to competition. It argued that, given the undesirable structure of industry, government regulation of oligopolies was necessary to preserve the public interest and to obtain reasonably adequate performance.

However, the emphasis of the structural approach represents a different "liberal economic" point of view. If a competitive system can be maintained in the structural sense, then the market place will be the regulator of economic activity. This then makes it possible to dispense with the "visible and heavy hand" of government to do society's regulating of individual industry.

The second liberal position is based on the view that performance of government regulatory agencies has been poor in protecting the public interest or in achieving efficient economic performance of industries regulated. The advantage argued for the structural standard, therefore, is that the alternative, the performance standard, is essentially a regulatory concept. The structural standard relies on competition and on the market place to achieve behavior and performance representing desirable achievements from the standpoint of the operation of the industry and the economy.

The relationship between structure, performance, and behavior was developed in the following terms: It was suggested that structure and behavior have one element in common—they tend mainly to be prohibitory standards. Performance, on the other hand, is regarded as a regulatory standard. Structure and behavior are prohibitory standards seeking to prevent undesirable conditions or events from occurring. Performance, on the other hand, is a result.

In stating the case for the use of the structural standard, it was argued that the performance record of an industry would not necessarily be ignored. It was suggested that the antitrust authorities should make some sort of judgment as to the performance record of an industry. A ranking of industries could then be achieved on the basis of these judgments of their performance. The antitrust authorities should then move vigorously against mergers and other acts which would tend to result in deteriorated structure for those industries that rank low by the criteria of performance. On the other hand, industries with good performance records, even though they may not meet structural tests, would be less subject to antitrust action in response to mergers and other events.

Thus, performance is not ignored but rather used as a device for setting priorities in connection with selecting among those industries and events that would receive the main attention of the resources of the antitrust agencies. A judgment of a relative performance record would be used as a relative priority for allocating the time, attention, and resources of the antitrust agencies.

EVALUATION OF STRUCTURAL APPROACH

Some mergers would have an adequate legal defense if they met certain general tests. The two general acceptable legal defenses of mergers are (1) the failing firm doctrine and (2) *de minimus* effects —cases in which the size of firms involved was so small that the effects on structure could not be great.

But aside from these two defenses on which there was general agreement, a number of reasons were presented why strict application of the structural standards could have undesirable effects. The arguments could be placed under the general rubric of efficiency. How elements of efficiency were created or enhanced by a merger were spelled out in a number of ways, and some illustrations from specific industries were used as a vehicle for conveying the concepts. In the brewing industry, many firms merged. One of the reasons appeared to be that some of the firms were below minimum efficient size. Their only hope for achieving minimal efficient size was by joining with other firms.

Another factor in the brewing industry was that for a period of years the total demand for beer was relatively constant. Some firms were efficient, aggressive, growing, and obtaining a larger portion of the relatively fixed demand. Thus inherently some of the individual firms had to fall by the wayside. They could preserve more of their values by selling out to the more successful firms.

Another possible efficiency of a merger was illustrated by the Von's merger. It was argued that the effects on concentration ruled out any plausible probability that monopoly was the motive. The discussion suggested the possibility that there was a management problem in Shopping Bag. A merger which pooled Von's relatively more efficient management into Shopping Bag would thereby increase over-all efficiency.

Related to this consideration is the possession by one of the firms involved in a merger of a wide range of managerial abilities, engineering skills, or historical experience which were not possessed by the other firm and which could be achieved by the other firm only with considerable time lags and with large outlays whose success would be uncertain. An extreme form of such an advantage would be the possession by one firm of patents which would prevent the other firm from entry. But this was cited merely to illustrate the point as an extreme form of an important economic or managerial advantage that might be possessed by one of the firms.

Another argument was that if one of the firms involved in the merger had started out as a small firm and was highly efficient, it would have a motive in selling out for tax considerations. There are advantages to the new, small firm selling out on a capital gains basis: (1) A future stream of potential (uncertain) earnings is realized on an immediate capital gains basis. (2) A tax on ordinary income is changed to a tax on capital gains, with a much lower rate. These two aspects of the capital gains form of return represent private advantages with little justification from a social standpoint. However, social advantages are also involved. The creation and vigor of a market in capital assets stimulates both the availability of entry capital and entry into any given industry. Since entry or potential entry has desirable competitive effects, a vigorous market for capital assets is desirable.

The computer industry was cited as another example of why mergers might perform desirable public functions from an economic performance standpoint. It was suggested that firms below a certain size do not have the resources necessary to invest and stay in the computer industry. This represents a problem of critical mass. A relatively small number of large firms is thus implied as the final structural characteristic of the industry. And again, to reach this end result without serious losses to smaller firms that initially entered the industry, mergers would play a socially useful function.

DEFENSE OF THE STRUCTURAL STANDARDS

Supporters of the structural tests offered rebuttal against the foregoing arguments. Where it is argued that economic justification for a merger is to achieve efficiencies or economies, the strict application of structural tests may not necessarily have harmful effects. If the achievement of efficiencies or economies of scale by merger are prevented, the firm has an escape hatch. It can grow internally to achieve economies of scale or reassess and improve its operations in order to achieve efficiencies.

A specific example was cited in connection with the prohibition of the Bethlehem and Youngstown merger. The companies had argued that the merger was necessary to enable them to compete more effectively with the larger firms in the industry. The merger was prohibited. Then it was stated that Bethlehem, "for the first time in its history," built a new plant in a new location. The argument was made further that the prohibition of acquisition of Kinney Shoes by Brown did not prevent Brown from setting up a chain of retail stores on its own. Also, it was pointed out that Von's Grocery had established new supermarket locations as well as having bought existing locations.

Counterarguments were made to these points. The efficiency argument is not destroyed by the fact that Bethlehem built a new plant: we do not know whether what was accomplished by building the new plant could have been accomplished more efficiently or cheaply by the merger. In the Von's Grocery case it was argued that clearly monopoly considerations were not involved. Therefore, the only factor involved must have been business efficiencies. Indeed, differences in relative efficiencies between the managements of Von's and

Shopping Bag would have resulted in increased over-all efficiency by a merger of the two companies.

Another line of criticism directed against the structural approach pointed out that the yardsticks for applying a structural test for evaluating mergers have not been developed. The items to be measured were: the size of firm, its rank in the industry, its market share, and the conditions of entry into the industry. But no specific standards were formulated for any of these four criteria of (1) size, (2) rank, (3) market share, and (4) conditions of entry. If measurement standards are not formulated, the structural approach cannot be operational. Furthermore, it was argued that it was difficult to specify when a merger has undesirable effects in terms of structure. If a market consists of 100 equal-sized firms, a merger by any two could be assumed not to have anticompetitive effect. At what point anticompetitive effects would be discernible could not be specified. Is the critical number 50 firms? 30 firms? or 20 firms?

The answer to this position given by the proponents of the structural approach reflected the arguments made in a series of Supreme Court decisions. It was urged that the discussion missed the emphasis of Section 7 of the Clayton Act in seeking to arrest "a tendency toward substantial lessening of competition." The spirit of Section 7 of the Clayton Act is to prevent mergers that result in an industry structure moving in the wrong direction. Thus it was argued that it was unnecessary to specify the precise point at which an industry structure results in the undesirable economic consequences that have been proscribed. It was argued that the case for the structural test is that although it is imperfect, it is a better proxy for potential restriction of output than any kind of performance test that could be devised. "Neither economists nor lawyers are able to measure efficiencies or restrictions of output directly. Nor do we know how to weigh efficiencies or possible restrictions of output against one another directly."

This view argued further that although a change from five to four or from four to three firms might not be demonstrably a change in the market for the worse, "every time oligopoly is made a little tighter, it makes it possible for the parties to engage in collective but noncollusive decisions." Oligopolistic awareness and spontaneous collusions are thereby facilitated. Furthermore, every time the number of decision-making centers is reduced, the dispersion of power over decisions is decreased. Thus, the random forces operating on innovation are also diminished. The effects both on competition under static assumptions and on the long-run growth of the economy through technical dynamism and innovation are diminished.

IMPLICATIONS OF STRUCTURAL STANDARDS FOR INDUSTRIES ALREADY CONCENTRATED

But if industry structure per se is of such vital importance in determining industry performance; indeed, if it is of such great significance that a movement in the direction of concentration is undesirable, this leaves the structural approach open to another line of criticism. The emphasis of the structural approach on prohibiting mergers that move industries in the direction of greater concentration is internally illogical in that it does not at all get at industries whose structure is already concentrated and therefore undesirable from the standpoint of the criteria of the structural approach. In this regard it was argued that a wide variety of industries would be presumed to have undesirable performance and behavior if the implicit assumptions of the structural test were valid.

The examples were then cited of two industries in which concentration is relatively high and therefore rate low by the structural tests. Furthermore, these two industries, autos and steel, have been subject to a considerable amount of criticism from some sources. With regard to the auto industry, it was argued that, despite very high concentration, both the performance and behavior record were excellent except for safety. And it was argued that consumer demand demonstrated that consumers did not want safety and were unwilling to buy it. Indeed, now when the installation of safety devices is required by government, in many cases consumers do not utilize them. With regard to the steel industry, it was suggested that its behavior would probably not have been changed by adding 10 or 20 more firms.

Counterarguments to these points stated that the auto industry's performance record was not absolved by consumer attitudes toward safety; in fact automobile companies determine or control consumer attitudes through their heavy advertising expenditures. In rebuttal, it was argued that a rational approach to advertising expenditures would emphasize those elements to which the consumer would respond. The automobile companies could achieve higher profits by selling safety devices in their advertising, if consumers would respond to such appeals.

With regard to the steel industry, the proponents of the structural test argued that more efficiency could be forced through opening up the industry to increased foreign competition by reducing tariffs, etc. Others suggested that this was not necessarily a complete answer for a number of reasons. Given that the steel industry operates with heavy fixed costs and relatively small marginal costs, foreign competition may represent a form of dumping. The dumping problem is further aggravated by the tendency of some foreign governments to subsidize their steel industry in order to have a basic steel industry. Given the large ratio of overhead to total costs in the steel industry, the existence of a foreign steel company in itself might encourage various forms of price discrimination in international trade. The many forms of potential price discrimination make it difficult to determine the relevant costs, making antidumping laws impossible to enforce and rendering uncertain whether foreign imports represent competitive or discriminatory pricing.

The issues opened by the foregoing exchange were pushed further by critics of the use of structural standards. It was argued that a wide variety of industries in which concentration is high and structure by any type of structural standard would be judged undesirable had favorable performance records. Attention was called to many forms of nonprice competition which take place. It was argued that an important expression of the competition is in the form of product improvement. Thus, even conventional measurements of price performance did not adequately measure industry performance because of continuous and steady quality improvement.

FORMULATION OF INDUSTRY STANDARDS

Documentation of excellence of performance and behavior of highly concentrated industries over a wide range of the United States industrial spectrum would raise an even more fundamental series of questions for the use of structural standards. What is really the norm for competitive industry? The structural test implies that the norm is industries composed of many small firms. But given technological and economic trends throughout the world, it was argued that industries composed of many small firms are not the norm. The aircraft industry was pointed to as one in which, for any generation of commercial aircraft, the size of the market in relation to the fixed costs involved was such that it was unlikely that more than two firms could be supported and highly probable that not more than three firms could be supported. The computer industry was pointed to as another example.

It was argued similarly that in the automobile industry the most we could hope for in terms of efficiently operated enterprises would be two or three additional firms, in which case the automobile industry would still rate low by strict application of structural tests. It was further suggested that the addition of two or three firms to the automobile industry could not make much difference to the performance or behavior of the industry.

A related line of argument follows from the inconsistency between the implications of the structural standard and the performance of highly concentrated industries. To determine whether effects of structure are appreciable and to know whether they are in the wrong direction, it is necessary to have an understanding of industry processes. But if an understanding of industry processes is developed, most of what is required for application of performance and behavioral tests has been accomplished. Thus a meaningful application of structural standards would require sufficient understanding of industry processes to make performance and behavioral tests readily applicable.

This view was reinforced by another stream of observations. It was pointed out that technology is destroying traditional industry classifications and makes nonsense out of concentration ratio measurements and the structural tests. Is there a chemical industry or is there a petroleum industry? Perhaps it is now a petrochemical industry. But entry by firms from other industries into the petrochemical industry would require redefinition of that industry. Concentration ratios in the aluminum industry are traditionally measured in terms of the firms that are predominantly aluminum producers. But the aluminum association has almost as many copper producers in it making aluminum products as it has aluminum producers. A fundamental trend is that basic materials are disappearing. The steel industry is now making materials to specification. It is developing new alloys which use much less steel. Some plastics are stronger than heavy steel. With these kinds of trends structural tests become less and less relevant to market reality.

More specifically it was argued that structural tests and the law are designed as negative prohibitories to remove interferences with competition. But the structural tests put blinders on and do not analyze what is interfering with competition. The only way to determine whether anything is interfering with competition is to look at the market place. "You cannot determine what the interferences to competition are by indirection—it cannot be done by structural mirrors."

It was argued further that application of performance and behavior tests was not as difficult as sometimes argued. Empirical behavior experience can be utilized. An example cited by one of the discussants referred to the second American Tobacco Case. Three firms in the tobacco industry had over 90 percent of the market. At a time when demand and cost were both reportedly falling, prices were increased. If the firms had been behaving oligopolistically they would have been behaving oligopolistically before the price increase. Such price behavior, it was suggested, could be taken as an indication of the shift from competitive relations between oligopolists to collusion among them.

The defense made to these criticisms by proponents of the structural test, or standard, was a restatement of the spirit of Section 7 of the Clayton Act. It was argued that mergers which result in increased concentration are moving industry structure in an undesirable direction. The issue was not joined as to whether the delays in achieving an efficient industry structure for international competition might have irremediable losses in terms of relative efficiency of large international firms. It could not be assumed that the individual firms could develop economies and efficiencies internally at a rate of speed or at a cost that would enable them to maintain their position in various domestic and international markets. The well-known difficulty of displacing a firm once it has developed a market share position and consumer allegiance is multiplied in foreign markets. A wide variety of government, social, and cultural relations must be established before effective operations are on stream in a foreign market. A firm which has a number of years head start over other foreign firms in such markets has a position which may, from a practical standpoint, be recognized as impregnable.

POTENTIALLY UNDESIRABLE EFFECTS OF
APPLICATION OF STRUCTURAL STANDARDS

Finally, arguments against the structural test were mounted in terms of specific undesirable economic consequences. A number of illustrations were given, in part hypothetical, of how the application of structural standards would not only delay and impair movements toward economies of scale and efficiency but have specific negative economic consequences as well. Suppose, for example, that three firms in the automobile industry are highly efficient and the fourth is less efficient. If the fourth disappears, the remaining three firms are subject to increased antitrust attack on structural grounds, whether the fourth firm is merged into one of the three or whether it disappears from the industry. With this kind of antitrust atmosphere there is pressure on the three efficient firms to preserve, under some umbrella, the fourth firm. As a consequence, such antitrust atmosphere may, in fact, produce output restriction and higher prices in order to make it possible for the fourth firm to survive. Thus, such an antitrust atmosphere might produce consequences similar to oligopolistic collusion or monopoly behavior, which, in a more enlightened public policy environment, would not have occurred.

Another undesirable consequence of the emphasis of the structural test was illustrated by the brewing industry. Human and physical resources used by firms in the brewing industry are somewhat specialized to the industry. To the extent that firms fearing antitrust attack take the path of internal growth rather than merger, the resources of the unsuccessful firms must be transferred to some other industries. To the degree that specialization of resources exists, these transferred resources are somewhat less productive than they would have been if transferred to another brewing firm.

CONCLUDING APOLOGY

The foregoing summary of the discussion on the relationship between structure, performance, and behavior is not intended to be comprehensive or complete. There were time limitations to the discussion. Furthermore, the proponents of the structural approach were necessarily in the position of the affirmative side of a debate, defending a positive position subject to attack from a variety of approaches. In concluding this discussion with a mounting array of criticisms of the structural approach, the intention is not to convey that this was the consensus of the group, nor is it intended that this is a final or definitive evaluation of the structural approach.

What this summary of the discussion has sought to do is simply to delineate the numerous issues that were opened and the many possibilities that were identified. Only limited empirical information on the conflicting propositions was brought to bear on the discussion. An agenda for further additional empirical research and analysis was developed.

IMPLICATIONS OF PROFITABILITY STUDIES

7

industry structure and price-cost margins

by NORMAN R. COLLINS AND LEE E. PRESTON

It is a fundamental proposition of economic theory that prices and profits are higher, and price-cost margins wider, under conditions of monopoly than under conditions of competition, all other things being equal. This proposition is unassailable on its own terms, but its substantive relevance for the explanation of price and profit results in a world of oligopolists and monopolistic competitors has been repeatedly questioned. In particular, scholars and policy-makers have asked whether there was any connection between the closeness of an industry to monopolistic structure—as indicated, for example, by concentration data—and its closeness to monopolistic behavior in the form of output restriction and price increase.

We have been engaged for some time in the study of this question, with a special focus on the concentration statistics prepared by the Bureau of the Census for the Senate Subcommittee on Antitrust and Monopoly, and on profit indicators that can also be computed from census data. The present paper is a summary report on our results to date and a presentation of selected findings from our current work. In the first section we set forth our principal hypothesis and examine the average percentage price-cost margin as a profit indicator. In the second section we summarize the main results of our analysis of concentration and margin data for 1958, and present some findings from a study of 1963 census data now in progress. The final section points out a few general conclusions and questions for further study.[1]

THE RESEARCH HYPOTHESIS

We began these investigations several years ago with the question: Does measured concentration really explain anything? In particular, we asked ourselves whether the high-prices-and-profits prediction of economic theory would be borne out if measured shares of a small number of large firms were taken as indicators of the closeness of industry structure to the theoretical condition of monopoly. This question, of course, has been raised by others, but a survey of previous studies revealed a great variety of research approaches and findings with no general and clear conclusion. The previous studies varied in time periods covered (both dates and length), in size of sample and method of selection, in concentration measure and profit indicator selected for analysis, and in other respects. The results range from the finding of a strong association between measured concentration and profitability to the opposite extreme. In brief, it appeared that an attempt to analyze all of the available recent data on a comprehensive and comparable basis would be justified.[2] We therefore began with the hypothesis, simply

[1]An earlier, published report dealing with a single industry group is Norman R. Collins and Lee E. Preston, "Concentration and Price-Cost Margins in Food Manufacturing Industries," *Journal of Industrial Economics*, XIV, 3 (July 1966), 226–242. A complete report on our analysis of the 1958 data, together with a detailed comparison of results from previous, related studies, is contained in Collins and Preston, *Concentration and Price-Cost Margins in Manufacturing Industries* (Berkeley: University of California Press, May, 1968). This latter publication is drawn upon extensively, and without detailed footnoting, throughout.

[2]The principal previous studies are summarized and a secondary analysis of them reported in Collins and Preston, *Concentration and Price-Cost Margins in Manufacturing Industries*, Chap. II.

stated, that interindustry differences in measured concentration would be positively related to interindustry differences in the relationship between prices and cost and, therefore, to differences in profitability.

In the selection of data for analysis, choice is effectively limited to the SIC category system and the concentration ratios computed by the Bureau of the Census if a large collection of comparable observations is to be obtained. In addition, the comprehensiveness and prominence of these data suggested that their specific explanatory and predictive relevance should be carefully examined. The profitability indicator to be examined presented more difficult selection problems. Most of the previous studies had used some measure of rate of return on assets or equity as the basis for analysis. However, rate-of-return data are not available on a comprehensive basis for the same defined industries as the basic concentration data (SIC four-digit industries). Thus, previous investigators have resorted either to (1) developing their own series of profit data from miscellaneous sources or (2) averaging basic concentration data in order to produce a series comparable to available rate-of-return data, or (3) some combination of these procedures.

It appeared to us that all of these approaches were subject to serious question in themselves, and that they gave rise to doubt as to the significance of particular research results and to ambiguity about their mutual consistency or inconsistency. Therefore, it seemed desirable to compute a profitability indicator from the source data underlying the concentration ratios themselves. The indicator selected was the average percentage price-cost margin, computed as the ratio of total direct costs to total value-of-industry shipments. The details of this computation are set forth in Appendix A, at the end of this chapter.

The percentage price-cost margin was selected both for its computability and for its more general conceptual relevance. As a profitability indicator for our purposes, it has some obvious attractions as well as some disadvantages. In principle, the market structure model we are trying to test deals with the relation between prices and costs, and with the discrepancy between them that gives rise to profits. The profitability of the firm as a fiscal unit—involving debt-equity ratios, degree of financial consolidation, intertemporal shifts of income and expense for tax purposes, etc.—is a different matter. The margin is, if anything, the simpler concept, and its computation is subject to a smaller number of essentially arbitrary or extraneous adjustments. The major deficiency in the margin as a profit indicator arises from the varying importance of fixed costs among industries. Under equally competitive long-run conditions, margins over variable costs would be higher in industries with higher fixed-variable cost ratios. Thus, if there are substantial variations in the importance of fixed or capital costs among industries, these variations must be specifically taken into account in the interpretation of margin data.

Margins and Other Profit Measures

An immediate question arises as to the relationship between percentage margins computed on this basis and more orthodox measures of profitability, such as rates of return on sales, assets, and equity, both before and after taxes. A formal comparison of these several series can be made only on the basis of two-digit industry data, for which all of the series can be readily obtained. The relevant data are shown in Table 1, for both 1958 and 1963, and simple correlations between margins and other indicators for each year are tabulated there.[3]

The rate-of-return data for the two periods are substantially comparable, and most industries show increases in one or more rate-of-return measures for 1963 as compared to 1958. The increases in margins between the two periods cannot be taken at face value, however, because the 1958 data have been adjusted to take account of some additional cost elements which are not removed from the 1963 data. (If unadjusted data are compared, however, margin

---

[3]These correlations, and some of the results presented below, exclude data for SIC 29—petroleum and coal products. Data for this industry are reported on a quite different basis for SEC and census purposes. For example, reported census industry shipments are approximately one-half of reported SEC industry sales, by far the greatest discrepancy in the data and a clear indication that the financial profit record of the constituent firms contains substantial contributions from their nonmanufacturing (e.g., crude oil production and transportation) activities. Because profits in this industry are accounted to the earlier stages of the production process, the industry shows very low value added by manufacture (relative to shipments) and, therefore, low price-cost margins as we compute them, in spite of high over-all rates of profit on capital. The special tax position of the industry also results in an unusual discrepancy between rates of return before and after taxes, as compared to the pattern in other industries.

TABLE 1

Profit and Price-cost Margin Data for Twenty 2-digit Industry Groups, 1958 and 1963

SIC Code	INDUSTRY GROUPS	1958 PROFITS						1958 Price-Cost Margin (adjusted)	1963 PROFITS						1963 Price-Cost Margin (unadjusted)
		Before Taxes as % of:			After Taxes as % of:				Before Taxes as % of:			After Taxes as % of:			
		Sales	Assets	Shareholders' Equity	Sales	Assets	Shareholders' Equity		Sales	Assets	Shareholders' Equity	Sales	Assets	Shareholders' Equity	
20	Food and kindred products	4.48	11.30	17.42	2.24	5.64	8.70	14.50	4.74	11.14	18.03	2.36	5.55	8.99	19.24
21	Tobacco manufactures	11.20	17.07	28.22	5.35	8.16	13.49	27.33	12.13	18.23	27.57	5.87	8.83	13.35	29.86
22	Textile mill products	3.36	5.02	7.39	1.57	2.35	3.46	11.70	4.77	7.82	12.36	2.34	3.84	6.06	17.39
23	Apparel and related products	2.25	6.21	11.63	.96	2.64	4.94	14.66	3.02	8.01	16.81	1.37	3.65	7.67	20.10
24	Lumber and products	5.12	6.86	10.46	2.80	3.75	5.72	10.49	5.14	7.53	12.93	3.27	4.78	8.21	18.28
25	Furniture and fixtures	4.43	8.93	13.67	2.04	4.11	6.29	16.28	4.87	10.46	16.98	2.37	5.08	8.26	22.80
26	Paper and allied products	9.26	10.93	15.72	4.74	5.60	8.06	17.64	8.64	10.39	15.56	4.51	5.42	8.12	23.76
27	Printing and publishing	6.85	10.81	18.19	3.13	5.33	8.97	23.07	6.51	10.17	18.92	3.15	4.92	9.15	30.69
28	Chemical and allied products	12.76	14.44	20.86	6.95	7.87	11.37	31.45	14.02	16.04	24.14	7.49	8.58	12.91	39.70
29	Petroleum and coal products	10.06	7.94	10.77	9.26	7.32	9.92	5.63	12.08	9.52	12.92	10.55	8.31	11.28	14.42
30	Rubber products	7.15	11.37	18.55	3.50	5.58	9.10	18.73	6.86	10.67	17.62	3.58	5.57	9.20	25.11
31	Leather and leather products	3.77	7.85	12.72	1.68	3.50	5.66	15.33	3.66	7.82	14.24	1.78	3.79	6.90	20.20
32	Stone, clay, & glass products	12.44	13.62	18.77	6.76	7.40	10.20	24.60	9.95	11.28	16.38	5.29	6.00	8.71	31.17
33	Primary metal industries	9.85	9.09	12.93	5.16	4.76	6.77	14.51	8.91	8.60	7.46	5.00	4.83	4.19	20.47
34	Fabricated metal products	6.34	10.07	15.07	3.06	4.87	7.28	16.20	6.35	10.32	16.40	3.21	5.21	8.28	23.43
35	Machinery, except electrical	7.76	9.42	14.53	3.65	4.44	6.85	17.54	9.48	12.32	19.39	4.70	6.10	9.60	25.39
36	Electrical machinery	7.65	12.18	20.42	3.82	6.09	10.22	20.73	7.42	11.49	19.88	3.75	5.81	10.05	25.89
37	Transportation equipment	6.21	9.63	16.49	3.34	5.17	8.86	15.08	10.80	17.76	30.82	5.33	8.76	15.21	19.67
38	Instruments & related prods.	11.31	15.03	22.13	5.43	7.22	10.63	23.79	11.95	15.79	24.08	6.00	7.92	12.08	33.99
39	Miscellaneous manufactures[a]	6.30	10.53	16.95	3.03	5.06	8.15	16.17	6.71	9.39	17.91	3.30	4.62	8.82	23.72
	r^2—margin with each profit measure, respective years (SIC 29 excluded)[b]	.625	.748	.686	.589	.745	.715	—	.549	.346	.229	.523	.378	.268	—

Source: Federal Trade Commission and Securities and Exchange Commission, *Quarterly Financial Report for Manufacturing Corporations*, and Census data. Quarterly data were aggregated to obtain annual figures.

[a] Data include Ordnance Group.

[b] All values significant at 5 percent level or better.

increases are shown in all but two groups.) In spite of the adjust-ment problem, the two margin series are highly correlated between the two dates ($r = .96$).

For each year taken separately, margins show a significant cor-relation with every other profit indicator examined. The correla-tions between margins and profits as a percent of sales, which would be expected to be the strongest on a priori grounds, are roughly comparable between the two periods. The correlations with returns on assets and equity, however, are much stronger for 1958 than for 1963. An averaging of rates of return over several years reduces these discrepancies somewhat, but it does seem clear that margins were more closely associated with other profit measures (other than rates of return on sales) in the earlier than in the later period.[4] Rather than argue which, if either, of these patterns repre-sents the typical relationship between margins and rates of return, we simply note two points: (1) even the weakest associations found in the data are far from negligible—thus, to a considerable extent, both types of measures are indicative of similar underlying condi-tions; and (2) on conceptual grounds, the margin is a valid measure of the price-cost discrepancy, which is the focal point of the simple market structure model under investigation.

Some Qualifications

Whatever the profitability indicator selected for analysis, any attempt to relate profitability to industry structure is subject to a number of important qualifications. Four of these requiring brief mention are: (1) the short-run nature of the observations, (2) the presence of monopoly costs which may distort the price-cost rela-tionship, (3) interindustry differences in the elasticity of demand, and (4) the industry classifications and reporting procedures used to generate the data.

[4]Inspection of the data shows that the difference in the correlation results is due primarily to SIC 37—transportation equipment—which experienced a very substantial increase in rates of return in 1963 as compared to 1958. A secondary effect is the failure of SIC 21—tobacco manufactures—to participate in the general expansion of margins and profits during the post-1960 years. It is notable that these two two-digit groups are peculiarly dominated by in-dividual four-digit industries (motor vehicles and cigarettes, respectively), both of which are highly concentrated, but which experienced roughly opposite changes in over-all demand and general market development during the period under study.

The problem of testing long-run models with short-run observations is typical in economic research. Fortunately, neither concentration nor measured profitability on an industry basis is subject to erratic short-term fluctuations. In addition, the basic protection against an erroneous short-run finding is the repeated analysis of similar data at different time periods. This, of course, is another reason for attempting to focus on a comprehensive analysis of census data, which do permit the comparison of successive studies over time.

The possibility that costs, rather than profits, might rise as a result of protected market positions is perhaps more serious, because if such a phenomenon were widespread, it could completely obscure the expected monopoly-profit relationship. Costs might rise either because of the organizational slack and loose management that might grow up within a protected market, or because of expense preferences on the part of managers and owners of large firms. Several studies have attempted to estimate and take account of such possible cost elements, and they can be accepted as a priori of some significance. However, there is no indication that such behavior would result in costs great enough to offset totally any underlying profits relationship. In any event, to the extent that monopoly costs do arise, then the measured profit relationship would understate the true effect of market structure on price levels.

A particularly troublesome and intractable problem is the effect of interindustry differences in elasticity of market demand. Although two perfectly competitive industries, with identical cost structures, should show the same (i.e., "normal") profitability regardless of interindustry differences in demand elasticity, two monopolized industries will not. On the contrary, under conditions of monopoly, margins and profits should vary systematically and inversely with elasticity of industry demand. If reliable and appropriate estimates of industry demand elasticities were available, they might be introduced into our analysis as explanatory variables. Failing that, we may examine our results to see whether observed differences in profitability appear to reflect elasticity differences that might be inferred a priori. An alternative approach would be to assume that when the number of firms of significant size is greater than three or four, the elasticity of *firm* demand is only loosely related to that of the relevant industry, and, thus, that the elasticity-margin relationship found in the monopoly case is not to be expected.

A final group of qualifications arises with respect to the industry classifications and reporting procedures used to generate the data, and particularly with respect to geographic coverage. Although detailed geographic data have been tabulated on occasion for a few industries, the main body of available concentration data shows shares of certain numbers of large firms in the total national activity of their industries. If all of the firms operate on a nationwide basis, the computed ratio will be a representative indicator of average concentration levels throughout the country. However, if each of the major firms operates primarily in a different regional market, then the typical level of concentration in any market area will be higher than the nationwide ratio. Other investigators of these problems have adopted a variety of means of taking these possible discrepancies into account. Our own approach is based upon a crude index of geographic market dispersion, explained in detail in Appendix A.

Research Hypothesis: Summary Statement

The research hypothesis under analysis may now be formally stated as follows: Interindustry differences in the relationship between gross revenues and current costs will be positively associated with the relative concentration of industry activity among a few firms, when account is taken of differences in capital requirements and the geographic comparability of industrial markets. In other words, the higher the level of concentration, the more nearly actual profitability results will approach the monopoly solution.

As noted above, this hypothesis does not formally take into account the impact of differences on the demand side or a detailed consideration of the effect of monopoly on costs. Nor does it specify the behavioral mechanism by which these profit results might be brought about. It may be, as Adam Smith suggested so long ago, that the smaller the number of large firms, the greater the ease of their conscious coordination or conspiracy; or it may be that the greater the relative size of firm, the more closely its *independent* behavior approximates monopoly behavior, regardless of the activities of other firms. There is also the question of whether the larger firms in an industry coordinate directly or simply recognize a leadership pattern; and whether they hold an umbrella so as to encourage mutually appropriate behavior for the small firms in the industry, or simply leave them to form a competitive fringe which does not follow the pattern of the larger units but simply declines in statistical importance as concentration increases.

A final point to be raised in this introductory section concerns the form of the hypothesized concentration-profitability relationship: Is it expected to be a continuous function or should we anticipate a distinct break between less concentrated and more concentrated industries? There is support for both expectations in the theoretical literature, and we have considered both in our analysis. However, we have placed primary emphasis on the search for a continuous, functional relationship because this approach provides the most general basis for a study, and because a particular level of concentration at which a break in the profits relationship should be expected cannot be deduced from theoretical reasoning. When continuous relationships are not found, we can then re-examine the data on an ad hoc basis for evidence of a distinct break.

CONCENTRATION AND PRICE-COST MARGINS, EMPIRICAL RESULTS

In this section we summarize the principal findings from our analysis of the relationship between measured concentration and price-cost margins for 1958 and 1963. Similar procedures were used in the analysis of both periods, but data are available for a larger group of industries in the later year. There was a significant revision of SIC industry definitions in 1957, but the concentration data for 1958 were computed on the basis of pre-1957 definitions in order to permit comparability with earlier tabulations. Thus, in combining the 1958 concentration data with other census data for that year, it was necessary to select industries that were comparable on the old and revised definitions. This discrepancy in industry definition was not substantial at the two-digit level of classification but was an important factor to be considered in selecting the set of four-digit industries to be included. Out of 426 four-digit industries reported in 1958, comparable concentration and industry data are available for 288 industries, which are, therefore, the total population of industries available for analysis in 1958. In 1963, on the other hand, concentration data are available on the same industry definition base used in the 1963 Census of Manufactures, and a group of 415 four-digit industries was, therefore, subject to analysis in that year.

Our summary of the statistical analysis focuses on three topics:

1. Relationship between concentration and margins among two-digit industry groups in 1958 and 1963; in addition, we analyze the relationship between concentration and other profit indicators for these groups.

2. Relationship between concentration and margins among four-digit industries *within* individual two-digit industry groups.

3. Relationship between concentration and margins among four-digit industries, irrespective of their two-digit industry identification.

Concentration and Margins Among Two-digit Industry Groups

Two-digit major industry groups are not generally thought to be appropriate categories for the analysis of competitive forces. With few exceptions, each of them is too large and diverse to be considered even roughly comparable to the economic concept of a "market" within which monopolistic and competitive forces might be expected both to operate and to be observed. Concentration figures for these groups can only be computed by aggregating in some manner the basic concentration data for their constituent industries or products. It is a striking result of previous studies, however, that fairly strong associations between concentration and profitability indicators have been observed using two-digit data.[5] Therefore, an analysis of the relationship between concentration, margins, and other profit measures among two-digit groups appears worthwhile.

Results of statistical analysis for the several profit indicators and concentration at the two-digit industry level for 1958 and 1963 are shown in Tables 2 and 3, respectively. Concentration is defined

[5]For example: H. M. Levinson, *Postwar Movement of Prices and Wages in Manufacturing Industries*, Study Paper No. 21, U. S. Congress, Joint Economic Committee (Washington, January 1960) ; Howard J. Sherman, *Macrodynamic Economics* (New York: Appleton-Century-Crofts, 1964), Chap. 8; and L. W. Weiss, "Average Concentration Ratios and Industrial Performance," *Journal of Industrial Economics*, XI, 3 'July 1963) , 237–254.

TABLE 2

Results of Regression Analysis: Average Concentration
Ratios and Profit Rates, Two-digit Industry Groups, 1958

Dependent Variable	Regression Coefficient for Independent Variable, Average Concentration Ratio	Constant Term	r^2
Profits before taxes:			
Percent of sales	.11[a]	3.54	.34
Percent of assets	.12[a]	6.26	.41
Percent of shareholders' equity	.19[a]	9.47	.43
Profits after taxes:			
Percent of sales	.05[c]	2.03	.18
(excluding SIC 29)	(.06)[a]	(1.60)	(.33)
Percent of assets	.06[a]	3.21	.37
Percent of shareholders' equity	.10[a]	4.78	.45
Price-cost margin	.16[b]	12.00	.20

[a]Significant at 1 percent level.
[b]Significant at 5 percent level.
[c]Significant at 10 percent level.

TABLE 3

Results of Regression Analysis: Average Concentration
Ratios and Profit Rates, Two-digit Industry Groups, 1963

Dependent Variable	Regression Coefficient for Independent Variable, Average Concentration Ratio	Constant Term	r^2
Profits before taxes:			
Percent of sales	.14[a]	2.96	.50
Percent of assets	.16[a]	5.44	.65
Percent of shareholders' equity	.21[a]	10.54	.39
Profits after taxes:			
Percent of sales	.07[b]	1.89	.25
(excluding SIC 29)	(.07)[a]	(1.47)	(.49)
Percent of assets	.08[a]	3.10	.56
Percent of shareholders' equity	.10[a]	5.81	.39
Price-cost margin	.11	20.52	.07

[a]Significant at 1 percent level.
[b]Significant at 5 percent level.

as the share of total four-digit industry shipments accounted for by the largest four firms, and average concentration within each two-digit group is computed as a weighted (by value of shipments) average of concentration in the constituent four-digit industries. Simple regression results, with concentration as the independent variable and each of the several profit indicators as the dependent variable, are reported in these two tables.

In the 1958 data (Table 2), concentration is shown to be positively and significantly related to each of the profit measures. The least substantial coefficient (for profits after taxes as a percent of sales) is due to the previously discussed anomalous position of SIC 29—petroleum and coal products—and the reliability of this coefficient increases substantially when this industry is removed from the analysis. In the 1963 data (Table 3), the concentration-profits relationship tends to be stronger, except in the case of margins, for which the results are not statistically significant at the 10 percent level.

Taken altogether, these results are consistent with the findings of previous studies that there is a systematic relationship between profits and concentration, when data at the two-digit level of aggregation are analyzed. However, the association between concentration and margins at this level of aggregation is weaker in the earlier data and not observed in the later. It might be suspected that this discrepancy was due to differences in capital intensity among industries, which would be expected to distort the relationship between margins and other measures of profitability, for the reasons previously discussed. Results shown in Table 4, however, reveal that this is not the source of the discrepancy. On the contrary, when industry capital-output ratios are introduced as an additional explanatory variable, they prove to be significant in the case of profits as a percent of sales, both before and after taxes, in both years, but they do not alter substantially the results with respect to margins.

Concentration and Margins Within Industry Groups

The large collection of data available on a four-digit industry basis makes it possible to cross-classify the observations and examine the concentration-profitability relationship within groupings that share some common characteristics. Some of these potentially

TABLE 4

Results of Regression Analysis: Average Concentration
Ratios, Profit Rates, and Capital Output Ratios,
Two-digit Industry Groups, 1958 and 1963

Dependent Variable and Year	Regression Coefficient for Independent Variable		Constant Term	R²
	Concentration Ratio	Capital-output Ratio		
1958				
Profits before taxes as percent of sales	.08[a]	.08[a]	—1.44	.68
Profits after taxes as percent of sales	.03[c]	.08[a]	—2.39	.78
Price-cost margins	.17[b]	—.02	12.66	.21
1963				
Profits before taxes as percent of sales	.14[a]	.09[a]	— .48	.76
Profits after taxes as percent of sales	.07[a]	.07[a]	— .79	.59
Price-cost margins	.11	.09	17.60	.13

[a]Significant at 1 percent level.
[b]Significant at 5 percent level.
[c]Significant at 10 percent level.

important characteristics are measurable; others are essentially qualitative. For example, the age, record of technological change, level
and pattern of change of demand, and interindustry position of
the component firms in each industry are, in part, unique and not
readily comparable. A qualitative analysis suggests, however, that
these industry characteristics are apt to be more similar among
industries closely related in terms of products, technology, or
sources of demand than among the industrial population as a
whole. It therefore appears plausible that some of these sources of
interindustry diversity might be taken into account by grouping
the available four-digit industries into their respective two-digit
industry groups for the purpose of cross-section analysis.

The relationship between price-cost margins and three characteristics of industry structure was analyzed within a regression framework, with linear functions fitted by the method of least squares.
A separate cross-section study was made for the component four-digit
industries within each two-digit industry group analyzed. In each
such analysis, two linear regression equations were fitted, as follows:

(1) $$Y_1 = a + bX_1$$

(2) $$Y_1 = a + bX_1 + cX_2 + dX_3$$

where:

Y_1 = price-cost margin

X_1 = concentration ratio

X_2 = index of geographic dispersion

X_3 = capital-output ratio

The price-cost margin as used in this analysis has been explained. Concentration is taken as the share of the four largest firms in the total shipments of each four-digit census industry. Using census data, we have computed the capital-output ratio as the ratio of gross book value of assets to value of shipments. As an index of geographic dispersion, we have attempted to measure the extent to which productive facilities and output in various industries are centralized in a few locations or scattered throughout the country. This index has been constructed so that the *lower* its value, the *greater* is the degree of geographic dispersion of the industry, and thus the *greater* the likelihood of local and regional markets. We therefore hypothesize that the lower this index, the higher the expected price-cost margins for any given level of national concentration. A more detailed description of all these computational procedures is given in Appendix A. (It may be noted here, however, that slightly different methods were used in computing the index of geographic dispersion for 1958 and for 1963.)

As mentioned above, concentration and other census data for 1958 were available on a comparable basis for 288 four-digit industries. When these data were classified into two-digit industry groups, 10 such groups contained 15 or more industries, which we felt was a sufficient number to merit analysis. These groups contained in total 213 of the 288 industries. The same 10 groups, containing in total 309 of the 415 industries available in 1963, were also analyzed for the later year.

Results of the analysis of the 1958 data are shown in Table 5. A statistically significant and positive association between margins and concentration was observed in six cases:

SIC Code	Industry
20	Food and kindred products
32	Stone, clay, and glass products
33	Primary metal industries
34	Fabricated metal products
36	Electrical machinery
39	Miscellaneous manufacturing

The concentration-margin relationship was observed whether or not additional variables were included in three instances: food and kindred products; stone, clay and glass products; and miscellaneous manufacturing. The relationship was found only when concentration alone was included in two cases: primary metal industries and fabricated metal products. In the electrical machinery group the relationship was evident only in conjunction with the two other explanatory variables.

Results for 1963, shown in Table 6, are closely similar. One industry group—SIC 33, primary metals—which showed a significant positive concentration-margin relationship in 1958 failed to do so in 1963. Among the five groups indicating a positive relationship, the association between concentration and profits was observed whether or not additional variables were included in three instances: food and kindred products; stone, clay, and glass products; and electrical machinery. The relationship was found only when concentration alone was included in two cases: fabricated metal products and miscellaneous manufacturing.

Certain differences also appeared with the relationship between margins and the index of geographic dispersion and capital-output ratios. With the 1958 data, a statistically significant negative relationship was found between price-cost margins and the index of geographic dispersion for four two-digit groups. In the case of the 1963 data, however, such a relationship was observed only for two two-digit groups: food and kindred products and textile mill products.

We hypothesize a positive relationship between margins and capital-output ratios. This variable was positive and statistically significant in the 1958 data only for food and kindred products. In the analysis of the 1963 data, however, the positive relationship

TABLE 5

Results of Regression Analysis: Ten Two-digit Groups, 1958

SIC No.	Industry Group	Number of 4-Digit Industries	Equation	Regression Coefficients of Independent Variables			Constant Term	R^2
				Concentration Ratio (X_1)	Geographic Dispersion (X_2)	Capital-Output Ratio (X_3)		
20	Food and kindred products	32	1	.31[a]	—	—	6.05	.40
			2	.41[a]	—.13[a]	.19[b]	5.06	.69
32	Stone, clay, & glass products	23	1	.16[b]	—	—	15.93	.25
			2	.15[b]	—.09	.07	15.99	.42
33	Primary metal industries	15	1	.20[b]	—	—	4.74	.34
			2	.14	—.03	.08	4.66	.38
34	Fabricated metal products	20	1	.13[b]	—	—	14.73	.21
			2	.05	.20[a]	—.20[b]	13.59	.81
36	Electrical machinery	18	1	.11	—	—	16.36	.12
			2	.15[b]	—.14[c]	—.18[c]	28.99	.40
39	Miscellaneous manufacturing	23	1	.11[b]	—	—	16.42	.22
			2	.09[b]	—.05[a]	.004	20.83	.46
22	Textile mill products	17	1	.05	—	—	11.47	.04
			2	.06	—.09[a]	—.11	22.76	.66
23	Apparel & related products	24	1	—.02	—	—	15.50	.004
			2	.06	.05[b]	.03	9.15	.23
28	Chemicals & allied products	19	1	—.09	—	—	32.13	.03
			2	—.06	.12	—.02	25.10	.13
35	Machinery, except electrical	22	1	.07	—	—	15.54	.05
			2	.04	.06	—.06	15.04	.08

[a]Significant at 1 percent level.　[b]Significant at 5 percent level.　[c]Significant at 10 percent level.

96

TABLE 6

Results of Regression Analysis: Ten Two-digit Groups, 1963

| SIC No. | Industry Group | Number of 4-Digit Industries | Equation | Regression Coefficients of Independent Variables | | | | |
				Concentration Ratio (X_1)	Geographic Dispersion (X_2)	Capital-Output Ratio (X_3)	Constant Term	R^2
20	Food and kindred products	42	1	.31[a]	—	—	10.77	.31
			2	.33[a]	—.12[a]	.22[a]	10.73	.53
32	Stone, clay, & glass products	27	1	.11[c]	—	—	24.82	.13
			2	.09[b]	.01	.14[a]	16.26	.58
34	Fabricated metal products	28	1	.16[b]	—	—	20.57	.20
			2	—.03	.31[a]	—.09	17.39	.69
36	Electrical machinery	33	1	.14[a]	—	—	21.84	.25
			2	.16[a]	—.03	—.06	24.09	.27
39	Miscellaneous manufacturing	27	1	.13[b]	—	—	21.05	.16
			2	.01	—.03	.34[a]	19.79	.50
22	Textile mill products	29	1	—.04	—	—	19.81	.03
			2	—.05	—.06[a]	.11[c]	21.94	.32
23	Apparel & related products	33	1	—.02	—	—	20.47	.003
			2	—.02	.02	.06	17.73	.08
28	Chemicals & allied products	28	1	.05	—	—	32.27	.01
			2	.02	.93	.03	30.52	.03
33	Primary metal industries	24	1	—.06	—	—	22.29	.04
			2	—.14[a]	.01	.21[a]	15.12	.64
35	Machinery, except electrical	38	1	.05	—	—	24.86	.05
			2	.05	.01	.02	24.47	.05

[a]Significant at 1 percent level. [b]Significant at 5 percent level. [c]Significant at 10 percent level.

appears for five two-digit groups: food and kindred products; textile mill products; stone, clay, and glass products; primary metal industries; and miscellaneous manufacturing.

On the basis of this analysis of both the 1958 and 1963 data, it is evident that there is a clear and significant tendency for concentration to be associated with profitability, as reflected in price-cost margins, in some industries. The pattern of association is varied, however, and there are some instances in which no association is found. An ad hoc analysis of the data reveals little evidence of a "distinct break," rather than a continuous relationship, nor does the "break" hypothesis receive any support from those data samples in which no significant relationship was found.

Concentration and Margins Among All Four-Digit Industries

Statistical analysis has also been made of the relationship between price-cost margins and the same structural features for the entire collection of 288 four-digit industries for which 1958 data are available, and of 415 four-digit industries for 1963. In the analysis of the 1958 data, we also cross-classified industries by broad capital-output and geographic dispersion categories. These latter computations were made to allow for the possibility that our estimates of both of these variables may be overly precise. That is, it may be relevant to separate high capital-intensive industries, or geographically concentrated industries, or their opposites, from all others, but not to attempt to take account of fine (and possibly ill-measured) distinctions among the values of these variables for individual industries.

Inspection of the 1958 data indicated that major clusters of values could be identified as follows:

Index of Geographic Dispersion—low (under 30), medium (30-89.99), and high (90 and over)

Capital-Output Ratio—low (under 50 percent) and high (50 percent and over).

More than 60 percent of all the 1958 industries are in the "medium" geographic dispersion class, and 78 percent are in the "low" capital-output class. Almost exactly one-half (141) of all industries fall into both of these classes, and this group of industries has also been segregated for analysis.

The results of these computations are shown in Table 7. The

TABLE 7

Results of Regression Analysis, All Four-digit Industries, 1958 and 1963

Group of Industries and Year	Number of 4-Digit Industries	Equation	Regression Coefficients of Independent Variables			Constant Term	R^2
			Concentration Ratio (X_1)	Geographic Dispersion Ratio (X_2)	Capital-Output Ratio (X_3)		
1958 Industry Data							
All available 4-digit industries	288		.13[a]		.01	13.90	.12
			.12[a]	−.02		14.60	.13
All industries classified by index of geographic dispersion							
less than 30	40	1	.10[c]			15.92	.09
		1a	.03		.18[a]	10.59	.40
30–89.99	180	1	.12[a]			14.13	.11
		1a	.13[a]		−.03	14.76	.11
90 and over	68	1	.14[a]			12.22	.19
		1a	.17[a]		−.07	13.12	.21
All industries classified by capital-output ratio							
under 50	225	1	.13[a]			13.60	.13
		1b	.13[a]	.002		13.45	.13
50 and above	63	1	.10[b]			15.81	.06
		1b	.11[b]	−.08[b]		20.24	.13
All industries with geographic dispersion 30–89.99 and capital-output under 50	141	1	.14[a]			13.75	.12
1963 Industry Data							
All 4-digit industries	415	1	.12[a]			20.27	.10
		2	.10[a]	−.03[b]	.09[a]	19.57	.18

Equation 1a: $Y_1 = a + bX_1 + dX_3$ Equation 1b: $Y_1 = a + bX_1 + cX_2$

[a]Significant at 1 percent level.   [b]Significant at 5 percent level.   [c]Significant at 10 percent level.

regression coefficients between concentration and price-cost margins are significant at the 5 percent level or better in all but two of the fifteen statistical analyses. The coefficients of determination range from .06 to .40, the latter involving an association between capital-output ratios and margins for the forty industries with very low indexes of geographic dispersion (i.e., highly regionalized industries). The only other instance of a variable other than concentration showing a significant relationship with margins in the 1958 data is the negative association between margins and the geographic dispersion index in the sixty-three industries with capital-output ratios above 50 percent. In the 1963 data, margins were found to be positively and significantly related to concentration, with an increase of 10 percentage points in concentration being associated with an increase of 1.0 to 1.2 points in margins. These results are similar to the coefficients obtained for 1958 data. However, our measures of geographic dispersion and capital-output ratios are significantly related to price-cost margins in 1963, which was not true with the 1958 all-industry data.

As we expected, the grouping of the industries into broad classes, with respect to the other two explanatory variables, has a substantial impact on the statistical results. Only relatively weak associations between concentration and margins are found for the industries with low indexes of geographic dispersion (regional industries). By contrast, relatively strong associations were found for the industries with high indexes. These are industries in which production is relatively concentrated in a few locations and which are, therefore, presumed to serve interregional, or roughly "national," markets from relatively concentrated sources of supply. It is precisely for these industries that we would expect the measured concentration data to be most relevant to economic concepts of industry structure, and thus it is significant that the results for these industries (which constitute less than 25 percent of the total) are comparable to the median cross-sectional results.

The results for the industries with indexes of geographic dispersion in the medium range, for industries with capital-output ratios under 50 percent, and for industries with both of these characteristics are very close to the results for the 288-industry collection for 1958 as a whole. This similarity would be anticipated because of the large bulk of these industries in the total collection. However, it is reassuring to find that the relationships observed in the total collection are not due to the extreme values but are, in fact, found in a large subsample of data containing what might be called the normal range of values of the geographic and capital variables.

CONCLUSIONS

The results of our statistical analysis of 1958 and 1963 data tend to confirm the findings of previous studies that there is frequently a statistically significant, but not always strong, association between measured concentration and indicators of profitability in manufacturing industries. This association was observed both in highly aggregated two-digit industry data and in more refined classifications, although not in every subsample of the latter.

The magnitude of the association found is of some interest. In the two-digit industry group data, and combining the results of both years, it appears that an increase of, say, 10 percentage points in the weighted average concentration index for a group would be associated with the following *percentage-point increases* for the several profit variables:

Profits Before Taxes
    Percent of sales: 1.1 to 1.4
    Percent of assets: 1.2 to 1.6
    Percent of shareholders' equity: 1.9 to 2.1
Profits After Taxes
    Percent of sales: .5 to .7
    Percent of assets: .6 to .8
    Percent of shareholders' equity: 1.0

These percentage-point increases would amount to 10 percent or more of the corresponding reported rates of return for most industries in the two years.

When attention was shifted to concentration and margins in the more narrowly defined four-digit industries, widely varied results were obtained from different subsamples of the data. In both years, large samples containing highly diverse industries revealed a significant association between concentration and margins. In addition, out of ten subsamples of four-digit industries within the same major industry groups, significant concentration-margin relationships were found in six cases in 1958 and in five cases in 1963. Concentration alone, however, never explained as much as one-half, and only rarely as much as one-fourth, of the variation in margins among four-digit industries.

The central tendency (median) of the significant regression coefficients for the concentration variable in the industry group subsamples, whether or not other variables were included in the analysis, was .14–.16 (considering each group in each year as a single observation). This is approximately the same as the coefficient for concentration and margins in the two-digit groups in 1958 (.16–.17), and slightly larger than the coefficients for concentration and margins in all four-digit industries in each of the two years (.10–.13). On the basis of these findings, we would predict that in samples of comparable four-digit industries, differences of as much as ten percentage points in the share of the four largest firms in total industry shipments tend to be accompanied by differences of something over one percentage point in price-cost margins, as we compute them. We should not be surprised, of course, if this prediction is wide of the mark in any specific instance, since the coefficients obtained are only best estimates within a range of probable values, and the relationship is not observed at all in some samples of data. It should be noted, however, that the range of probable values includes values larger as well as smaller than these specific estimates.

The median level of concentration among the four-digit industries is in the 30–40 percent interval, and the median price-cost margin around 15 percent in 1958 and 25 percent (unadjusted) in 1963. Approximately 18 percent of all four-digit industries had four-firm concentration ratios of more than 60 percent in each year. Neither high levels nor increases in concentration are rare, and the finding that differences in concentration are more likely than not to be positively associated with differences in price-cost margins should strengthen support for public policies directed against both high levels and increases in industrial concentration.

From an analytical viewpoint, the diversity of our statistical results is somewhat perplexing. Although no one would expect that a few crudely identified and possibly ill-measured variables would explain *all* of the variability in profit margins among industries, one might expect that the explanatory power of these variables might be roughly the same within any appropriate sample of data. Having found this not to be true, we may now both (1) question whether all of our samples are appropriate—i.e., whether they lack appropriate dimension, or are nonrepresentative for some other reasons— and (2) further examine the sample groupings to see whether there are differences among them that account for the diversity of results. The selection of other sample groupings and addition of other explanatory variables are obvious next steps in this analysis. One variable to be added is "marginal" concentration, as suggested by Miller: the difference between the shares of the four and eight (or more) largest firms.[6] Additional analysis in terms of differences in demand elasticity, interindustry technological and financial movements, and other variables is also called for.

An obvious, and particularly troublesome, group of problems arises from the relationship among industry size, firm size, and rates of growth, on one side, and both profits and concentration on the other. In some analyses, profitability is shown to be positively associated with firm size, regardless of market or industry context; and the firms accounting for high concentration in specific industries tend, on the average, to be relatively large firms in the economy as a whole. Thus, the *source* of greater profits in the larger and concentration-causing firms is not clearly established; and the association among concentration, absolute firm size, and profitability has not been fully investigated. Further, concentration tends to be lower in larger (total shipments) industries and to decrease with industry growth, although profit opportunities would be expected to increase under growth conditions (and growth rates and profit indicators typically show positive statistical associations). If growth and other factors favoring profitability simultaneously tend to reduce or offset the effects of concentration, then a fundamental concentration-profitability association might be obscured by changes in these additional variables, particularly in periods of general prosperity.

A final point concerns the timing of data observations. Concentration and related census data are available only for relatively few and widely separated time periods. Economy-wide changes in scale, technology, and tastes and changes in the relative importance of individual industries seriously reduce our ability to make comparisons among the sequence of census observations. In addition,

---

[6]R. A. Miller, "Marginal Concentration Ratios and Industrial Profit Rates," *Southern Economic Journal*, **XXXIV** (October 1967), 259–267.

cross-sectional analysis of data from any single census runs the risk of obtaining results that are specific to that particular time period. Previous studies have shown a tendency for the 1954 concentration data to yield clearer evidence of a concentration-profitability association than that found in the 1947 data; and the different cyclical positions of the two dates have been offered as a possible explanation for this result. The year 1958 is cyclically similar to 1954 (both years of recession), and thus the similarity of our 1958 results with those obtained by others for 1954 is a specific confirmation of the concentration-profitability association in such periods. The greater cyclical variability of profits of smaller firms and, by implication, less concentrated industries might, however, serve to wipe out, or conceivably reverse, this association in periods of peak prosperity (e.g., 1947). On the other hand, it could be that the stronger concentration-profits association found for 1954 and 1958, as compared to 1947, is a secular phenomenon and will in the future be observed at all stages of the business cycle. There is no possibility of discriminating definitively between these two hypotheses at the present time. However, the similarity of our results for both 1958 and 1963, the latter being a year of general prosperity, gives us some reason to believe that the concentration-profitability relationship is not primarily a cyclical phenomenon.

Our analysis thus appears to justify the continued accumulation and analysis of concentration data as a significant dimension of industry structure. The generally assumed correspondence between the concentration measures and the "degree of oligopoly," including the behavioral implications of the latter, is, at least in part, substantiated by the finding that there is a significant association between concentration and indicators of profitability in numerous and varied samples of industries based upon various classification systems. On the other hand, concentration does not explain everything, and in some cases it appears to explain nothing at all. Thus, not surprisingly, the answer seems to lie somewhere between the extremes. Concentration is more likely than not a significant variable in the analysis of industry profit and price-cost performance, but other variables are also important and in some cases they appear to outweigh or offset completely the effects of concentration. The identification of these other variables and their careful integration into a more refined theory of market behavior remain tasks for future research.

APPENDIX A

Data Employed in Statistical Analysis, Explanatory Notes

1. *Four-digit industries included in 1958 analysis.* Census data for 1958 are available on the basis of the revised 1957 Standard Industrial Classification. The 1958 concentration data are available for industries as defined for the 1954 Census of Manufactures. Therefore, only those four-digit industries were selected for which the 1957 SIC definitions were wholly or substantially unchanged from the pre-1957 definitions. In some cases, census data from two or more four-digit industries could be combined to obtain comparability with an industry for which concentration data were available. A total of 288 four-digit industries was included in the cross-section analysis. There were 213 four-digit industries included in the 10 two-digit groups specifically analyzed.

2. *Four-digit industries included in 1963 analysis.* Census data for 1963 are available on the same industry classification basis as that employed in the presentation of concentration statistics. A larger number of four-digit industries could be used, therefore, in the cross-section analysis of 1963 data than was possible for 1958. A total of 415 four-digit industries was included. There were 309 four-digit industries included in the 10 two-digit groups specifically analyzed.

3. *Computation of the 1958 price-cost margin.* The price-cost margin is defined as:

$$\frac{\text{value added (adjusted)} - \text{payroll} - \text{other costs}}{\text{value of shipments (including resales)}}$$

The numerator is an estimate of the margin between total receipts and total direct costs for each four-digit industry. Value added is obtained by the Census Bureau by subtracting from the value of shipments the following costs: materials, supplies and containers, fuel, purchased electric energy, and contract work. From value added is then deducted total payroll costs. Also, subtraction is made of estimates of selected supplementary employee costs, maintenance and repair costs (other than salaries and wages to own employees), insurance premiums, rental payments, and property taxes. Data on these latter costs were obtained from the special sample survey, "Supplementary Inquiries for 1957," conducted by the Census Bureau as part of the 1958 Census of Manufactures program. Data were estimated on the basis of three-digit totals when not available for four-digit industries. The total of these costs in 1957 was related to the total 1957 payroll figure. This factor was then applied to the total 1958 payroll to obtain an estimate of these costs in 1958. Dividing the total margin figure by the 1958 total value of shipments gives the price-cost margin used in the 1958 analysis.

It should be pointed out that this margin figure does include certain additional expenditures. Among the items remaining in the aggregate are advertising, developmental and research services provided by other establishments, and services of outside consultants. (For a detailed explanation, see *U. S. Bureau of the Census, U. S. Census of Manufactures: 1958. Vol. II, Industry Statistics, Part 1, Major Groups 20 to 28*, 1961, Appendix D, p. D-12.) Although the inclusion of some of the latter items in the total may be arguable, three points, at least, may be adduced to justify this procedure: (1) many of the items (e.g., services of outside consultants) are extremely small in relation to the totals involved; (2) others (e.g., advertising expenditures) are likely to be profit-determined to an important degree; and finally (3), a more refined measure of margins suitable for comparison with sales and concentration figures seems impossible to obtain on an interindustry basis from available data.

Source of data for value added, payroll, and value of shipments: U. S. Bureau of the Census, *U. S. Census of Manufactures: 1958. Vol. II, Industry Statistics*, 1961.

Source of data for estimating other costs: U. S. Bureau of the Census, *U. S. Census of Manufactures: 1958, Vol. I, Summary Statistics*, 1961, pp. 9-3 to 9-23.

4. *Computation of the 1963 price-cost margin.* The price-cost margin is defined as:

$$\frac{\text{value added (adjusted)} - \text{payroll}}{\text{value of shipments (including resales)}}$$

The computation procedure for the 1963 price-cost margin differs from that used in determining the 1958 statistic in that data are not available in 1963 for the "other cost" component (selected supplementary employee costs, maintenance and repair costs, insurance premiums, rental payments, and property taxes). The effect of using this slightly less refined price-cost margin measure does not appear to be very great, judging from regression results using 1958 price-cost margins with and without the exclusion of these other costs. We have seen above (Table 2) that in the 1958 analysis of two-digit group data the relationship between concentration and price-cost margins (excluding other costs) was:

$$Y_1 = 12.00 + .16 \, X_1 \qquad\qquad r^2 = .20$$

where

Y_1 = price-cost margin (excluding other costs)
X_1 = four-firm concentration ratio.

The corresponding regression equation where price-cost margin (Y'_1) is computed without deducting the other costs is:

$$Y'_1 = 16.56 + .16 \, X_1 \qquad\qquad r^2 = .18$$

The latter regression coefficient for concentration is significant at the 10 percent level, and the former is significant at the 5 percent level.

Source of data for value added, payroll, and value of shipments: U. S. Bureau of the Census, *U. S. Census of Manufactures: 1963. Vol. II, Industry Statistics,* 1966.

5. *Concentration.* Concentration is computed as the share of the four largest firms in the industry's total value of shipments.

Source of data on 1958 concentration: U. S. Congress, Senate, Subcommittee on Antitrust and Monopoly, Committee on the Judiciary, *Concentration Ratios in Manufacturing Industry, 1958,* Part I, 87th Congress, 2d Session, 1962, Table 2.

Source of data on 1963 concentration: U. S. Congress, Senate Subcommittee on Antitrust and Monopoly, Committee on the Judiciary, *Concentration Ratios in Manufacturing, 1963,* Part I, 89th Congress, 2d Session, 1966, Table 2.

6. *Computation of the 1958 Index of Geographic Dispersion.* The index of geographic dispersion is computed as follows: The percentage of each four-digit industry's 1958 value of shipments accounted for by establishments in each of the four census regions was computed; also, the percentage of United States population in each census region. The index of geographic dispersion for each industry is the sum of the absolute differences between the percentage of value of shipments accounted for by establishments in each region and the percentage of population in that region. The greater the geographic dispersion, the smaller the numerical value of this index.

Source of data on geographic distribution of value of shipments: U. S. Bureau of the Census, *U. S. Census of Manufactures: 1958. Vol. II, Industry Statistics*, 1961. (Estimates were made where census regional totals were not published.)

7. *Computation of the 1963 Index of Geographic Dispersion.* In the 1963 analysis, the index of geographic dispersion was computed in a slightly different manner: The percentage of each four-digit industry's 1963 value added accounted for by establishments in each of the four census regions was computed; also, the percentage of total manufacturing value added accounted for by each census region. The index of geographic dispersion for each industry is the sum of the absolute differences between the percentage of value added accounted for by establishments in each region and the percentage of total manufacturing value added accounted for by that region. Again, the greater the geographic dispersion, the smaller the numerical value of this index.

Source of data on geographic distribution of total manufacturing value added: U. S. Bureau of the Census, *U. S. Census of Manufactures: 1963. Vol. I, Summary and Subject Statistics*, 1966, Table E, p. 10.

Source of data on geographic distribution of four-digit industry value of shipments: U. S. Bureau of the Census, *U. S. Census of Manufactures: 1963. Vol. II, Industry Statistics*, 1966.

8. *Computation of 1958 capital-output ratio.* The capital-output ratio is computed by dividing the gross book value of assets as of December 31, 1957, by the total 1958 value of shipments.

Source of data on gross book value of assets: U. S. Bureau of the Census, *U. S. Census of Manufactures: 1958. Vol. I, Summary Statistics*, 1961, pp. 9-3 to 9-23. (Data were estimated on the basis of three-digit totals when not available for four-digit industries.)

Source of data on value of shipments: U. S. Congress, Senate, Subcommittee on Antitrust and Monopoly, Committee on the Judiciary, *Concentration Ratios in Manufacturing Industry, 1958*, Part I, 87th Congress, 2d Session, 1962, Table 2.

9. *Computation of 1963 capital-output ratio.* The capital-output ratio is computed by dividing the gross book value of assets as of December 31, 1963, by the total 1963 value of shipments.

Source of data on gross book value of assets: U. S. Bureau of the Census, *Annual Survey of Manufactures: 1964, Book*

Value of Fixed Assets and Rental Payments for Buildings and Equipment, M64(AS)-6, 1967.

Source of data on value of shipments: U. S. Bureau of the Census, *U. S. Census of Manufactures: 1963. Vol. II, Industry Statistics,* 1966.

10. *Computation of 1963 average price-cost margins for the four largest firms and the remaining firms for each four-digit industry.*

Source of data: U. S. Congress, Senate, Subcommittee on Antitrust and Monopoly, Committee on the Judiciary, *Concentration Ratios in Manufacturing, 1963,* Part II, 90th Congress, 1st Session, 1967, Table 27.

8

significance of profit data for antitrust policy

by YALE BROZEN

The antitrust division of the Justice Department pays less attention to profits as an indicator of monopoly power than to concentration ratios, despite Fritz Machlup's observation that the view which apparently prevails among economists is that profits are the "monopoly index *par excellence*."[1] The division has used profit data (or allegations concerning profits) on a few occasions. In the American Tobacco, Sugar Institute, Eli Lilly, Alcoa, Cellophane, and General Motors cases, either profit data were used or statements were made about uses to which profit data would be put.

In a General Motors case the antitrust division argued, without any information

[1] Fritz Machlup, *The Political Economy of Monopoly, Business Labor and Government Policies* (Baltimore: Johns Hopkins Press, 1952).

George Stocking believes that profit data are a substitute for cost-price data. "Because economists rarely have access to cost data they may be forced to rely on profit data in determining the existence of monopoly." "Economic Tests of Monopoly," *Workable Competition and Antitrust Policy* (Nashville: Vanderbilt University Press, 1961), p. 280.

on profits, that the "high" profits GM derived from the manufacture of common-carrier buses indicated monopoly. When it found that GM's profits were not "high" in this business, it then shifted to arguing that GM's "higher" profits (and lower costs) than its competitors demonstrated an ability to lower prices. This "discretionary" price-setting power meant that GM had monopoly power, according to the division.[2] Also, the division argued that different profit rates on different models of common-carrier buses would show "selective pricing policies with respect to specific types of common-carrier buses which had detrimental effects on competition."[3]

The latter argument is, of course, based upon the notion that "predatory" pricing may be used to gain control of a market. It harks back to the old Standard Oil case.[4] In this instance, it is "low" profits which presumably indicate an attempt to monopolize. Here we come full circle from high or above-average profits presumably indicating the existence of monopoly to low or below-average profits indicating monopolizing activity, both monopoly and monopolizing being illegal under present law (except where the industry has been exempted from the application of the antitrust statutes).

If, given these contentions, we are to use a profits test for determining whether to prosecute for an antitrust violation, businesses would be forced to be sure that their profits (total and by model, product, and market) are neither "high" nor "low" if they are to avoid prosecution. Inasmuch as most businesses are not in a position to control their profits, particularly in view of the aphorism that we

---

[2]The argument was apparently another version of the "deep pockets" hypothesis. That is, the government argued that GM's lower costs made it possible for GM to lower prices and force other firms from the market if it chose to do so. The government did not make it clear as to how GM would recoup its lost revenues from the lower price. Judging by the fact that Mack Truck bid on and won the San Francisco bus contract in 1962 after having been out of the bus manufacturing business for five years, re-entry and new entry would occur with great rapidity if GM were ever to try the tactic of raising prices to recoup foregone revenues after forcing others out. See W. L. Leeman, "The Limitations of Local Price-cutting as a Barrier to Entry," *Journal of Political Economy*, 64 (August 1956) , 329–334.

[3]Affidavit of A. I. Jacobs, November 5, 1962, p. 8, Civil Action 15816, U.S. District Court for the Eastern District of Michigan.

[4]For an analysis of the improbability of predatory pricing, see J. S. McGee, "Predatory Price Cutting: The Standard Oil (N.J.) Case," *Journal of Law and Economics*, I (October 1958) , 137.

cannot measure or know their profits until they are liquidated, such an index would expose every firm to the threat of prosecution by the antitrust division. Thus what has been called by some the "new tyranny" would be carried to its extreme limits.

The primary reason that the antitrust division places more reliance on concentration data than on profit data lies in the attitude of judges. They have been friendly to the use of concentration data but not profit data. Judge Learned Hand, in the Alcoa case, made it clear that his decision was reached without the use of the profit data which the government had submitted. Judge Wyzanski rejected United Shoe Machinery's use of its profit data in defense against the charge of monopolization. Judge Leahy said of the antitrust division's charge that high profits showed the existence of monopoly power in cellophane: "Years of profit do not establish monopoly power over prices. They establish this: du Pont was an efficient business company. Monopoly cases do not rest on such insubstantial evidence to support complete power over price."[5]

Economists, however, have accorded profits a more important role. "There is no more important proposition in economic theory than that, under competition, the rate of return on investment tends toward equality in all industries."[6] It would seem, then, that the persistence of an above-average rate of return in an *industry* could be construed as evidence of the existence of barriers to entry into the industry. "Entrepreneurs will seek to leave relatively unprofitable industries and enter relatively profitable industries."[7] —which should reduce high rates of return and raise low rates of return. However, Stigler warns us that

> ... a lack of desire for profits or a lack of knowledge of returns in alternative ventures could render any tendency toward equality of rates so negligible as to be wholly unimportant .... [Also,] if ... unexpected and large disturbances occurred frequently within the period necessary to bring about a reasonably full adjustment to one disturbance—the equality of rates of return would never be approached even distantly. Almost any amount of dispersion of rates of return in competitive

[5]*United States* v. *E. I. du Pont de Nemours & Co. et al.*, 118 F. Supp. 41, at p. 208 (U.S.D.C. Delaware, 1953).

[6]G. J. Stigler, *Capital and Rates of Return in Manufacturing Industries; A Study by the National Bureau of Economic Research*, (Princeton: Princeton University Press, 1963), p. 54.

[7]*Ibid.*

industries would be consistent with the basic theoretical proposition.[8]

That is, given these circumstances, the *tendency* to equality found under competition could be operating persistently without producing a detectable movement toward equality.

Stigler also points out that "equilibrium rate of return ... [may] be lower [in some] than in other industries" and this may be a source of continued dispersion in rates of return despite a tendency toward equality of "the total of all advantages and disadvantages—nonmonetary as well as monetary—of using resources in various fields .... Dispersion would arise because of differences among industries in monetary and nonmonetary supplements to the average rate of return."[9]

COMPANY VS. INDUSTRY PROFITS

Economic theorists seldom point to accounting profits in individual companies as a possible indicator of existence of monopoly.[10] Their discussions, exemplified by the remarks cited above, have been in terms of industry rates of return.[11] The antitrust division and congressional committees have, on the other hand, seldom pointed to industry profit rates in their indictment of any industry or any company. In the various cases cited above, it was always the profits of the defendant that were entered in evidence or discussed in briefs. In the 1958 majority report of the Senate Subcommittee of the Committee on the Judiciary, the level of General Motors' accounting rate of return on net worth was cited as an indication that the antitrust division should do something.[12]

8*Ibid.*, p. 56.

9*Ibid.*, pp. 56, 57.

10Corwin Edwards argues that "... prices, price discrimination, limitation of output below capacity, and the level of profit are all unreliable guides for the identification of monopoly power." *Maintaining Competition; Requisites of a Governmental Policy* (New York: McGraw-Hill Book Company, 1949), p. 125.

11Professor Stocking seems to believe that the profit data of a single company are relevant: "... the aspects of performance most relevant to determining whether a firm possesses monopoly power are its pricing policy and its profit record." *Op. cit.*, p. 279.

12General Motors' rate of return was compared with Ford Motor Company's rate of return, which, in turn, was said to be "impressive when compared to the earnings of most manufacturing companies." *Administered Prices: Automobiles.* Report of the Subcommittee on Antitrust & Monopoly, Senate Judiciary Committee, 85th Congress, 2d session (1958), pp. 110–111, 126.

Calculated rates of return, adjusted to match economic concepts, earned by a single company are no guide to whether it has a monopoly. This is aside from the thoroughly discussed inadequacies of accounting rates of return for individual companies as an indicator of economic profits[13] (such as the understatement of current values of existing assets after a period of inflation, the arbitrary allocation of costs over time, and the expensing of capital outlays). Although it is an economic truism that in pure competition minimum average costs of all companies will be identical if rents are calculated and entered in costs, such figures are never observed. The company which has long-term contracts or ownership of resources in which the contract figure or book value is below market value will appear to be earning high accounting rates of return. This is what we observe in the available financial statements. Heroic assumptions are required to adjust accounting figures to match economic concepts, and these assumptions can be validated, or invalidated, only by future events. On the other hand, accounting returns for monopolists may be reduced to what might be expected under competitive circumstances as the result of the capitalization of monopoly profits if a transfer of assets has occurred.

When a company has a high rate of return per books, and it is asserted that this may possibly be the result of monopoly power or oligopoly conspiracy, then other companies in the industry should be enjoying high rates of return also. They are either shaded by the monopoly price umbrella or share in the conspiracy's return. This ought, then, to show in the industry's return being much above average. Presumably, then, we should be able to detect monopoly (partial) or conspiracy by persistent above-average industry returns.

Unfortunately, the umbrella held by a partial monopolist or an oligopoly conspiracy may shelter inefficient companies as well as efficient companies enjoying monopoly returns in the form of high accounting profits. A monopolized industry may, then, show lower returns than a continuously innovating competitive industry, a continuously disturbed (continuously pleasantly surprised) competi-

---

[13]G. E. and R. D. Hale, *Market Power: Size and Shape under the Sherman Act* (Boston: Little, Brown and Co., 1958), pp. 78–79, 188–190; J. S. Bain, "The Profit Rate as a Measure of Monopoly Power," *Quarterly Journal of Economics*, 55 (Feb. 1941), 271–293.

tive industry, or a high-risk competitive industry.[14] Industry accounting returns serve as no better guide to the existence (or nonexistence) of monopoly (or conspiracy) than company accounting rates of return, even when we assume that the monopoly occurs under market circumstances which would make it possible to extract large monopoly profits. In some market circumstances, of course, the possession of monopoly power does not yield large profits (economic or accounting) despite even the most effective use of such power.

PROFITS AND CONCENTRATION

Despite the lack of acceptance by judges of profit data and the conceptual difficulties of using such data, they have entered indirectly into antitrust policy. The faith displayed by economists in concentration ratios as a basis for suspecting monopoly or collusion, a faith shared by antitrust division lawyers and by judges, is in part a result of correlations of accounting rates of return with concentration ratios which have been found in various studies.[15]

---

[14]This is not to say that the industry will not on the average earn higher than competitive rates of return, but that the economic rate of return on required assets will be depressed by the presence of marginal firms earning only the competitive rate of return.

[15]See, for example, J. S. Bain, "Relation of Profit Rate to Industry Concentration, American Manufacturing, 1936–1940," *Quarterly Journal of Economics*, 65 (August 1951), 293–324; N. R. Collins and L. E. Preston, "Concentration and Price-Cost Margins in Food Manufacturing Industries," *Journal of Industrial Economics*, 14, 3 (July 1966), 226–242; W. S. Comanor and A. Wilson, "Market Structure, Advertising, and Market Performance: An Empirical Analysis," presented at the Econometric Society Meetings, December 1965 (mimeographed); J. R. Felton, "Concentration, Condition of Entry, and Profit Rates," *Mississippi Valley Journal of Business and Economics*, I, 2 (Spring 1966), 1–35; Fuchs, "Integration, Concentration, and Profits in Manufacturing Industries," *Quarterly Journal of Economics*, 75 (May 1961), 278–291; F. J. Kottke, "The Relations of Measurable Characteristics of Industry Structure and Experience to the Profitability of Industry Leaders" (mimeographed); H. M. Levinson, *Postwar Movement of Prices and Wages in Manufacturing Industries*, Joint Economic Committee, Study of Employment, Growth and Price Levels, Study Paper No. 21 (Washington: G.P.O., 1960), pp. 1–139; H. Mann, "Seller Concentration, Barriers to Entry, and Rates of Return in Thirty Industries, 1950–1960," *Review of Economics and Statistics*, 48 (August 1966), 296–307; R. A. Miller, "Marginal Concentration Ratios and Industrial Profit Rates: Some Empirical Results of Oligopoly Behavior," *Southern Economic Journal*, 34, 2 (October 1967), 250–267; H. J. Sherman, *Introduction to the Economics of Growth, Unemployment and Inflation* (New York: Appleton-Century-Crofts, 1964), Ch. 8; W. Weiss, "Average

The correlations have been interpreted as signifying that highly concentrated industries can and do price their products above competitive levels and thereby earn the higher accounting rates of return on assets or net worth found to be associated with higher concentration ratios. Other hypotheses could account for higher rates of return being associated with higher concentration ratios, but few tests have been made of these. One group of possible hypotheses springs from the possibility of systematic accounting bias increasing with increases in concentration. Larger firms, for example, are likely to be older than smaller firms on the average. Since larger firms are found in more highly concentrated industries, the higher average age of these firms may result in a greater understatement by accounting data of the true market value of their assets than for the younger firms composing less concentrated industries.[16]

Larger firms tend to be more research-intensive than smaller firms.[17] Since research outlays are charged to expense rather than capitalized despite the fact that present outlays are expected to bring most or all of their return in the future, the current net worth and net assets of larger firms tend to be more understated than that of smaller firms. Current income is also more understated,[18] but the relative understatement in this item is somewhat less than the relative understatement in net worth. The result is

---

Concentration Ratios and Industrial Performance," *Journal of Industrial Economics*, 11 (July 1963), 237–254.

[16]One test to determine the "newness" of assets of larger firms relative to those of smaller firms used the ratios of net to gross book values. Seven industries had positive rank correlations of the ratio of net to gross book values with size, and twelve showed little or no association. J. R. Moroney and J. W. Duggar, "Size of Firm and Capital-output Ratios: A Comparative Study in U.S. Manufacturing," *MSU Business Topics* (Summer 1967).

N. R. Collins and L. E. Preston have found a correlation between ratios of excess of price over "variable" cost to price and concentration.

[17]Smaller firms which did research were more research-intensive than larger firms prior to World War II, judging from the sketchy data available in National Resources Planning Board, *Research—A National Resource* (Washington: U. S. Government Printing Office, 1941), pp. 124–125. The relationship reversed in the 1950's. See the various reports of the National Science Foundation. However, it has apparently been true for some time that a much greater proportion of large companies than of small companies do research.

[18]Since research outlays have been growing, current expenditures exceed the depreciation of past expenditures, which causes current income to be understated.

an overstatement of the rate of return[19] in larger firms (and in more highly concentrated industries) relative to rate of return in smaller firms (and in less highly concentrated industries).[20]

Larger firms are also more likely to have tool-rebuilding capacity in their maintenance departments and to have construction departments. If they do more rebuilding of tools and construction under the accounting guise of maintenance and repair, their assets and net worth will be relatively more understated than those of small firms which buy rebuilt second-hand tools to replace worn and obsolescent equipment and contract for new construction without jacking up the roof of an old building to build a new structure under it. Even where large firms capitalize tool rebuilding and construction turned out by their construction departments, book values will be understated by the cost of equity capital used in the rebuilding and construction process. Again, the result is an overstatement of the rate of return in larger firms (and in more highly concentrated industries).

We can also expect large firms to perform more of other services for themselves besides tool rebuilding and construction than do small firms. Large firms invest in the development of service-performing departments, but the organizational and development investment required to launch these departments are not capitalized. Their net worths are further understated for this reason and their rate of return overstated. The use of capital-output ratios to adjust for differences in capital intensity underallows for the extra capital

[19]A recomputation of the accounting return on net worth in the chemical industry, capitalizing past and current research expenditures and restating current income, reduced the return on net worth in 1966 from 14.7 percent to 13.1 percent. A recomputation of the return for transportation equipment excluding aircraft and parts reduced the 1966 return from 15.6 percent to 13.5 percent.

[20]To the extent that advertising and other promotional and selling expenditures tend to be relatively larger in more concentrated than in less concentrated industries, this, too, will contribute to a relatively greater understatement of net worth in more concentrated industries, since advertising is almost always charged to expense, and will cause accounting rates of return to be more greatly overstated in concentrated industries. The evidence on the relationship of concentration and advertising is mixed. L. Telser, using three-digit industries, finds no relationship. "Advertising and Competition," *Journal of Political Economy*, 72 (December 1964), 537–562. H. M. Mann, J. A. Henning, and J. W. Meehan, Jr., using four-digit industries and selected firms, find a fairly strong relationship. "Advertising and Concentration, An Empirical Investigation," *Journal of Industrial Economics*, 16, 1 (Nov. 1967), 34–45.

intensity in more concentrated industries and tends to attribute a spuriously greater return to concentration.[21]

Another set of hypotheses consistent with higher rates of return for larger firms and more concentrated industries springs from economic considerations. Larger firms (and more concentrated industries) may own riskier assets than equivalent-size collections of smaller firms. If larger firms use larger plants with more specialized, larger-scale equipment than smaller firms, the resultant loss of flexibility or adaptability may result in higher risk. The findings of S. Hymer and P. Pashigian are consistent with this hypothesis.[22]

Risk is, in itself, a reason for higher concentration. Many risks cannot be insured except by self-insurance. In order to spread the risks in high-risk industries and, in effect, reduce the cost of self-insurance, firms in high-risk industries must be somewhat larger relative to their markets than is necessary in low-risk industries. In this case, profits and concentration may be associated because of the association of risk and concentration, concentration being the method for reducing the costs of risk. Weiss's finding that increases in concentration between 1947 and 1954 were significantly related to the rapidity of style and model changes[23] is consistent with the hypothesis that higher-risk industries will tend to be more highly concentrated, *ceteris paribus*, as a method of providing self-insurance.

Another possible hypothesis consistent with higher accounting rates of return correlating with higher levels of concentration is that the varieties of entrepreneurial talents required in some industries are much scarcer than those required in others. This might be true in the more rapidly evolving industries with complex technologies and marketing structures. To the extent that these talents are relatively scarce and scale economies are perhaps appreciable—or, at least, there are no diseconomies of scale—the more efficient use of resources by firms with these scarce talents leads to their more rapid growth and ultimate concentration of output in a few hands. Accounting rates of return will appear high and continue high until

21N. R. Collins and L. E. Preston's unpublished study, "Industry Structure and Price Cost Margins" (1968), is subject to this deficiency.

22S. Hymer and P. Pashigian, "Firm Size and Rate of Growth," *Journal of Political Economy*, 70 (Dec. 1962), 567–569.

23L. W. Weiss, "Factors in Changing Concentration," *Review of Economics and Statistics*, 45 (Feb. 1963), 70–77.

the rate of evolution slows and others learn the methods which *have* worked in the large, successful firms.

An alternative hypothesis with which the correlations found are consistent, and which follows to some extent from the preceding, largely untestable hypothesis, is that the higher returns in more concentrated industries are simply a manifestation of a disequilibrium situation. Just as research-intensive industries were once found to be relatively more profitable than other industries when large-scale research and development was a fairly new activity and an equilibrium rate of investment had not been approached, the industries where the optimum scale of operation was large compared to the size of the market may have been relatively more profitable in part because of the relative newness of these industries and/or of the economies realizable from increased or larger-scale operations. To the extent that this was a disequilibrium situation, correlations could be expected to deteriorate, as they have in the case of the research-intensive industries,[24] unless there continue to be surprise discoveries of ways to economize in large-scale operations which are not applicable to the small-scale operations typically more economical for less concentrated industries.

When we examine a list of 39 industries in the four-digit group (except three-digit sugar, dairy products, meat products, drugs and medicines, and iron and steel foundries) for which company data could be found and in which companies had a large share of their activity concentrated in the industry of their classification, we find the correlations of profitability and concentration deteriorating through time. The rank correlation for Bain's 42 industries, using 1935 concentration ratios, was 0.31. The rank correlation of accounting rates of return on net worth with 1954 concentration ratios using the 39 industries mentioned above deteriorates to 0.12. Using 1963 concentration ratios and 1961–64 accounting the rates of return on net worth, the correlation deteriorates further to 0.05, a statistically nonsignificant level.

The deterioration of the correlation gives some support to the hypothesis that the relationships found earlier of concentration and accounting profits were a manifestation of disequilibrium rather than of oligopoly conspiracy or partial monopoly. It also supports

[24]Y. Brozen, "The Future of Industrial Research, *Journal of Business*, 34 (Oct. 1961), 434–441.

Harold Demsetz' argument "... that the asserted relationship between market concentration and competition cannot be derived from existing theoretical considerations and that it is based largely on an incorrect understanding of the concept of competition or rivalry."[25]

CONCLUSION

Although our theory tells us that economic profits are more likely to persist under monopoly circumstances, it does not tell us that economic profits occur only because of monopoly. They may occur for many other reasons, ranging from disequilibrium to innovation, and they may persist for reasons other than monopoly. Our theory also tells us that a monopolist does not necessarily earn economic profits unless market circumstances are favorable, given cost conditions. The occurrence of persistent economic profits are not, then, helpful in determining whether antitrust action is appropriate.

Even if persistent economic profits were such a signal, we are faced with data which do not tell us whether or not persistent economic profits are occurring. Accounting rates of return may be persistently above average because of accounting conventions which bias reported rates of return persistently upward much more in some industries than in others.

Any attempt to use accounting profits by model, by product, or by market to determine whether a firm is engaged in monopolizing (predatory activity)[26] faces the insuperable problem of allocating joint costs, which is always arbitrary and for which there is no theoretical basis. A model on which the reported margin on sales or return on investment is lower than all others produced may actually be the most profitable in the line (see Appendix A following this chapter).

Accounting profits can never be a guide to antitrust action or policy. The corroboration they have appeared to give in the past to concentration ratios as a guide to antitrust action also is ap-

[25]Harold Demsetz, "Why Regulate Utilities," *Journal of Law and Economics*, 11 (April 1968) , 55–65.

[26]See J. S. McGee, *op. cit.*, pp. 142–143, for a discussion of *price* differences which are "often taken to be symptomatic of predatory price cutting, when in fact they may be nothing of the sort."

parently spurious.[27] Even where economies of scale make it more economic to use a single production facility to supply a market, there is no ground for believing that monopoly profits will be earned.

APPENDIX A

Are Differing Profit Margins by Model Evidence of "Selective Price Cutting" and Monopolizing Activity or Monopoly Price Discrimination?

The antitrust division has alleged that "selective pricing policies with respect to specific [models cause] ... detrimental effects on competition" and that such "selective pricing policies" can be demonstrated by differing profit margins on different models of a product. Whereas to the division differing profit margins are evidence of monopolizing, to Professor Clemens they are evidence of price discrimination.[1] Since persistent price discrimination is possible only under monopoly conditions, persistent differing profit margins can, then, be taken as evidence of monopoly if they are truly evidence of price discrimination.

The data available on profit margins by model, however, are accounting data. With the normal indivisibilities that lead to joint cost situations, accounting profit margins by model are meaningless. The production of a model that is low-margin or money-losing according to the accounting statements, in the presence of high-margin models, is not evidence of the practice of predatory pricing or of price discrimination.

[27]Peter Asch finds no relationship between concentration (1958) and accounting rates of return on equity (1951–60) in a multiple regression of profit rates on concentration, entry barriers,, industry growth rates, and stability for 21 four-digit industries despite a simple correlation of 0.38 between concentration and accounting rates of return for these industries. "Industry Structure and Performance: Some Empirical Evidence," *Review of Social Economy*, 25 (Sept. 1967) , 175–176.

[1]E. W. Clemens, "Price Discrimination and the Multiple-Product Firm," *Review of Economic Studies*, 19, 1 (1951) , 1–11; reprinted in *Readings in Industrial Organization and Public Policy*, A.E.A., R. B. Heflebower and G. W. Stocking, eds. (Homewood, Ill.: Irwin, 1958) , p. 266. Clemens is not concerned with persistent "price discrimination," remarking that "Price discrimination ... emerges ... as the most common means of competition."

It is probably evidence only of the fact that there is no conceptually valid method of allocating joint costs among models and that the accounting formulas used for this purpose are arbitrary exercises in imagination. There are numerous accounting formulas and different formulas produce results which may contradict each other. One formula may result in a high-profit margin for one model and a low one for a second model. Another formula, equally acceptable (and equally arbitrary), may reverse the relationship.

Leaving aside the accounting situation which makes comparisons of budgeted or reported accounting profit margins on different models meaningless, the profit margin on a given model may be lower than that on others and yet not be "unnaturally" low if it returns the cost of (the yield required to attract) incremental capital necessary to produce the model in question. If the incremental capital was in the form of idle capacity on equipment only partially employed for other purposes, which would be available whether or not the model in question was produced and idle if the model is not produced, the yield required to attract such capital is zero or less (less to the extent that if the model in question returns any part of the depreciation, it is better to earn, let us say, minus 5 percent than to let the equipment sit idle and earn, let us say, minus 10 percent).

It should be added that the production and sale of a low-yielding (as determined by the accountants) model in these circumstances increases the yield on other models, thus making them appear to be high-return models relative to this low-yielding (as measured by accountants) model. The apparent yield of high-margin models would be much lower in the absence of the production of the presumed low-yielding model because the depreciation (and investment base) assigned as a cost against the low-yielding model would be allocated to the other models in the absence of production of the low-return item. The low-return model, then, actually provides not only its stated accounting yield but also additional returns on other models. This additional return should be assigned to the low-return model since its production and sale produced the increased yield on other models as well as its own presumed low yield.

Perhaps the best way to demonstrate the point is to consider the following situation. Suppose a firm produces one model of an airplane. (To simplify the situation, we will assume that the only indirect cost is depreciation.) It sells 100 airplanes at $1,000 each for a total sales volume of $100,000. It has direct costs (materials and labor) of $80,000 and indirect costs (depreciation) of $15,000. Its pretax profit, then, will be $5,000 or 5 percent of sales (see Table 8).

The firm now adds a second model to its line. This model, let us say, is a smaller and cheaper airplane usable by airlines which do not find the larger model economic. The firm sells 100 of the second model at $500 each for a total dollar volume of $50,000. No additional capacity is required because present equipment used for the first model has sufficient idle time. Producing the second model adds $45,000 to direct

TABLE 8

One-model Aircraft Firm

Total sales	$100,000
Less	
Direct costs	80,000
Depreciation	15,000
Profit (pretax)	5,000
Profit % of sales	5%

costs but causes no increase in depreciation. The aircraft company's total sales are now $150,000 and total direct costs are $125,000. With $15,000 of depreciation, its pretax profit is now $10,000 or 6.7 percent of sales. The pretax profit has increased from $5,000 to $10,000 and its pretax profit percent of sales has increased from 5 percent to 6.7 percent (see Table 9). Adding a second model has made the company more profitable and has increased its profit percentage of sales.

TABLE 9

	One Model	Two Models
Total sales	$100,000	$150,000
Less		
Direct costs	80,000	125,000
Depreciation	15,000	15,000
Profit (pretax)	$ 5,000	$ 10,000
Profit% of sales	5%	6.7%

Let us now examine the profit margin by model. To do so, using a conventional accounting approach, we will allocate the indirect costs according to the amount of direct cost caused by each model.

Total direct costs are $125,000. Total indirect costs are $15,000. We have twelve cents (12¢) of indirect cost for each dollar of direct cost.

The first model has $80,000 of direct costs. Allocating 12¢ depreciation for each dollar of direct cost, the allocation of indirect cost to the first model is $9,600. Total direct and allocated indirect cost amount to $89,600. With sales of the model amounting to $100,000, pretax profit is $10,400 and pretax profit percent of sales is 10.4 percent. By producing and selling the second model, the pretax profit margin on the first model has been increased to 10.4 percent from 5 percent (see Table 10). This is the result of assigning some of the depreciation against the second model when it is produced.

TABLE 10

Profits on First Model Without and
With Production of Second Model

	First Model (No Second Model)	First Model (With Second Model)
Total sales	$100,000	$100,000
Less		
Direct costs	80,000	80,000
Depreciation	15,000	9,600
Profit (pretax)	$ 5,000	$ 10,400
Profit % of sales	5%	10.4%

The second model has $45,000 direct cost. Allocating 12¢ depreciation for each dollar of direct cost, the allocation of indirect cost to the second model is $5,400. Total direct and allocated indirect cost amount to $50,400. With sales of the second model amounting to $50,000, there is an accounting loss of $400 and an accounting profit percent of sales of minus 0.8 percent (see Table 11).

TABLE 11

Profits on Second Model

Total sales	$50,000
Less	
Direct cost	45,000
Depreciation	5,400
Profit (Loss)	(−$400)
Profit % of sales	(−0.8%)

Now suppose we examine a company whose statements show that pretax profit margins on two models are 10.4 percent and minus 0.8 percent. Does the negative (or much lower) profit margin on one model mean that the company is practicing predatory pricing? Is it trying to "unnecessarily exclude actual and potential competition? Is it erecting an "unnatural barrier?"

Presumably, "unnecessarily exclude" means to exclude a competitor who would not be wasting manpower, capital, and materials in producing the model. It means excluding someone who is an efficient or more efficient producer. It is "natural" to exclude inefficient competitors and "necessary" if the market is to be well served. Efficient competitors should grow and inefficient decline if our society is to progress and grow.

To sell the second model at an accounting profit margin of minus 0.8 percent is not an "unnatural barrier" if the company adds to its total profits (or reduces its losses) by doing so. It is not doing this to exclude efficient competitors from the aircraft business. It is doing this to increase its own efficiency (better utilize its capital) and to increase its profits. By adding the second model, the company has doubled its profits, increasing them from $5,000 to $10,000. It has lifted its over-all profit percentage of sales from 5 percent to 6.7 percent.

What is "unnatural" here is the appearance presented by the accounting data. Why should a model whose price, sales volume, direct costs, and use of machine and plant time have not changed suddenly apparently become more profitable? Why should extra profitability be attributed to the first model when a second model is introduced? This is a result of the arbitrary nature of accounting conventions. I would argue that the profitability of the first model has not changed. It is still making 5 percent on sales.

The cost of the second model is not $50,400. Its cost is $45,000, and it is returning 10 percent on sales, not minus 0.8 percent. The cost of doing or producing anything is what you give up (sacrifice) to do it. To produce the second model, we give up $45,000. The $5,400 depreciation will occur whether or not we produce the second model. It is not caused by the decision to produce the second model. It was caused when we decided to purchase plant and equipment to produce the first model.

Any good manager realizes this and, therefore, pays little attention to what the accountants tell him are profit margins on various models. He looks at models in terms of what they contribute to covering present burden and to profits. The accounting and budget statements do not tell us what was in the manager's mind when he made the decision to produce a model, which, according to these formal statements, would yield or did yield a low or negative rate of return on sales. The manager was probably well aware that the actual margin was 10 percent on the second model even though the budget statement indicated a probable profit margin of minus 0.8 percent. He is well aware of the fact that some high-return models (according to the formal accounting statements) may not be worth continuing because the high return is actually a result of the allocation of depreciation or other indirect costs to the low-return models or a result of special tools and dies for this model having a very low book value because they are nearly fully depreciated.

Only by finding what was in a manager's mind when he made his decisions can we tell what was the intent in producing low-return (according to the formal statements) models. The accounting statements are *pro forma* and yield no illumination with respect to the contributions to profit expected or obtained from any given model. They are not evidence which relates in any relevant or competent way to the question of whether any given price was a predatory price. They do not tell us what the alternatives were which a manager faced when he made his decisions to produce or not to produce any given model at the price he could obtain. They do not tell us whether the manager had any latitude in establishing a price on any one model.

Of course, we should also consider the company's reasons for adding a second model rather than increasing the output of the first model. It may appear reasonable to argue that it could equally well add an additional $50,000 of output of the first model instead of $50,000 worth of the second model, and that the additional direct costs would amount to only $40,000 rather than $45,000, thus tripling accounting profits rather than only doubling them. This is not necessarily the case, but let us assume that it is if there were a market for the additional fifty aircraft. Implicitly, given these assumptions, we are assuming that there is what has been called a "natural monopoly" in the first model. The available market can be more efficiently served by a single producer than by more than one, and indivisibilities led to the idle capacity situation.

With this limited market and "natural monopoly," does it follow that the manufacturer of the first model has a monopoly in the sense that he can set prices higher than long-run marginal costs? I would argue that the manufacturer probably got the business producing the first model because he set prices lower than the long-run marginal cost of a single model producer. Manufacturers bid for the business of airline companies, for example, on the basis of a proposed design and price before they go into production. There are many bidders, which prevents a monopoly price despite the fact that we end up with a single producer. The recent competition between Lockheed and McDonell-Douglas for the air bus business of American Airlines is illustrative of the situation. The successful bidder may be the one who takes into account the possibilities of earning his cost of capital only by the addition of an apparently money-losing model which makes it possible for him to earn a sufficient total accounting profit to return his cost of capital.

9

profit data and public policy

by SAM PELTZMAN

Economic theory suggests that there is some
relationship between the competition that
public policy seeks to promote and profits.
More precisely, it states that a firm will earn
more profits in the absence of any present
or prospective competitors than in their
presence. With much less precision, theory
suggests that a firm will earn more profits
in the presence of few actual or potential
competitors than it would if it had many
rivals. The statement of theory poses an
immediate problem for the economist who
seeks to verify it or the lawyer who wishes
to apply it to public policy: we are not
able to observe the same firm operating in
alternative states of competition at the same
time. And economic theory does not imply
that a monopoly in industry X will earn
more profits, or a higher rate of return,
than a competitive firm in industry Y. What
it suggests is highly qualified: in long-run
equilibrium, under suitable demand and
cost conditions, and if its accountants do
not properly account for economic rents,

the X-monopoly will have a rate of return which is no lower than that of the Y-competitor.

FUNDAMENTAL PREMISES

In spite of the necessary qualifications and the still weaker statement that can apply to an X-oligopolist, we are left with a *ceteris paribus* presumption that the class of noncompetitive industries will contain more industries with above-average rates of return than the class of competitive industries. Economists have attempted to verify this theoretical presumption by relating some index of profitability to some index of industry competitiveness. By and large, the relationships they have generated conform to the theoretical presumption. As the Collins-Preston paper and their several previous studies indicate, the relationship between profitability and market structure is typically not very strong, but it is usually significantly in the expected direction. My analysis will focus on the usefulness for public policy of this by now well-established relationship. To what extent can the antitrust agencies use the conjunction of high profitability and high concentration to select cases or areas for investigation? Which problems associated with the use of such a relationship can be overcome and which are irreducible?

One point must be made clear at the outset: we shall discuss the extent to which high profitability *combined* with high concentration can be used to imply a departure from competition. Few would argue that profitability alone is a sufficient index of competitiveness. Surely nothing in economic theory denies the possibility of a particular competitive industry's having above-average profits for a long period of time, or a monopoly's having low profits for a long time. Therefore, we are compelled to select the class of possibly-noncompetitive industries on some structural criterion, for example the degree of market concentration. If profit data are useful at all, they may help us to identify particular noncompetitive industries within this class.

I will, with most writers in this field, assume that market concentration is a sufficiently good measure of market structure. This assumption is itself a matter of no small controversy, and it is made here only to narrow the discussion. Surely, the developing literature on the relationship between profitability and market structure is the poorer for not having as yet attempted to assess the independent influence of numbers of firms, the relative size of the largest firms, etc. We shall, by implication at least, discuss some defects of the concentration ratio as a measure of market structure, but the main focus will be on the particular information provided by profits. So, for convenience, concentration and oligopoly are often used interchangeably.

I shall consider two broad interrelated classes of objections to the use of profit data for public policy: (1) the profitability measures that we have are so liable to error that this compromises their usefulness as a measure of monopoly power; (2) common forces, unconnected with market power, affect both profits and concentration in the same way, and so produce a spurious association between the two. I hope to show that both classes of objections can be met, but, particularly the second class, not entirely met.

ERRORS IN MEASUREMENT OF PROFITABILITY

It is well known that current tax laws and accounting practices lead to serious discrepancies between reported profitability data and the "true" measures that are relevant to a study of market structure. This fact alone is not, however, a critical objection to concentration-profitability relationships, unless we are willing to believe that measured profitability is totally unrelated to true profitability. Further, many of the factors that lead to discrepancies between measured and true profitability apply as much to competitive firms as to oligopolies. Therefore, a positive relationship between measured profitability and concentration implies a positive relationship between the latter and true profitability.

For similar reasons, one cannot argue that the defects of true profitability, were we ever to know this datum, as a measure of monopoly power destroy the usefulness of concentration-profitability relationships. A strong market position may enable a firm's managers to trade profits for executive benefits. A competitive firm may enjoy high profits because its industry is in dynamic disequilibrium, or because it is earning a risk premium. Differences in cost and demand conditions can lead to wide differences in profitability among the most highly concentrated industries. However, all of this leaves intact the theoretical presumption that the *class* of non-competitive industries will be more profitable on average than the class of competitive industries, and all of these sources of error do not obviate the significant empirical relationship between concentration and profitability.

Although these measurement errors do not destroy the usefulness of concentration profitability relationships, they do seriously limit its usefulness for public policy. The cumulative result of these measurement errors is that the over-all relationship between profitability and concentration is fairly weak. This means that, in practice, only in the class of industries with very high concentration will a conclusion that high profitability is attributable to that concentration be warranted. The same conclusion for less highly concentrated industries will be subject to too much statistical error to be acceptable. Thus, the concentration-profitability relationship may give the policy maker little more information than he has already.

If concentration-profitability relationships are to be made more useful, more accurate and relevant profitability measures must be developed. Economic theory can be helpful here. Consider, for example, the error that is introduced when a competitive industry is earning unusually high profits because of some recent increase in demand to which full adjustment has not been made. If this industry is truly competitive, these profits will be eroded by new entrants and the expansion of existing firms. Economic theory suggests, then, that the crucial difference between competition and oligopoly will be found in *permanent* or long-run profitability, not profitability as of every moment in time.

The distinction between short- and long-run profitability is worth emphasizing, because it may critically affect the usefulness of concentration-profitability relationships as they now stand. To illustrate, I ranked each of the 20 two-digit manufacturing industry groups by profitability (rate of return on invested capital) for each of three years of economic expansion, 1955, 1959, and 1964. The coefficient of rank correlation between profitability in 1955 and 1959 is .672, which is statistically significant; the rank correlation between 1955 and 1964 profitability is .319, which is insignificant.

This deterioration would be even more pronounced without the considerable averaging of errors involved in using such broad industry classes. Now, even if 1955 concentration were perfectly correlated with 1955 profitability, which it is not, 1955 concentration would, at best, be insignificantly related to 1964 profitability. Yet, it is something like the latter relationship that we are really interested in. Who, after all, would wish to assign to the Justice Department the task that is accomplished by the market within the gestation period of an antitrust case? In a very real sense, then, concentration-profitability relationships are irrelevant; they relate concentration to the wrong variable, namely current profitability.

The irrelevancy may be avoided by use of measures that better reflect permanent profitability. One such measure that might be investigated is the market value of the firm's shares, where that is available. Stock market values capitalize all future expected earnings, and economic theory suggests that it is precisely this whole earnings stream that concentration should affect. For example, consider two companies with identical, above-normal current profits; one firm is competitive, the other noncompetitive. The market value of the latter will exceed that of the former to take account of the temporary nature of the competitive firm's profits.

Stock market values will, in other cases, reflect the relevant net advantages accruing to an industry's owners where current profits will not. Current profits may be higher in one industry than another solely on account of risk differences. An industry's measured profits might be low only because depreciation is being overstated; again stock prices will be unaffected.

Of course, stock market values are only estimates of the future, and they are often wrong. However, they are statistically unbiased estimates, and they accord more closely with what economic theory tells us is the relevant effect of concentration: permanent profitability. As such, their use may improve our knowledge of the effects of concentration. The only evidence I have for this belief is fragmentary: for a sample of 17 industries, Stigler found the rank correlation of the rate of return on invested capital with concentration to be .507. On substitution of the ratio of stock market value to invested capital, the correlation improves to .642.[1]

1See G. J. Stigler, "A Theory of Oligopoly," *Journal of Political Economy*, 72 (Feb. 1964), 58. Our contention is that stock prices are superior here because they contain fewer transitory elements. This view is strengthened by some independent evidence. Lawrence Fisher has constructed stock price indexes for each of the 20 two-digit manufacturing industries. See his "Some New Stock-Market Indexes," *Journal of Business*, 39 (Jan. 1966), 191–205. The rank correlation of the 1955 and 1959 indexes is .859. When 1955 and 1959 rates of

Surely, in view of the limited usefulness of existing concentration-profitability relationships, futher investigation of market values is warranted. Some attempt to distinguish long-run from short-run concentration is also in order, perhaps by averaging concentration ratios over time. A competitive industry which has experienced a recent increase in demand will have both unusually high profits and high concentration. That is, new entry will tend to reduce both over time. In the absence of some measure of permanent concentration, the conjunction of high profits and high concentration could be doubly misleading.

THE IDENTIFICATION PROBLEM

If some factor were related in the same way to profitability and to concentration, the inference that concentration caused high profitability might be misleading. This sort of statistical problem may lead to far more serious limitations on the usefulness of concentration-profitability relationships than the problems I have just discussed.

On initial analysis, the limitations do not seem formidable. Professor Brozen suggests, for example, that age of firm, concentration, and measured profitability are all positively related. If this is so, a simple concentration-profitability relationship is merely incomplete. The appropriate statistical function should include age of firm as a separate variable. However, this approach may be pursued only so far before certain intractable problems in interpretation are encountered. I shall illustrate this point by discussing two factors which give rise to such problems: firm size and advertising.

The one primary motive in using concentration-profitability relationships for public policy is that we wish to distinguish cases where high profitability is due to the absence of competition from all other cases. Since there is no a priori reason to believe that an old firm is by that fact alone in a noncompetitive or competitive industry, we can add age of firm to the statistical function explaining profitability and suffer no ambiguity in interpretation. Age of firm takes account of a bias in measured profitability; concentration takes account of market structure.

---

return are converted to indexes with the same base (1960 = 100) as the stock price indexes, their rank correlation is .503.

However, consider the effects of firm size. It is well known that the most concentrated industries also tend to have firms which are the largest absolutely. Further, any profitability measure which uses aggregated industry data will accord larger firms a greater weight than smaller firms. In consequence, the more concentrated the industry, the more will aggregate industry profits be dominated by large-firm data. These considerations suggest that existing profitability-concentration relationships may be capturing effects attributable to advantages of large absolute size. This suspicion is strengthened by a very interesting finding of the Collins-Preston study. They find that wherever an industry group exhibits a significant profitability-concentration relationship, the largest firms within the group tend to have a substantial profitability advantage over the smaller firms. No such large-firm advantage is present where concentration and industry profitability are unrelated. This finding suggests strongly that the high industry profitability that comes with high concentration is attributable entirely to some advantage specific to the largest firms in the industry.

Let us suppose for the moment that it is really large absolute size that accounts for higher profitability and not concentration. How should we interpret this? On the one hand, large size may bring about certain economies, which raise profitability because smaller firms cannot merge quickly enough to take advantage of them. On the other hand, it has been suggested that large absolute size may constitute a barrier to entry: the cost of large units of capital is higher to entering than to existing firms.[2] This second kind of large-firm advantage contains, as the first kind does not, the same sort of policy implications that any concentration-induced profitability does. But we cannot tell what the source of a large firm's advantage is merely by observing the effect of size on profitability. Thus, the relationship of size to profitability provides no useful information for public policy. The point may be put more generally: statistical accuracy compels us to account separately for the effects of size and concentration. Having done so, however, we necessarily obscure the distinction between the noncompetitive sources of high profitability and other sources.

Advertising is another variable whose inclusion in a profitability relationship is both called for and certain to lead to difficulties in

[2]See J. S. Bain, *Industrial Organization* (New York: John Wiley and Sons, 1959), pp. 251–53.

interpretation. A recent study of advertising found that advertising and concentration were each positively related to each other and to profitability. However, once the effects of advertising on profitability were accounted for, concentration proved to be uncorrelated with profitability. The authors conclude from this: "It is likely . . . that much of this profit rate differential due to advertising is accounted for by the entry barriers created by advertising expenditures and by the resulting achievement of market power."[3]

If this is really all there is to advertising, the finding that concentration is really a proxy for advertising leads to few ambiguities. An industry with either high concentration or high advertising combined with high profitability would be presumptively noncompetitive. Unfortunately, matters are not so simple. At least part of the positive relationship between advertising and profitability is spurious; it arises from an error of measurement and has nothing to do with market power or entry barriers. The effects of advertising are cumulative, and a true measure of a firm's capital ought to include its investment in advertising. However, accountants treat advertising as a current expense and not as investment in a depreciable asset. This leads to a systematic bias: the more a firm advertises the more its measured capital understates its true capital. This understatement of capital increases the measured rate of return and, thus, produces a positive association between the latter and advertising. For all we know at present, this spurious correlation may account for all of the observed positive relationship between advertising and profitability. Because advertising and concentration are positively related, it may account for some of the observed positive relationship between concentration and profitability. In any case, our ability to distinguish noncompetitive sources of high profitability is weakened.

These examples illustrate a general point. Part, probably all, of the observed positive relationship between profitability and concentration is in fact attributable to other factors which happen to be correlated with concentration. However, we cannot be sure whether or to what extent these other factors are manifestations of or causes of noncompetitive behavior. Therefore, no unambiguous implication for public policy follows from the relationship of these other factors to profitability.

[3] W. S. Comanor and T. A. Wilson, "Advertising, Market Structure and Performance," *Review of Economics and Statistics*, 49 (Nov. 1967), 437.

At best, when we have adjusted for these other factors, we may be left with some effect on profitability due to concentration alone, which is smaller than the already small effect that has been detected in past studies. This is certain to reduce the usefulness of concentration-profitability relationships for public policy. The more likely possibility is that concentration will prove to have no independent effect on profitability; the other factors such as advertising and size will explain all that concentration now explains. In that case, whatever usefulness we now think that concentration-profitability relationships have for public policy will be vitiated.

This conclusion, however, represents empirical judgments which may not be verified. The obvious challenge to future research is to refine existing profitability-concentration relationships. Some index of permanent profitability should replace current profitability; the separate effects of variables like absolute size and advertising should be measured; etc. Even then, should concentration prove to explain nothing, other aspects of market structure should be investigated. Until this is done, we have to conclude that the positive relationship of profitability to concentration conceals more than it reveals.

ASPECTS OF VERTICAL
INTEGRATION THEORY
AND POLICY

10

vertical integration and competitive processes

by ROBERT H. BORK

Antitrust law has always been concerned about the effects of vertical integration upon the competitive process, and of late that concern has become so intense that many forms of vertical integration are probably illegal per se. It may be helpful at this point to outline the varieties of vertical integration which exist in the economy and the present attitude of the antitrust law to them.

FORMS OF VERTICAL INTEGRATION

Vertical integration by ownership may be created either by acquisition or by growth. Since the passage of amended Section 7 of the Clayton Act vertical acquisitions have been subjected to so many successful attacks by the Antitrust Division of the Justice Department and by the Federal Trade Commission that it sometimes appears the government can win almost any case it chooses to take to the Supreme Court. The usual theory of such cases is that the acquisition may foreclose either the acquiring or the acquired firm as a supplier or a customer for rivals of one or the other.

By contrast, vertical growth has almost never been subjected to antitrust attack. (In fact, I do not recall any such attack.) There is, however, no doctrinal reason why Section 2 of the Sherman Act might not be used to attack vertical growth on a foreclosure theory.

Vertical integration also occurs by contract. Often the integration is not complete but involves control by each firm over certain activities of the other. When the integration takes the form of a requirements contract or an exclusive dealing contract the law's objection, based either on Section 1 of the Sherman Act, Section 3 of the Clayton Act, or Section 5 of the Federal Trade Commission Act, is the foreclosure-of-rivals theory. When the integration takes the form of resale price maintenance or division of dealer territories, the objection, based on Section 1 of the Sherman Act, is usually that competition between the outlets has been suppressed. Exclusive dealing and requirements contracts are highly vulnerable under the law, resale price maintenance (except where a state Fair Trade Law is complied with) is illegal per se, and vertical division of dealer territories is dangerous, though the law is now in a highly confused state concerning the criteria by which such division is judged.

The field of vertical integration thus displays antitrust's two major theories of the ways in which competition may be injured to the detriment of consumers. (For purposes of this discussion I leave out of account the supposed noneconomic purposes of antitrust and confine myself to a standard consumer welfare analysis.)

✓ THEORIES OF INJURY BY VERTICAL INTEGRATION

These two major theories of mechanisms by which the competitive process may be injured are fundamentally distinct:

1. Agreements (including mergers) by which consenting parties remove all or some of the competition existing or likely to exist between themselves.
2. Practices (including contracts and mergers), undertaken singly or in concert, by which one or more parties inflict injury upon competitors and thereby ultimately injure the competitive process.

The theory which explains how agreements in the first category may injure consumers is quite well known and generally accepted. The typical price-fixing cartel provides an example. When the members of an industry agree to set prices they are able to maximize the industry's net revenues, and hence the size of the slices taken by each member of the cartel, by restricting the industry's output to a level below that which would be produced under competition. (Under competition each firm maximized independently by setting its output so that marginal cost equaled the market price, with the result that the entire industry produced at the intersection of the summation of all marginal cost curves and the demand curve. The cartel enables the firms acting jointly to take into account the fact that the addition revenue, shown by the marginal revenue curve, declines more rapidly than does the price shown on the demand curve, so that by restricting output to the point where summation of all marginal cost curves intersects the marginal revenue curve, the industry increases its net revenue or decreases its net loss.)

The loss to consumers from restriction of output arises from the fact that some of the industry's resources now lie idle or are employed in competitive industries where their value to consumers is less. (The discrepancy between marginal cost and price in the cartelized industry and the equation of marginal cost and price in the competitive industries indicates that the value of the marginal product of resources is greater in the former than in the latter.) Consumers would be better off if more resources were employed in the cartelized industry and fewer in the competitive industries.

This theory does not suggest that all elimination of competition between firms or persons is bad for consumers. Obviously elimination of competition accompanies much integration which is essential to the achievement of economic efficiency. The law holds price-fixing cartels illegal per se because there do not appear to be significant efficiencies associated with that form of elimination of competition. Until recently, antitrust was not terribly severe with respect to horizontal mergers because of their obvious capacity for creating efficiency. Section 7 of the Clayton Act, however, is currently being interpreted with a severity which overlooks the importance of this factor.

When this first theory of antitrust is applied to vertical integration, whether by acquisition or contract, it is difficult to understand the objection of the law. I will begin with vertical integration by acquisition.

Monopoly power is usually defined as the ability to alter the market price for a product or service. A firm effects the alteration of market price through changes in its own output that significantly change the total output of the industry. Monopoly power, therefore, depends upon the percentage of the market occupied by the firm, and the ease of entry into that market. Vertical integration does not, of itself, increase the percentage of the market controlled by a firm. If a manufacturer with 50 percent of the national market acquires 100 percent of the distributors of the product, the problem is not the vertical nature of the acquisition but the putting together of a monopoly at the distributor level. The objection to the acquisition would be the same if one distributor acquires all the others. If the manufacturer acquires only 50 percent of the distributors, and sells only through them, there would be no increase in his power to affect price.

Though this much seems plain, it is often asserted that vertical integration causes or permits a firm to behave differently than it would in the absence of integration. But it also seems clear that vertical integration, aside from the case in which it creates new efficiencies, does not affect a firm's pricing and output policies. If, for example, a firm operates at both the manufacturing and retail levels, it maximizes over-all profit by setting the output at each level as though the levels were independent. Where both levels are competitive, the firm maximizes by equating marginal cost and price at each level; each level makes the competitive return. Where the firm has a monopoly at the manufacturing level but is competitive in retailing, it will of course exact a monopoly profit at the first level. And the manufacturing level should sell to the retail level at the same price as it sells to outside retailers. The integrated firm would have no incentive to price its manufactured product lower to outsiders. At best, if the marginal costs of retailing were constant, the result would be the same total profit as if the owned retailers had been charged the same as independent retailers. But if, as is certainly the case in a competitive market, the marginal costs of retailing were rising, the self-deception involved in selling more cheaply to the affiliated retailers would result in an increased output by those retailers, and the integrated firm would be paying more for the service of retailing than it would if it operated at a smaller scale on the retailing level.

If the integrated firm has monopolies at both the manufacturing and retail levels, however, the levels will not maximize independently. This is true because vertically related monopolies can take but one monopoly profit. A single monopoly, say in manufacturing, would set its price so that the price to the ultimate consumer would be at the point returning the greatest net revenue to the monopolist. That is, the monopolist manufacturer would attempt to set his output and price so that the appropriate monopoly price would be charged to the final consumers. The manufacturer would leave a competitive return to the retailers; if he allowed them less, the level of investment and activity in retailing would be too low; if he allowed them more, the additional return would be money out of the manufacturer's pocket. The purchase of all retailers would not change the calculations in any way. The manufacturer, still dealing with the same costs of production and retailing and with the same consumer demand, would arrive at the same profit-maximizing output and price decisions. After the acquisition the retail level would not act independently and restrict output further than the manufacturing level had already restricted it because such a course of action would result in an output lower and a price higher in the final markets than the maximizing monopoly price. The net revenue to the firm would decline.

The foregoing analysis demonstrates that a vertical acquisition can never create or increase a restriction of output. By cutting costs and creating efficiencies it can result in an increase in output. So far as we have gone, therefore, a vertical acquisition appears incapable of injuring consumer welfare and capable of furthering it. There have been a variety of objections to this analysis, but before turning to these, it may be convenient to set out the analysis of vertical integration by contract, which parallels what has been said so far.

ANALYSIS OF VERTICAL INTEGRATION BY CONTRACT

The relevant types of vertical integration by contract under this first major theory of antitrust (the consensual elimination of competition) are primarily resale price maintenance and vertical market division. Here too, I believe, it can be shown that the only real problems are horizontal and that vertical control should be lawful. That is to say, when dealers collude and force a division of their territories or a resale price maintenance policy upon manufacturers, we are confronted with an ordinary cartel whose primary purpose appears to be restriction of output. Similarly, it is conceivable that colluding manufacturers should agree to employ resale price maintenance as a way of minimizing the temptation for any one of them to cut prices and to provide a visible indication of such cheating on the cartel. Each of these cases involves a horizontal agreement which should be illegal.

Resale price maintenance desired by an individual manufacturer, however, is a different thing. The antitrust law on the subject made a fundamental mistake 57 years ago when Justice Hughes in the 1911 *Dr. Miles* decision laid down the incorrect premise that there is no more valid reason to permit a manufacturer to eliminate price competition among his retailers than there is to permit the retailers to fix prices themselves. Since a price-fixing cartel among the retailers would be per se illegal, it follows, on this premise, that vertical price fixing by the manufacturer must be a per se offense as well, and it is. Curiously, the law of vertical market division is not symmetrical. On Hughes' premise one could say that there is no more reason to permit a manufacturer to divide his retailers' territories than there is to permit the retailers to divide territories themselves. Since a market-division cartel among the retailers would be per se illegal, it follows that vertical market division must be a per se offense as well, and it isn't. I will not attempt to follow the tortured criteria being employed by the Supreme Court for the legality of vertical market division, but will instead argue that both vertical price fixing and vertical market division should be lawful.

When a manufacturer eliminates some or all of the competition existing among his retailers he does not thereby increase his own share of the market and so does not create any ability in himself to restrict output. The objection, if there be one, must be that the suppression of competition among the resellers creates an ability in them to restrict output at that level. But this seems extraordinarily unlikely. Why should a manufacturer ever wish his retailers to sell less at a higher profit to themselves? Such a result would decrease the manufacturer's net revenues. Since our theory does not predict such behavior on the part of manufacturers, we must seek some other hypothesis to explain why many of them do in fact seek to maintain their retailers' prices and divide their marketing areas.

The obvious explanation is that the manufacturer using such a device expects to gain efficiencies at the retailer level. There are a number of possible efficiencies which may be so gained, but I will mention only one here. If the manufacturer thinks his product is best sold by a certain level of retailer service, promotion, etc., he has the problem of inducing the appropriate amount of retailer activity. If there were only one retailer, his interest would coincide with the manufacturer's and there would be no problem. But when there are a number of retailers the problem of the "free ride" may arise. Customers will frequently go to the retailer who provides a complete line, information about products, and the like, and then purchase from the retailer whose price is lower because he does not incur the cost of providing those things. Retailers who do not get paid for providing such activities will soon cease to provide them, or provide less, and the manufacturer will discover that his retailers' sales effort is less than he finds appropriate. Resale price maintenance and vertical market division are techniques for solving the "free ride" problem and inducing each retailer to provide the appropriate sales effort. The absence of restriction of output and the presence of identifiable efficiencies in these forms of vertical contractual integration suggests that they too should be lawful.

But now one comes to a range of objections to vertical integration which are of a different nature: theories of ways in which vertical integration, whether by contract or acquisition, may injure rivals to prevent their appearance. These are the theories which underlie the law's strictness with vertical mergers, exclusive dealing contracts, and similar arrangements. It is difficult to understand these theories for they do not seem logically complete.

FORECLOSURE THEORY OF VERTICAL INTEGRATION

The major theory of this sort is that vertical integration "forecloses" competitors and thereby renders their competition less effectual. So virulent has this theory become that the government appears able to win almost any case against a vertical corporate acquisition and has equal success against long-term requirements or exclusive dealing contracts. The economic theory underlying the doctrine of "foreclosure" appears fallacious.

Let us take the example of a vertical merger to illustrate the point. Firm M manufactures shoes and has ten percent of industry sales. Neither M nor any other shoe manufacturer is integrated into shoe retailing. M then buys shoe retailer R, which makes ten percent of retail sales and has never purchased from M. One explanation for this behavior on M's part is that the integration of manufacturing and retailing will lower the total costs of getting M's shoes to the public, thus expanding M's output and increasing its net revenues.

The theory of foreclosure advances an alternative explanation, however. M may force its shoes on R, and this will foreclose other manufacturers from selling to R. If M acquires enough shoe retailers and repeats this tactic it may eventually lever itself to a monopoly position in this manner. The theory states an impossibility. First, whatever reasons caused R not to want M's shoes before the merger are still valid reasons after the merger. When M forces an inappropriate product on its new subsidiary R, it must injure R at least as much as it benefits M. Nothing has been gained. In fact, something has been lost. M could have accomplished the same result, getting its shoes in R's stores, by offering R a lower price to compensate R for whatever disadvantages M's shoes had in R's markets. By buying R and forcing the shoes on it, M has done the same thing except that the loss will appear on R's books rather than M's.

Nor is there any reason to suppose that M can monopolize in this way any more easily than it could by initiating a price war. The bidding for customers through lowered prices would merely be translated into the bidding for retailers through higher purchase bids. But let us suppose that it is argued that a series of vertical mergers disguises the predatory intent of M more successfully than would the cutting of prices at the manufacturing level. First, I do not see why the disguise should be any more difficult to penetrate. Second, it is highly unlikely that M would gain anything, for as its merger program reached culmination the price for retailers would skyrocket. The last retailer to sell out, for example, would in effect be selling M a monopoly and could be expected to charge M for it. It is doubtful that M would be left with any monopoly return after paying for all the retailers. This makes it unlikely that M would regard the course of conduct described as rational. Third, the real objection to what is postulated is that M has put together a monopoly at the retail level. The problem is horizontal merger, not vertical merger. The situation would be equally bad if someone previously unconnected with the shoe industry bought all the retailers or if *M* sold its manufacturing facilities and merely engaged in retailing. Thus, the law should focus on market share at the horizontal level and ignore altogether the accident that the firm acquiring the retailers is vertically related to them. All of this suggests that *M*'s acquisition of *R* should be perfectly lawful.

Up to this point I have not even mentioned the problem of entry. *M*'s program makes even less sense as a foreclosing mechanism because entry will undoubtedly occur at the retailing level, either independently or by other manufacturers of shoes. But the problem of entry is usually argued the other way in vertical integration cases. The argument is that entry is made more difficult if vertical integration becomes complete since the new entrant would have to enter on both levels at once. Thus, the law is particularly concerned about *M*'s acquisition of *R* if it appears that other manufacturers are also integrating vertically, the theory being that if the industry becomes completely integrated potential entrants will be discouraged. Even if that were true, there would be no occasion for concern in cases where the number of firms already in the industry is sufficient to give competitive results. I would suppose that competitive results are likely to be achieved whenever there are more than two or three firms, but I need not argue this point in the present context for it seems very improbable that vertical merger could impede entry.

Let us take the extreme case and suppose that *M* is a complete monopoly and so is the retail level. *M* wishes to block entry at the manufacturing level. The argument is that it can do so by purchasing the retail monopolist, thus imposing upon entrants the necessity of entering at both levels at once. There are a variety of possibilities here. If retailing is a natural monopoly, then it does not matter whether manufacturing is monopolized or who owns the retail level. The full monopoly profit will be extracted from the consumer, and entry at the manufacturing level would only affect the division of the spoils between the two levels. In fact, if the manufacturing entrant were more efficient than *M*, the retail level, whether owned by *M* or someone else, would maximize net revenues by purchasing from the new entrant.

If retailing is not a natural monopoly, then we have a case of curable horizontal monopoly and the retail level should be dissolved into several firms. But this is on a horizontal rather than a vertical theory. In general, if greater than competitive profits are to be made in an industry, entry should occur whether the entrant has to come in on both levels at once or not. I know of no theory of imperfections in the capital market which would lead suppliers of capital to avoid areas of higher return to seek areas of lower return.

We have dealt with an extreme case, in any event, and the improbability that vertical integration would be used to block entry—except by the desirable means of making the existing firm more efficient—is so great that the law, which operates on general rules, should discount it altogether.

OTHER OBJECTIONS TO VERTICAL INTEGRATION

Brief mention should be made of two other arguments sometimes advanced against vertical integration. The first is that such integration may confer upon a monopolist the ability to discriminate in price. A monopolist may have two classes of customers making different products, one of which class of customers is willing to pay more than the other, and yet, because of reselling between the classes, be unable to take advantage of the situation by discrimination. If, however, the monopolist should integrate with one of the classes, leakage would stop and discrimination become feasible. I doubt that the law should concern itself with this means of maximizing revenues from a monopoly position. The phenomenon of vertical integration for this purpose is probably uncommon and the existence of price discrimination would often be hard to prove, requiring difficult, if not virtually impossible, measurements of costs and rates of return. More important, however, price discrimination by a monopolist may increase or decrease his output. Its effect upon consumers, therefore, cannot be stated in advance or form the basis for general rules about vertical integration.

The second objection is that vertical integration may be used to evade price regulation at one level. This problem arises primarily in the case of a regulated monopoly integrated with an unregulated supplier on customer level. By inflating the costs of the goods the monopolist purchases or by taking the monopoly return at the downstream unregulated level the integrated supplier or customer, respectively, may defeat the purposes of the regulation. This is a special case, not adequate to form the basis of general antitrust rules, and should be dealt with within the regulatory context. The decision to be made is whether or not the increased costs of regulation are greater than the efficiencies the integration is likely to produce. That complex issue is outside the scope of this paper.

The analysis set forth here suggests that in the antitrust context the law should not concern itself at all with vertical integration by acquisition, growth, or contract. This is to say that there should be no antitrust law about vertical mergers, exclusive dealing contracts, requirements contracts, resale price maintenance or dealer market division imposed by individual manufacturers or suppliers, or any other vertical relationships.

11

public policy toward vertical mergers

by WILLARD F. MUELLER

Vertical integration refers to the linking of successive stages in the production and distribution of a particular product. The *degree* of vertical integration refers to the number of stages which have become integrated under the ownership or control of a single enterprise. Vertical integration may take various *forms*, ranging from direct ownership of successive stages to various kinds of contractual or other integrating or coordinating devices which fall short of complete ownership.[1] This discussion will deal only with ownership integration.

Firms integrate vertically because they believe doing so enhances their profits. Economists have identified a number of ways in which vertical integration presumably increases the profitability of the firm engaging in it:[2]

[1]Friedrich Kessler and Richard H. Stern, "Competition, Contract, and Vertical Integration," *Yale Law Journal*, 69 (Nov. 1959), 1–129; W. F. Mueller and N. R. Collins, "Grower-Processor Integration in Fruit and Vegetable Marketing," *Journal of Farm Economics*, 39 (Dec. 1957), 1471–1483.

[2]A. R. Burns, *The Decline of Competition* (New York: McGraw-Hill Book Co., 1936), p. 619; C.

1. Vertical integration may cut production costs because of technological considerations. Simply, the costs of operating two successive stages of production are lower under combined than under separate ownership.

2. It may result in economies associated with coordinated control of the production process.

3. In imperfectly competitive markets firms may find it preferable to avoid selling costs by developing "captive" outlets for their products.

4. Ownership of successive stages may permit entrenchment of a monopoly position at one stage.

5. Partial vertical integration may enable a seller to engage in discriminatory pricing.

6. Integration may enable a firm to share in or erode the monopoly profits of a related stage of production.[3]

Although these and other considerations may encourage firms to integrate into related stages of production, our concern is not with the causes but with the competitive effects of vertical integration.

HOW MAY VERTICAL INTEGRATION AFFECT COMPETITION?

Vertical integration, as such, does not confer market power on the integrated firm. After all, few American enterprises are more vertically integrated than the farmer selling his apples at a roadside stand. But he gains no market power merely because he controls all stages of production and distribution from the orchard to the ultimate consumer.

Edwards, "Vertical Integration and the Monopoly Problem," *Journal of Marketing,* 17 (April 1953), 404–410; M. A. Adelman, "Concept and Statistical Measurement of Vertical Integration," *Business Concentration and Price Policy* (Princeton: Princeton University Press, 1959), pp. 201–321; J. Markham, *The Impact Upon Small Business of Dual Distribution and Related Vertical Integration,* Hearings before Select Committee on Small Business, House of Representatives, 88th Cong., 1st Sess., Vol. I, p. 50; G. E. Hale and R. D. Hale, *Market Power: Size and Shape under the Sherman Act* (Boston: Little, Brown and Company, 1958); E. A. G. Robinson, *The Structure of Competitive Industry* (New York: Pitman Publishing Corp., 1948).

[3]Vertical integration may at times occur for reasons entirely unrelated to efficiency or market power reasons, being simply the product of historical accident or chance.

The competitive effect of vertical integration is to be found in the impact which it has on market structure and/or conduct. Under certain circumstances it may be a "source" or "carrier" of economic power.[4] Control of limited sources of supply at one stage of production may serve as an important barrier to entry at successive stages. When entry into two separate stages of production is already difficult because of large capital requirements or for other reasons, combining successive stages will further raise entry barriers, because new entrants must enter two stages rather than one. Vertical integration also may raise entry barriers when it "forecloses" part of the market. Such foreclosure will shrink the "open" portion of the market, thereby raising the economics of scale barrier to entry.[5]

In addition to the above structural effects, vertical integration may enable firms which already have a degree of market power to enhance or entrench such power through the use of various competitive strategies not available to nonintegrated firms. The firm with a strong market position in one level of production may place a price "squeeze" on its nonintegrated competitors at a successive stage. This behavioral strategy may, of course, have long-run implications for market structure. Additionally, the mere threat of a price squeeze may cause the nonintegrated firm to behave in a less aggressively competitive manner. Integrating successive stages of production may eliminate the kind of "cross-market competition" which may induce competitive rivalry, even among hard-core oligopolists. When oligopolists in one industry sell to a related industry which is asymmetrically structured, competitive rivalry may be engendered as the oligopolists strive to obtain the patronage of the "prize" customers.[6]

---

[4]C. Kaysen and D. F. Turner, *Antitrust Policy* (Cambridge: Harvard University Press, 1959) , pp. 121–122; R. E. Caves, *American Industry: Structure, Conduct and Performance* (Englewood Cliffs, N.J.: Prentice-Hall, Inc., 1964), pp. 50–51; and studies cited in previous footnotes.

[5]This is the so-called "percentage effect." Suppose the economies of scale in an industry are such that a new entrant must command 10 percent of industry demand. Should half of the market become foreclosed by vertical mergers, a new entrant must then dislodge 20 per cent of the "open" market from existing firms. See J. S. Bain, *Barriers to New Competition* (Cambridge: Harvard University Press, 1956) , for discussion of barriers to entry caused by economies of scale.

[6]De Chazeau and Kahn have concluded that this is one of the major stimulants to competition in the petroleum industry. Melvin G. de Chazeau and Alfred E. Kahn, *Integration and Competition in the Petroleum Industry* (New Haven: Yale University Press, 1959) .

Because vertical integration may affect competition in various ways, determination of its effects is necessarily a complex empirical matter. Insofar as vertical integration may affect market structure, industrial organization theory provides the appropriate framework for analysis. An especially fertile area for analysis in this regard is empirical inquiry into the ways in which vertical integration may raise various entry barriers, including capital requirements, economies of scale, and product differentiation.

A word of caution concerning the use of oversimplified theories in evaluating vertical integration: It can be demonstrated theoretically that a monopolist does not have a profit incentive for integrating into a competitive industry unless doing so results in economies of combined operations.[7] It can also be demonstrated that when each of two stages of production is occupied by separate monopolists, the price to consumers will be greater than if both stages of production were under the control of a single firm.[8]

Some persons have used these models to argue that vertical integration is rarely anticompetitive. They reason that it is likely to occur only when motivated by economies of coordinated operation or in response to the presence of monopoly power in a related industry.

Great care must be taken in generalizing from these two models. They are designed to explain market behavior under very exceptional structural situations. The first assumes a monopolist selling under conditions of blockaded entry to a perfectly competitive market, and the second assumes two monopolists operating under conditions of blockaded entry. In the real world vertical integration generally occurs in that broad range of structural situations between the polar extremes of perfect competition and monopoly.

It is wrong to equate the behavior of oligopolistically structured markets with the behavior of monopolistic ones. It is true that the models in some sophomore economic texts equate the performance of small-number oligopoly with the performance of a monopolist.

[7]S. Weintraub, *Intermediate Price Theory* (Philadelphia: Chilton Book Company, 1964), pp. 301–310; J. J. Spengler, "Vertical Integration and Antitrust Policy," *Journal of Political Economy*, 58 (August 1950), 347–352.

[8]*Ibid.* Machlup and Taber review the historical development of these theories. They take issue with those who would use these theoretical models as a reliable guide to public policy. Fritz Machlup and Martha Taber, "Bilateral Monopoly, Successive Monopoly, and Vertical Integration," *Economica*, 27 (May 1960), 101–117.

There is mounting empirical evidence, however, that oligopolistic markets behave more competitively as they depart from monopolistic markets. The works of Bain and others[9] clearly demonstrate, for example, that profit rates of industries with eight-firm concentration ratios of 50 percent are markedly lower than those of industries with eight-firm concentration ratios of 70 percent.

Quite clearly, then, it is inappropriate to use the monopoly model in attempting to evaluate performance engendered by vertical integration by oligopolistic industries. For example, whereas a monopolist selling under conditions of blockaded entry would not have a profit incentive to integrate into a competitive industry, firms in an oligopolistic industry would have an incentive to integrate into an imperfectly competitive industry if the effect were to raise entry barriers and thereby entrench a previously weak oligopolistic position.

Similarly, it is true that economic theory demonstrates that two vertically related industries would perform better if both industries were under the control of a single monopolist than they would if each industry were under the control of its own monopolist. But this model cannot be used to argue that two successive industries would perform better if both were under the control of one group of oligopolists than if each industry were occupied by its own group of oligopolists. For example, if each industry were performing in an "effectively competitive" manner (because of the level of concentration, the height of entry barriers, or because of buyer-seller rivalry), combining the successive stages could hardly be expected to improve performance. On the other hand, performance would very likely deteriorate if in the process of integration concentration were increased or entry barriers were raised.

This is not a new argument. As with so much economic wisdom,

[9]See, for example, Joe S. Bain, "Relation of Profit Rate of Industry Concentration: American Manufacturing, 1936–40," Quarterly Journal of Economics, 65 (August 1951); L. W. Weiss, "Average Concentration Ratios and Industrial Performance," Journal of Industrial Economics, 11 (July 1963); Norman R. Collins and Lee Preston, "Concentration and Price Margins in Food Manufacturing Industries," Journal of Industrial Economics, 14 (July 1966), 226; a report by the staff of the Federal Trade Commission, The Structure of Food Manufacturing, Technical study No. 8, National Commission on Food Marketing (June 1966), pp. 202–210; H. Michael Mann, "Seller Concentration, Barriers to Entry, and Rates of Return in 30 Industries, 1950–60," Review of Economics and Statistics, 48 (August 1966), 296–307; unpublished study by Collins and Preston, "Concentration and Price-Cost Margins in Manufacturing Industries" (Apr. 1, 1966).

Alfred Marshall recognized what has since been forgotten or has been ignored—that, under rigid assumption, "it may be reasonably argued that the public interest generally requires that complementary monopolies should be held in a single hand." He further observed, however:

> But there are other considerations of perhaps greater importance on the other side. For in real life there are scarcely any monopolies as absolute and permanent as that just discussed. On the contrary there is in the modern world an ever increasing tendency towards the substitution of new things and new methods for old, which are not being developed progressively in the interests of consumers; and the direct or indirect competition thus brought to bear is likely to weaken the position of one of the complementary monopolies more than the other.[10]

Precisely the same argument can be made, of course, with respect to successive or vertically related monopolies. It is more likely that monopoly will wither at one stage if successive stages are independent of one another than if all stages are controlled by a single enterprise.

The lesson I am trying to teach is this: Where vertical integration occurs in industries which lie between the polar extremes of perfect competition and monopoly—and this is almost always the case—we must evaluate the structure of the markets in which integration occurs and then determine how the integration may affect the structure and behavior of the industries involved. In sum, determining the effects of vertical integration is essentially an empirical, not a theoretical, question.

So much for our brief review of the causes and possible effects of vertical integration. My concern now is with public policy toward vertical integration achieved by merger. Let us, therefore, turn to the treatment of vertical integration under Section 7 of the Clayton Act.

PUBLIC POLICY TOWARD VERTICAL MERGERS

The Celler-Kefauver Act of 1950

Section 7 of the Clayton Act, as amended by the Celler-Kefauver Act of 1950, is designed to prevent mergers which may substantially lessen competition or tend to create a monopoly. This Act covers

[10]A. Marshall, *Principles of Economics; An Introductory Volume*, 8th edition (London: Macmillan & Co. Ltd., 1938), p. 494.

all forms of mergers—horizontal, vertical, and conglomerate. In each case, however, the legal test is the same: whether the merger may have an adverse effect on competition. It cannot be emphasized too strongly that the entire thrust of the Act is to prevent monopoly in its incipiency. The legislative history of the Act makes it clear that the Congress viewed mergers as posing a special threat to competition. In its view, American industrial experience demonstrates that mergers have been responsible for creating many existing positions of market power. Because mergers represented a unique threat to competition, the Celler-Kefauver Act was designed to place certain constraints on growth by mergers. Quite clearly, then, public policy has explicitly and purposefully created different legal standards for evaluating growth achieved by merger than for growth by internal means. Let us consider briefly how this standard has been applied to vertical mergers.

Supreme Court Decisions Involving Vertical Mergers

The first vertical merger case brought under the Celler-Kefauver Act to reach the Supreme Court was *United States* v. *Maryland & Virginia Milk Producers Association*.[11] This case involved foreclosure of 96 percent of all fluid milk sales in the Washington, D.C., metropolitan area. Because of the unusually great amount of foreclosure caused by this merger, the Supreme Court's decision in this case did not represent a very significant legal precedent under the new law.[12]

The Supreme Court's *Brown Shoe* decision in 1962 involved both horizontal and vertical aspects. Although the Court could have declared the merger illegal on horizontal grounds alone, it chose to rule on the vertical aspects as well.[13] Because of the apparently small market foreclosure resulting from the merger, *Brown Shoe* represents a strong precedent on the subject of vertical mergers.

Briefly, these are the facts surrounding the vertical aspects of the case. In 1956 the Brown Shoe Company acquired the Kinney Shoe Company. Brown was the country's fourth largest shoe manu-

[11]362 U.S. 458 (1960).

[12]The most significant aspect of this case was the Supreme Court's ruling that agricultural cooperatives were covered by Section 7 of the Clayton Act.

[13]The Court could have declared the merger illegal on horizontal grounds because the merger resulted in the achievement of substantial market shares in the retail sale of shoes in many metropolitan areas.

facturer, accounting for 4 percent of United States production. Kinney was the largest individual shoe retailer, with 1.6 percent of all retail shoe store sales.

Taken alone, these facts do not argue very persuasively that the merger could have had any significant anticompetitive effects— the vertical foreclosure involved appeared miniscule. But consider these additional facts: This merger was the most recent of a series of vertical mergers by Brown and other leading shoe manufacturers. Thirteen shoe manufacturers already operated 21 percent of all retail shoe stores. Although shoe manufacturing was quite competitively structured, the number of companies had been declining and concentration increasing. This suggested to the Court that the industry was already experiencing trends which threatened to lessen competition. The Court concluded that not only was Brown "a participant but also a moving factor, in these industry trends."

The question before the Court, then, was whether in this industrial setting the fourth largest shoe manufacturer should be permitted to acquire the largest remaining shoe retailer. If the line was not to be drawn here, where could or should it have been drawn? Summing up its reasons for finding the merger in violation of the Celler-Kefauver Act, the Court concluded, "We reached this conclusion because the trend toward vertical integration in the shoe industry . . . may foreclose competition from a substantial share of the markets for men's, women's, and children's shoes, *without producing any countervailing competitive, economic, or social advantages.*" [Emphasis added.]

What have been the effects of this decision? Time permits only a few observations. Subsequent events suggest that this case had an important effect on structural developments in the shoe industry. Although the number of shoe manufacturers has continued to decline—from 970 in 1954 to 785 in 1963—and mergers have continued, the action taken against Brown in 1956 resulted in halting substantial mergers by the industry. Since 1956 the top four shoe manufacturers have made no sizable shoe manufacturing or distribution acquisitions.[14] The top four shoe manufacturers' share of total shoe production rose from 28 percent to 30 percent between 1947 and 1954. Over the next nine years concentration declined—

---

[14]One of the largest of these was challenged by the Federal Trade Commission in 1965. *In the Matter of Endicott Johnson Corporation*, Docket No. C-1009 (1965).

to 25 percent by 1963.[15] It appears that well before the Supreme Court's *Brown Shoe* decision in 1962, enforcement policy had the effect of channeling merger activity away from the leading companies. This development doubtless played a significant role in the observable decline in concentration between 1954 and 1963. For had the top companies continued to merge at the pre-1956 rate, they might easily have forestalled this decline[16] and perhaps have expanded their share of shoe manufacturing. Apparently real economies of horizontal or vertical integration were not sufficient to enable these companies to expand their market share through internal growth alone.

Since 1956 companies ranking below the top 4 companies have made a fairly large number of mergers.[17] Partly because of their acquisitions, the 5th to 20th largest shoe manufacturers increased their share of United States sales from 15 percent in 1954 to 18 percent in 1963.

Vertical Mergers in the Cement Industry

The most intensive effort undertaken to date to challenge vertical mergers in a single industry involved cement manufacturers' acquisitions of their customers. The Federal Trade Commission has issued 13 merger complaints challenging forward vertical-type acquisitions of ready-mixed concrete or concrete product firms.[18] Five of these complaints challenged ten acquisitions of the country's

15These concentration ratios are for all "shoes, except rubber," SIC 3141.
16Whereas the four largest companies made at least 33 shoe manufacturing and retailing acquisitions during 1950–1956, they made only 19 during 1957–1966. Moreover, whereas the companies acquired during the 7 years 1950–56 had assets of at least $91 million, those acquired in the 10 years 1957–66 had assets of at least $9 million. Asset information was available for 17 companies acquired during 1950–1956 and 10 companies acquired during 1957–1966.
17According to *Moody's Industrial Manual* shoe manufacturers and retailers, other than the top four, acquired 11 shoe retailers and manufacturers between 1950 and 1956 and 26 such companies between 1957 and 1965.
18*In the Matter of Permanente Cement Co.*, FTC Docket No. 7939 (1960). This complaint challenged a vertical as well as a horizontal merger. The other companies challenged were *Martin-Marietta Co.*, Docket No. 8280 (1961); *Lone Star Cement*, Docket No. 8585 (1963); *American Cement Corp.*, Docket No. C-681 (1964); *Mississippi River Fuel Corp.*, Docket No. 8657 (1965); *National Portland Cement*, Docket No. 8654 (1965); *Texas Industries*, Docket No. 8656 (1965); *United States Steel Corp.*, Docket No. 8655 (1965); *Ideal Cement Co.*, Docket No. 8678 (1966); *Lehigh Portland Cement Co.*, Docket No. 8680 (1966); *Lone Star Cement*, Docket No. C-1159 (1967).

four largest cement companies—Ideal Cement, Lone Star, United States Steel (Universal Atlas), and Lehigh Portland.

These cases were a response to an accelerating merger movement which got under way in 1959, when four vertical acquisitions occurred (see Table 12). Over the next eight years an additional 65 vertical mergers occurred. Many of these acquisitions appeared to be of a defensive nature; that is, companies were responding to either actual or threatened acquisition of their customers.[19]

Very briefly, the vertical merger movement in this industry threatened competition because it promised to result in a significant degree of foreclosure in some markets.[20] This, in turn, would place

TABLE 12

Acquisitions of Cement Users by Cement Manufacturers 1950–1965

Year	Number of Acquisitions	Number of Commission Complaints[a]	
1950–55	2	0	
1956	1	0	
1957	0	0	
1958	1	0	
1959	4	0	
1960	9	1	(1)
1961	3	1 [b]	
1962	5	0	
1963	8	1	(2)
1964	10	1	(1)
1965	12	4	(7)
1966	12	4	(8)
1967	2	1	(1)
Total	69	13	(20)

[a]Numbers in parentheses show the number of vertical acquisitions challenged in the complaints.

[b]This complaint challenged the acquisition of 29 small concrete pipe companies and several aggregates and lime companies, as well as 5 cement manufacturers. *Martin-Marietta Corp.*, Docket 8280. None of these acquisitions is included in Column 2.

Source: W. F. Mueller, *The Celler-Kefauver Act: Sixteen Years of Enforcement*, A Staff report to the Antitrust Subcommittee, Committee on the Judiciary, House of Representatives (October 16, 1967), p. 23.

[19]See Bureau of Economics staff report to the Federal Trade Commission, *Economic Report on Mergers and Vertical Integration in the Cement Industry* (April 1966), hereafter cited as *Economic Report*.

[20]This discussion of the likely effects of vertical mergers in this industry is based on the *Economic Report*. It should not be inferred from this discussion that all vertical mergers by cement manufacturers violate Section 7. Each merger must be evaluated in its industrial context.

some manufacturers at a competitive disadvantage and would raise entry barriers. These results might occur because of the structure of the cement industry.

Market concentration is high in cement manufacturing, which is essentially a regional market industry.[21] Because there are substantial economies of scale at the manufacturing level, it is difficult to enter most markets.[22] Should a substantial part of a market become foreclosed by vertical mergers, entry barriers would be raised because of the so-called "percentage effect" mentioned earlier.[23] Moreover, unchecked vertical merger activity by leading firms almost certainly breeds more mergers. Those firms losing customers in the process would be forced either to seek new customers elsewhere or to make mergers of their own. Since some firms would be less successful in this respect than others, the losers would become less effective competitors and, perhaps, be forced to leave the industry—very probably via the horizontal merger route.

Although the Commission issued one complaint in each of the years 1960, 1961, 1963, and 1964, the merger movement continued unabated. In 1965 the Commission issued four additional complaints challenging seven acquisitions; in 1966 it issued four complaints challenging eight acquisitions; and in 1967 it issued one complaint challenging one acquisition.[24] Over the period 1960–67 the Commission issued 11 complaints challenging 29 ready-mixed concrete acquisitions (Table 12).[25]

In 1964 the Commission, in issuing its first opinion involving a vertical acquisition in this industry,[26] took cognizance of the industrywide character of the merger movement, observing that "vertical integration in the cement industry through merger is of growing importance and urgency and has apparently assumed indus-

---

[21]In most states the four largest cement companies account for 75 percent or more of cement shipments. In only three states do the top four firms control less than 50 percent of sales. *Economic Report*, p. 30.

[22]A 1-million-barrel cement plant is equal to between 2 percent and 4 percent of some of the largest regional markets. *Economic Report*, p. 43. The costs of a 1.2-million-barrel plant are 77 percent greater than those of a 5.9-million-barrel plant. (*Ibid.*, p. 34.) A plant of the latter size would account for between 10 and 20 percent of the consumption of even large markets.

[23]See p. 152, footnote 5.

[24]The challenged acquisition occurred in 1966.

[25]It also challenged the acquisition of 29 concrete pipe companies. (See footnote ᵇ, Table 12) .

[26]*In the Matter of Permanente Cement Co.*, Docket No. 7939.

trywide dimensions."[27] It subsequently announced its intention "to consider the problem on an industrywide basis to determine whether its current approach to vertical mergers in these industries was correct and effective, or whether it should be supplemented."

As a first step in informing itself on this subject, the Commission directed its Bureau of Economics to undertake an industrywide study, and on April 26, 1966, a staff *Economic Report on Mergers and Vertical Integration in the Cement Industry* was published. Thereafter public hearings were held in July 1966 and interested parties presented written and oral statements regarding the economic causes and consequences of vertical mergers. Based on its experience and the record developed at these public hearings, the Commission decided to spell out "insofar as possible, its future enforcement policy with respect to vertical mergers in the cement and ready-mixed concrete industries."[28] In essence, it set forth the circumstances in which it would challenge future vertical mergers.[29]

It appears that the vertical merger movement in the industry was halted by the Commission's various legal actions and its explicit announcement regarding future enforcement policy. The number of vertical mergers fell sharply after 1966. This decline appeared to be in response to the Commission's industrywide hearings in the summer of 1966 and the enforcement policy statement which it issued in January 1967. To my knowledge, no substantial ready-mix concrete companies have been acquired by cement companies since January 1967, and no ready-mix companies have been acquired since May 1967.

It is still too early to judge the long-range effects of the Commission's several-faceted enforcement policy in the cement industry. The pressure of excess capacity in the early 1960's and other factors tended to increase competition by broadening cement markets and eroding the competitive position of market leaders.[30] These pro-

[27]*Ibid.*

[28]Federal Trade Commission, "Enforcement Policy with Respect to Vertical Mergers in the Cement Industry" (Jan. 3, 1967), 2.

[29]The Commission also stated that henceforth it would require all Portland cement companies to notify the Commission at least 60 days prior to the consummation of any merger or acquisition of a ready-mixed concrete producer. *Ibid.*, 11–12.

[30]Between 1958 and 1963 the market position of the four leading hydraulic cement manufacturers declined in four of the six Census Regions for which this information is available. *Concentration Ratios in Manufacturing Industry, 1963,*

competitive factors apparently stimulated many of the vertical mergers occurring since 1960, as some companies attempted to entrench their existing positions against the new competitive pressures. Hence, insofar as vertical mergers have been deterred, chances seem good that competitive pressures will further erode the high levels of concentration still common to many markets. To date, cement companies have not entered ready-mix by the internal growth route. This suggests that there were no compelling real economies of integrated operations underlying the vertical mergers occurring in this industry.[31]

THE CRITICS OF VERTICAL MERGER POLICY

Vertical merger policy has recently come under severe criticism in some circles because it allegedly interferes with economic efficiency. Bork and Bowman have made the most strident attacks on the Supreme Court's *Brown Shoe* decision. They sum up their criticisms as follows:

> The Brown Shoe case employed the theory of exclusionary practices to outlaw vertical integration that promised lower prices, the theory of incipiency to foresee danger in a presumably desirable trend that was barely started, and the theory of "social purpose" to justify the fact that the decision prevented the realization of efficiencies by a merger which, realistically viewed, did not even remotely threaten competition.[32]

Let us examine the basis for each of their conclusions. First, what basis is there for the conclusion that the merger "promised

Part II, Report prepared by the Bureau of the Census for the Subcommittee on Antitrust and Monopoly of the Committee on the Judiciary, U.S. Senate (1967), p. 330.

[31]The Commission's staff study concluded that there were no such economies. The preponderance of industry testimony during the Commission's hearings on the subject bore out this conclusion.

[32]Robert H. Bork and Ward S. Bowman, "The Crises in Antitrust," in "The Goals of Antitrust: A Dialogue on Policy," *Columbia Law Review*, 65 (March 1965), 373. I shall not discuss their third point, namely, that the decision employed "a theory of social purpose." It is true that the Supreme Court did include some language which may be interpreted as meaning that the merger should have been prevented because it threatened the future of small independent businessmen. I consider this language largely irrelevant for our purposes because I believe the rule of law laid down in this decision can be defended entirely on the economic criteria.

lower prices"? They cite no evidence for this inference except that the Court observed, "Of course, some of the results of large integrated or chain operations are beneficial to consumers." The recognition that integrated and chain operations may result in benefits to consumers in no way proves that the Brown-Kinney merger actually resulted in such benefits;[33] or that the merger route is the only way to achieve such benefits; or, finally, that even if such benefits were, in fact, achieved by this merger, they would have been passed on to consumers.

Second, what evidence did Bowman and Bork muster in criticizing the Court's "incipiency" theory? Here they argued that concentration was still so low that there was no need to stop vertical mergers. After all, they argued, vertical mergers by large manufacturers could not injure competition because smaller manufacturers whose business was displaced by such mergers could easily find other customers, or, failing this, they could make mergers of their own. Consequently, shoe manufacturing must inevitably remain competitive. This argument rests on the assumption of an essentially frictionless and perfectly competitive market, in which all sellers have equal access to customers, capital, and other resources. Blake and Jones put it well when they say, "It is well recognized, Bork and Bowman notwithstanding, that the capital market does not operate like the textbook 'model'—providing unlimited funds to all comers, strictly in relation to profits and risk—particularly where very large amounts are involved."[34]

Bork and Bowman go so far as to argue that:

> Even if, as there was no reason to expect, complete vertical integration took place in the industry, there would obviously be room for hundreds of shoe manufacturers and, given the ease of entry into shoe retailing, no basis for imagining that any new manufacturer could not find or create outlets at any time he chose.[35]

[33]In fact, the Court stated explicitly that the merger did not produce "any countervailing competitive, *economic*, or social advantages." (Emphasis added.)

[34]Harlan M. Blake and William K. Jones, in "The Goals of Antitrust: A Dialogue on Policy," *Columbia Law Review*, 65 (March 1965), 392–393.

[35]Bork and Bowman, *op. cit.*, 371. They point out further that: "It is hard to conceive of a use of capital more fraught with uncertainty than an attempt to break into an industry occupied by vertically integrated firms enjoying the fruits of their fewness of number. And the stakes will often be high. It is elementary "game theory"—or what is the same thing, known to any poker-

They cite no authority for their assumption of perfect ease of entry. Although I believe the record is silent on this point, it is a fact that even large shoe manufacturers have made practically no entry into retailing via internal growth, even since being foreclosed from "entry" by merger. While it may be "easy" to enter shoe retailing by opening an isolated store here and there, it would be extremely difficult and costly for a shoe manufacturer to enter shoe retailing rapidly and on a sufficient scale to sell sizable portions of its output. Hence, were the industry to become largely integrated, it would become difficult for an entirely new entrant to enter retailing on a scale sufficient to operate an efficient size shoe-manufacturing establishment.

In the real world manufacturers cannot replace without cost substantial customers lost because of mergers. As a result, even the seemingly small foreclosure resulting from mergers of Brown-Kinney dimensions may very well trigger additional defensive vertical mergers. Nor are all firms equally capable of succeeding in the ensuing merger race. The largest firms almost certainly will have greater access to capital than will smaller firms, with the result that they will find it easier to gain merger partners. Because of the contagious nature of vertical merger movements, each merger creates pressures for additional mergers as sellers strive to make up for their lost accounts. For it is costly and time-consuming to pick up new customers. In imperfectly structured markets there are present varying degrees of product differentiation, personal ties, franchise arrangements, financial linkages, and other "imperfections" which make it difficult and costly to shift customers.[36]

Upon close inspection, even seemingly large national markets turn out to be segmented geographically and by product lines. The shoe manufacturer who loses a major part of his market because someone acquired his major retail outlet will disagree with Bork and Bowman's characterization of his plight. They argue, in effect, that all the disadvantaged manufacturer need do is compete aggressively and he will readily find a new outlet which is a good substitute for the old one. But in the real world, the shoe manufacturer will likely find that some retailers are outside his "natural market

---

player—that one does not knowingly enter into a "two-person, zero-sum" game or a poker game without having resources equal to the opponent's, or at least knowledge of their dimension."

36See *Federal Trade Commission* v. *Brown Shoe Co.*, 384 U.S. 316 (1966).

area," say on the West Coast. And if he sells a low or moderately priced line he must rule out those retailers now selling Florsheim and other high price lines with strong consumer franchises. And he would also find that, in addition to the "captive" outlets of the integrated manufacturers, he must rule out those retail outlets that have franchise agreements and other arrangements which tend to bind a manufacturer and "his" retailers together.

No, in the real world the shoe market is not the great big, frictionless market envisioned by Bork and Bowman. And this is precisely what industry witnesses testified to in the district court proceedings in this case. Such industry testimony cannot be dismissed blithely by labeling it as the special pleadings of injured private parties, or arguing that it be dismissed because to do otherwise is to be concerned solely with "competitors" rather than "competition."

The presence of the above factors causes vertical mergers to beget more vertical mergers, and causes those manufacturing companies weakened by vertical mergers to become parties to horizontal mergers. In this setting, financial and market power, not economic efficiency, may determine the winners in the competitive race. Nor are there any "natural" safeguards in this industrial setting to guarantee that vertical integration will not result in an industry's becoming unnecessarily concentrated and difficult to enter.

As I emphasized earlier, there is a different public policy standard for vertical integration achieved by merger rather than by internal growth. This distinction is not an anomaly arising from legislative oversight. It is rooted in sound economics. The important point to grasp in evaluating public policy with respect to growth achieved by vertical mergers is that it short-circuits the "market" test of growth. Professor Heflebower put it well when he said:

> When a corporation chooses to grow by building it expects to face tests in the market for the product over the years required to establish and develop a new operation. It must fight its way in, that is, compete to succeed, and not buy its way in. I consider this a far better market test, and a more immediately relevant one, than the "market test" involved in a merger for the market for firms is highly imperfect. . . .
>
> Second, in nearly all circumstances, a firm whose acquisition is apt to be challenged has the capacity to grow by building.

It has or can get the funds, it has the management capacity, and often already some of the needed market connections.[37]

It is for this reason that we have a different public policy toward vertical integration by merger than toward integration achieved by internal growth. It is for this reason that I believe the rule of law laid down in *Brown Shoe* is good public policy. Its effect has been to prevent the industry leaders from growing vertically via the merger route. It is true that, as economists, we may never be entirely satisfied that this policy prevented the emergence of high concentration in shoe manufacturing and retailing. But this policy will increase the probability that any substantial industry restructuring which does occur will have passed the market test and will therefore have been rooted in economies of integrated operations rather than in market power.

Doubtless there will be instances where public policy prohibits mergers which would not seriously injure competition. But industrial history argues persuasively that to err on the side of a too strict antimerger policy is preferable to the reverse. As Professor Heflebower has put it, "the social cost of error from being too easy in merger policy is far more serious and less easily reversed than from being too strict."[38]

---

[37]Richard B. Heflebower, "Comments on the F.T.C. Staff Document, *Economic Report on Mergers and Vertical Integration in the Cement Industry*," presented at the Federal Trade Commission public hearings on vertical mergers in the cement industry, July 11, 1966.

[38]R. B. Heflebower, "Corporate Mergers: Policy and Economic Analysis," *Quarterly Journal of Economics*, 77 (Nov. 1963) , 558.

12

issues in
vertical integration policy

by SAM PELTZMAN

Partly as a result of effective antitrust enforcement, horizontal mergers have decreased in importance relative to vertical
mergers. The increasing importance of vertical mergers has produced a parallel increase in concern by the antitrust agencies
and the courts. So great has this concern
become that the courts now stand ready to
accord the vertical aspects of a merger more
weight than the horizontal; *vide* Brown
Shoe. In this discussion, I shall attempt to
determine the extent to which vertical
mergers do pose special problems for antitrust policy that are not posed by horizontal
mergers.

In sorting out the relevant issues, we
must abstract from any efficiencies created
by vertical mergers. A vertical merger might
be attractive to a firm because it creates
efficiencies and/or because it increases the
firm's market power. My inquiry here is
directed entirely to the latter possibility.
That is, where it can be shown that vertical
integration has no anticompetitive effects,
I shall not try to specify the efficiency that

might have prompted the merger. Since the antitrust laws are prohibitory, such a specification would, in any case, be irrelevant for public policy. Conversely, where competition may be harmed by vertical merger, I shall not speculate on whether the harm might be outweighed by some efficiency created by the merger.

Two kinds of anticompetitive effects have been attributed to vertical merger: (1) the acquiring firm may foreclose the acquired supplier or outlet to rivals, or otherwise use the acquired entities to harm rivals; (2) vertical merger may discourage entry by raising the capital required by an entrant.

VERTICAL MERGERS AND MARKET FORECLOSURE

I shall contend that concern about possible market foreclosure is misplaced. A manufacturer may, in certain circumstances, improve his market position by buying retail outlets and foreclosing them to his rivals. But, wherever he can do this, there are alternative ways of enhancing his market power which are distinctly superior to foreclosure, which obtain all of the advantages of foreclosure and avoid the costs specific to this practice. This being so, we should not expect foreclosure to be important as a predatory tactic.

To understand why foreclosure does not make sense as a predatory tactic, consider the consequences to a manufacturer who attempts to use it so. In the simplest case, there would be no output effects. To use a familiar example, there are ten shoe manufacturers, $A, B, \ldots J$. Each is producing 2,000 pairs of shoes per year, and they are being sold through ten equal-sized, multi-brand retail outlets, I, II, $\ldots$ X. Each retailer thus sells 2,000 pairs, 200 of each brand. Now shoe manufacturer B buys retailer II, and, without changing his output, denies this outlet to the other manufacturers. B's foreclosure of 10 percent of their former market will impose costs on B's rivals: the foreclosed outlet may have been attractively located, there will be costs of transferring sales to new outlets, etc. B hopes that these costs will drive some rivals from the shoe industry and thus strengthen B's market position.

There is another aspect to this, however, which may frustrate B's intent. B's action has, at least initially, reduced the demand for the services of independent retailers by 10 percent. The independent retailers will react by accepting lower retail margins for non-B

shoes. This is, of course, the obverse of the so-called "percentage effect." Foreclosure, without any initial change in output, means simply that the "open" portion of the retail market expands exactly by the degree of foreclosure. The net result will not, however, be a mere shifting about of brands among retail outlets. There will be costs, but they will be borne by everyone concerned: B's rivals, independent retailers, consumers, *and B.*

This conclusion follows because if the shoe retail market was in equilibrium before B's intervention, the then existing distribution of brands among retail outlets was optimum. Retailers were, in this example, selling ten brands and selling them in equal proportions, because that is what their customers wanted. Presumably customers valued the ability to choose among ten brands without having to incur extra shopping trips, enough so that the costs of a larger inventory were offset in the retail price of shoes. The distribution of brand preferences among consumers accounted for the particular distribution of sales by brand among retail outlets. (If the previous brand distribution among stores was nonoptimal, there would have been a gain to any retailer who changed that distribution.) B's foreclosure, by changing the distribution of brands in a way not desired by customers, lowers the value of all retail outlets, his own especially.[1]

B incurs another cost specific to him: since B would not have entered retailing but for the possibility of engaging in foreclosure, his costs of operating the II division will be no lower, and possibly higher, than those of the independent II. Indeed, this last cost could be most significant: to the extent that there is some systematic division of function between manufacturing and retailing in this industry, there must be strong cost disincentives to combining the two. Otherwise, we would see a more or less random pattern of manufacturing-retailing relationships.

Now we come to the crux of the matter. This imposition of mutual costs by B may succeed in strengthening B's market position, if it is better able to stand the costs than $A, C, \ldots J$. That is, it may for one reason or another have to pay less than its rivals for the capital that is dissipated or foregone when B restructures the market. This could then result in some of B's rivals leaving the shoe industry. However, there is a better way for B to use such a cost advan-

---

[1]Especially, because B's retail division ends up handling fewer brands than independent retailers.

tage. B can simply buy his rivals out. This would save the costs of restructuring the retail market, and B can induce mergers with his rivals by sharing some of the savings with them. If the law rules out horizontal merger, he can simply reduce the wholesale price of shoes. In this way, he can displace rivals' shoes while maintaining an optimum apportionment of sales in the different parts of the retail market and avoiding the higher costs he faces in retailing.

We get to the same result if we relax the assumptions in the preceding analysis. Suppose, for example, that B buys II and simply forecloses it to $A, C, \ldots J$, but continues selling 200 pairs of shoes through each independent retail outlet. B may also increase his own output to make up for the sales of his II division that are lost by foreclosure. Whether B increases output or not, he will have created (avoidable) problems for himself.

Suppose B does not expand output. Then the following will happen: (1) B's competitors will suffer losses from two sources. They will absorb relocation costs, and independent retailers' margins will rise as shoe manufacturers bid for "space" in the "open" portion of the market. However, as in the previous case, the "percentage" effect has secondary consequences, namely (2), there will be entry into shoe retailing in response to its increased profitability. This entry will mitigate the losses to B's rivals. Finally (3), B's retail division will incur losses, both because its sales rate is now nonoptimal (it has been cut to 200 pairs from 2,000), and because it is offering a nonoptimal brand selection. Once again, if B is better able to stand these losses than are $A, C, \ldots J$, the foreclosure may be successful. But once again, B's presumed capital cost advantage can be used more effectively in strengthening his horizontal market position in manufacturing directly. In this way, the losses in (3) could be avoided and B could collect some of the losses in (1).

If B increases his total output in order to maintain the sales rate of his II division, one loss will only be replaced by another. The II division, it is true, will have smaller losses than otherwise. But, because total shoe output has expanded, the price of shoes will fall, and the manufacturing division will incur losses.[2] This situation is in every way analogous to predatory price cutting, except that B must incur the added losses due to a nonoptimal brand distribution at his retail division and his lack of expertise in retailing. In such

2More generally, the receipts from the additional output will not cover the costs of producing it.

a case, *B* is obviously better off if he simply cuts his wholesale price.

The general point that emerges here is that foreclosure imposes costs on the firm that practices it as well as on the intended victims. If the firm has a cost advantage which can make foreclosure a successful strategy, it can always use this advantage to achieve the same result by different means which avoid the costs of foreclosure. Therefore, the expectation that predatory market foreclosure is an important goal of vertical mergers has a very weak theoretical base.

This does not mean that the hypothetical events discussed above should be of no concern to the antitrust agencies. However, that concern ought to be properly focused: Company *B* may achieve *horizontal* market power in manufacturing, but the purely vertical aspects of *B*'s behavior are irrelevant to this. *Any* firm with a cost advantage in a particular market may achieve horizontal market power there, regardless of the structure of its vertical relationships. *Any* firm will use that power in the same way, since to do otherwise imposes unnecessary costs on it.

If, for example, *B* suddenly developed a new shoe retailing technique that gave it an advantage over existing retailers, it might well acquire monopoly of the retail market. But it would not foreclose that market to rival shoe producers and thereby damage the value of this monopoly. Rather, it would, like any monopolist in the retail market, charge manufacturers a sufficiently high retail margin for access to the market. Conversely, if a company could not achieve horizontal market power in some market, it cannot synthesize this ability by a vertical merger. This implies that current antitrust policy may well generate a paradoxical result: as it devotes increasing attention to vertical mergers, it misses more of what is really consequential, and thus weakens its over-all effectiveness.[3]

VERTICAL MERGERS AND PREDATORY PRICING

A companion to foreclosure in the demonology about vertical mergers is the price-squeeze against independent retailers. *B* buys II and imposes losses on I, III, . . . X by raising wholesale prices,

[3]Actually, this understates the case. We have deliberately ignored the possibility that there may be oligopoly at both the retail and manufacturing levels. In this case, economic theory shows a policy against vertical merger to be not merely irrelevant, but perverse. See M. Burstein, "A Theory of Full-line Forcing," *Northwestern University Law Review*, 55, 1 (March–April 1960), 62–95.

lowering retail prices, or doing both. *B* thus intends to achieve a monopoly at the retail level. This must first presume that *B* has some power to raise wholesale prices or that it has cheaper access to capital than independent shoe retailers. In either case, the price-squeeze is as pointless as foreclosure.

Where *B* has market power at the manufacturing level, achieving market power at the retail level is redundant. Retail margins are already competitive,[4] so the price-squeeze produces losses with no returns. Where *B* has cheaper access to capital than retailers, and uses that advantage to get a retail monopoly, the price-squeeze is simply another name for predatory price cutting, and is best considered in its horizontal aspects alone.

The more interesting kind of price-squeeze is a variant of foreclosure. The manufacturer seeks to squeeze retailers so as to reduce the number of retail outlets available to his rivals. Having discussed foreclosure at length, we need add little here. Suffice to say that all of the gains of the price-squeeze could be realized by horizontal merger at either the manufacturing or retail level, or, as a second-best, by predatory price cutting at the wholesale level. This would preserve intact an otherwise optimal network of retail locations. Once more, any antitrust problem that arises here will be rooted in some pre-existing ability of a firm to obtain horizontal market power, an ability that cannot be enhanced by vertical merger.

VERTICAL MERGERS AND BARRIERS TO ENTRY

Vertical mergers are alleged to engender horizontal market power by increasing barriers to entry. Even if a firm may not be able to damage its existing competitors by vertical merger, a series of vertical mergers might discourage entrants. An extreme example will bring out the essentials of this argument. Suppose that each of the ten manufacturers has bought a retailer, so that the whole shoe industry has become vertically integrated. Suppose further that the shoe industry is profitable to existing firms. An eleventh shoe manufacturer would like to enter the industry to share these profits, and he would in fact enter as a nonintegrated manufacturer. However, the vertically integrated nature of the shoe industry compels him

[4]Again, I emphasize that I am not considering the bilateral oligopoly cases, where vertical mergers have beneficial effects.

to enter at both levels. Beyond a certain point, new entrants, whether in retailing or manufacturing, may face rising costs of capital which established firms do not. In this example that point is presumably defined by the capital required to go into manufacturing (or retailing) alone. The higher cost of the larger capital required to enter at both levels simultaneously may be sufficient to deter the entrant.

This frequently stated argument[5] must be made more precise before it can be analyzed. Even if we assume for the moment (and we shall examine the assumption shortly) that every established integrated shoe manufacturer forecloses his retail outlets to the new entrant, it does not follow that the new entrant will be compelled to enter at both levels. He has the alternative of vertical integration by contract. That is, this new entrant, and possibly others, may enter into supply agreements with one or more new retail outlets, leaving to the latter the task of raising capital for the retail operation. This is hardly an uncommon form of vertical integration, and the supply agreements that sometimes accompany it seem designed specifically to obtain particular divisions of the capital-raising task.[6] Thus, an upward sloping supply schedule of capital is not necessarily a relevant barrier to entry here. If there is a barrier to entry it arises out of the transaction and information costs facing the new entrant as he seeks to establish a retail relationship. Such costs may be increased by market foreclosure in an amount exceeding the similar costs borne by established firms when they rearranged the industry's distribution system. Note also that any of the gains due to entry restriction must exceed all of the costs specific to foreclosure that we have alluded to previously.

Suppose that existing manufacturers do in fact have a compara-

[5]See, e.g., J. S. Bain, *Barriers to New Competition* (Cambridge: Harvard University Press, 1956).

[6]For example, a new manufacturer may grant exclusive territories to retailers, thus giving them an incentive to develop a local market for the unknown brand. In effect, the retailer assumes the function of raising the market development capital and is paid for this with an exclusive territory. An example of this type of vertical integration is found in the *Sandura* case, where a manufacturer, under financial duress, found it otherwise difficult to raise market development capital for an effective re-entry into the home flooring market. Antitrust policy toward vertical integration by territorial exclusive dealership contracts has been ambiguous. The FTC opposed Sandura's contracts, but the last head of the Antitrust Division has indicated that the Justice Department may look favorably upon this form of vertical integration. See Donald F. Turner, *Speech*, Department of Justice Press Release (August 10, 1965).

tive advantage in obtaining access to the retail market. Are they likely to use this advantage to deter entrants via vertical merger and foreclosure? Possibly, but only if the conditions for effective horizontal collusion are already present in the market for wholesale and retail information. In our example, note that there are *ten* low-cost producers of such information. Even were it in their collective best interests to use this cost advantage to limit entry, any one of the ten would be better off serving an entrant. He could, by selling the new entrant access to his retail stores, obtain a return on his superior position in the retail market. The costs of the increased competition would be spread among all ten existing firms.

The general point here is that if one unconcentrated industry integrates vertically into another unconcentrated industry, there will be no barrier to entry even if the integration is complete. Some existing firm would find it in its own interest to sell the newcomer the right to use its retail distribution facilities at some price which leaves both parties to the transaction with a net gain. The fact that there has been vertical integration by merger does not change this in the least. The situation might be changed if the vertical mergers were accompanied by expanded horizontal market power, but it is the latter phenomenon that is relevant here.

To see this more clearly, consider the behavior of any group of firms which possess a cost advantage obtaining access to the retail market, whether these be real estate brokers, shoe manufacturers, or (much more probably) shoe retailers. They will find it in their collective interest to restrict the output and raise the price of those services connected with providing access to the retail market. Up to a point, they may do this without provoking entry into retailing. This noncompetitive price may deter an entrant at the shoe manufacturing level.

However, unless there are few firms providing access to the retail market, this collective interest in output restriction will not be realized. Any one firm among many will find it attractive to break an output restriction agreement, for, if it does so, it will obtain a larger share of a profitable market. If many firms react to this incentive, the price for access to the retail market will decline, and entry into shoe manufacturing will become more attractive. If there are few firms, a collusive agreement may survive, because one firm can no longer assume that its own actions do not affect industry profitability. In this case, the high price for access to retail markets remains as a deterrent to entry in shoe manufacturing.

All of this is, of course, very familiar economic theory when applied to simple horizontal market relationships. Not one of these forces would be altered if the firms providing access to the retail market were vertically integrated into manufacturing. In the absence of horizontal market power at the retailing level, no barrier to entry into shoe manufacturing in the form of a noncompetitive price for access to the retail market will persist.

The foregoing analysis implies that vertical mergers cannot produce noncompetitive market structures. This in turn implies that the vigorous attack on vertical mergers may dilute the effectiveness of antitrust enforcement. The antitrust agencies obviously do not believe this. Yet, even if one is prepared to accept the theoretical underpinnings of their attack on vertical mergers, present policy must seem highly anomalous. Under current antitrust policy, only vertical merger and some forms of vertical integration by contract are subject to attack. Vertical integration by internal growth is not subject to such attack, and, indeed, is urged on offending firms as an acceptable substitute to vertical merger. By contrast, extension of horizontal market power by internal growth is subject to antitrust attack.[7]

This policy is grossly inconsistent. Whatever evil flows from vertical mergers inheres in internal vertical growth, and vice versa. Consider the model shoe market of this paper. That market is big enough to support ten manufacturers and ten retailers. Since we have abstracted from any efficiencies created by vertical integration, that market will not be widened by such integration. Indeed, the reason for the antitrust authorities' concern over manufacturer *B*'s purchase of retailer II is that other shoe manufacturers will now have access to only nine retail outlets instead of the previous ten. Suppose that, instead of buying II, *B* builds a new retail division, and forecloses it to rivals. Once *B* does this, there will be a decline in the demand for the services of independent shoe retailers, and one of them will leave the industry. *B*'s rivals will be left with but nine independent retail outlets just as surely as if there had been a vertical merger. If the shoe market can support only ten retailers,

[7]For example, one of Alcoa's offenses was its "building ahead" of the market.

that is how many there will be.[8] Of course, this effect of internal vertical growth operates more subtly than that of vertical merger, but their substance is identical.[9] Since internal vertical growth displaces independent retailers to no less an extent than vertical merger, it ought to be attacked no less vigorously.

CONCLUSIONS

Every firm is vertically integrated to some degree, and, no doubt, this degree changes continually. A consistent vertical integration policy must proceed from a theory which shows precisely at what point vertical integration, however accomplished, becomes anticompetitive. Presumably the antitrust agencies would not care to look upon the trimming of leather and the assembly of shoes by a single firm as a predatory tactic designed to foreclose the assembly market to potential leather trimming entrants.

Although the example may seem absurd, the plain fact is that the antitrust authorities have no theory which shows why it is absurd and what forms of vertical integration do reduce competition. This is a particularly serious deficiency in present policy. Even if some kinds of vertical integration are thought to have anticompetitive effects, it is by no means self-evident that present policy, proceeding on an ad hoc basis in a theoretical vacuum, has a lower social cost than no policy at all. Of course, the main thrust of this discussion is that the appropriate vertical integration policy is, in fact, no policy at all. To those who share this view, the failure of the antitrust agencies to press their vertical integration policy consistently may seem to be only a beneficial constriction of an erroneous policy.

[8]Unless, for some unfathomable reason, B is prepared to operate his new retail division permanently at a loss.

[9]Indeed, this illustration shows why firms may prefer vertical merger to internal vertical growth. Whatever makes vertical integration attractive to a firm need not be associated with growth in the total market. Thus internal vertical growth may waste resources by making some existing downstream investment redundant. An outright purchase of the existing investment avoids the redundancy.

V

THE RECENT TREND
TOWARD CONGLOMERATE
MERGERS

13

conglomerate mergers—theory and congressional intent

by JOHN M. BLAIR

We are approaching the end of the second decade of enforcement under the Celler-Kefauver amendment to Section 7 of the Clayton Act, signed into law by President Truman on December 29, 1950. Among students of the law there is a consensus that it has been an effective restraint against horizontal and vertical mergers. There is also a consensus that it has not been a significant deterrent to conglomerate mergers. On this point the facts leave little room for doubt. According to the Federal Trade Commission, mergers of the conglomerate type accounted for 71.0 percent of the assets of all "large" companies[1] acquired during 1960–1964.[2] According to a study based on a special survey of the Census Bureau:

Of the 820,000 workers involved in acquisitions during 1959–62, 305,000 or

[1] Companies with assets of over $10 million.
[2] Hearings on Economic Concentration before the Subcommittee on Antitrust and Monopoly, Pt. 2, "Mergers and Other Factors Affecting Industry Concentration, 89th Cong., 1st Sess." (1965), p. 516.

37 percent were engaged in facilities classified in the same industry as the acquiring company. One-sixth of the total, 130,000, were in other industries but within the same major industry group. But the biggest segment, nearly 400,000 workers, or almost half of the total, had been engaged in facilities which were not even within the same major industry group as the acquiring firm.[3]

It is thus clear that the recent and continuing wave of merger activity is made up largely of conglomerate acquisitions. The very term itself, formerly spurned by corporate management, has become something of an accolade, connoting growth, "dynamic" leadership, and stock appreciation, though not necessarily high dividends or particularly favorable stock-earnings ratios.

At long last it is now conceded that the amended Section 7 applied to all mergers—horizontal, vertical, and conglomerate. How then to explain its effectiveness against the first two forms and its ineffectiveness against the last? Is there a deficiency of the law itself? Or does the problem lie in the manner in which it has been administered? The point of view expressed here is that it is the latter—a failure of enforcement which is directly traceable to certain unfortunate interpretations. The reference is not to judicial interpretations, but rather to interpretations by eminent legal authorities, set forth in lengthy articles in leading law journals. The article which, because of its comprehensiveness,[4] best exemplifies these interpretations is by Donald F. Turner.[5]

To the extent that they have been accepted, these interpretations provide the intellectual bases for (1) a failure to utilize the tendency-toward-monopoly test of the law, (2) a failure to make effective use of theories based upon expectations of reactions, (3) an assumption that economies of scale must be "taken into account" in applying the law, and (4) a failure to comprehend that the congressional intent was not only the maintenance of competition but also the preservation of certain social and political values to which Congress, rightly or wrongly, attached great importance.

---

[3]*Ibid.*, p. 1011.

[4]The article has been described by an admiring colleague as "an all-encompassing exploration" (James F. Rill, "Conglomerate Mergers: The Problem of Superconcentration," *UCLA Law Review*, 14 [May, 1967], 1055) .

[5]Donald F. Turner, "Conglomerate Mergers and Section 7 of the Clayton Act," *Harvard Law Review*, 78, 7 (May, 1965) , 1316.

THE TENDENCY-TOWARD-MONOPOLY TEST

It is widely believed that Section 7 is concerned only with those acquisitions which have "anticompetitive effects." Thus, Turner has written: ". . . the House and Senate Committee reports . . . indicate that the amended statute was directed *only* at mergers after which there would be a reasonable probability of anticompetitive effects."[6] Further, "In theory, the ideal regulatory policy would be one that discriminated carefully on a case-by-case basis between those mergers that threatened substantial *anticompetitive consequences* and those which do not."[7] "Hence," in Turner's view, "rational lawmaking requires that we endeavor to establish some idea of the relative probabilities of *anticompetitive effects* as among the various types of mergers, so that our hierarchy of rules will at least make internal sense."[8]

There can certainly be no objection to distinguishing between those mergers that do and those that do not have *"anticompetitive consequences,"* or to establishing a rational order of priority among those that do. But there is very real objection to the assumption that those mergers that cannot be shown with reasonable probability to have such effects are therefore beyond the reach of Section 7. There is, it happens, a second test of illegality carried over from the original Clayton Act: mergers are prohibited which "may tend to create a monopoly." Although no cases based solely on this test were ever adjudicated, the fault lay not in the test itself but rather in the assets loophole which, it soon became evident, foredoomed to failure any case brought under Section 7.

The passage of the Clayton Act in 1914, as is well known, was a response to the dismay in Congress over the interjection in 1911 of the "rule of reason" into the Sherman Act. What is not so well known is that in framing this new law Congress used as its model tests which prior to the "rule of reason" decisions had been developing in the *Northern Securities* case, the *Trans-Missouri Freight* case, and the circuit court opinions in the oil and tobacco cases. Among them was a prohibition of consolidations and mergers

---

[6]*Ibid.*, p. 1316 (emphasis added).
[7]*Ibid.*, p. 1318 (emphasis added).
[8]*Ibid.*, p. 1320 (emphasis added).

between previously competing firms on the grounds that they would necessarily destroy previously existing competition. This standard was incorporated into Section 7 almost without change.[9]

Another test related to monopoly, per se. In arguing the *Standard Oil* case before the Supreme Court, the Attorney General emphasized that trade could be restrained by virtue of stock ownership alone. Pointing to the Court's previous decision in the *Northern Securities* case and to other precedents, he contended that the power to restrain trade "... which could be exercised by reason of stock ownership and control of the various corporations was as much in violation of the antitrust act as direct restraint by contract."[10] In keeping with the general purpose of the Clayton Act of seeking to "nip monopoly in the bud," this line of argument was given expression in the prohibition of mergers which *"may tend* to create a monopoly." These two tests, plus a prohibition against mergers which may "substantially lessen competition," thus formed the warp and woof of the 1914 law.

The Celler-Kefauver amendment deleted the "between the acquiring and acquired company" test partly on the grounds that, taken literally, it would prohibit all horizontal mergers, some of which might be promotive of competition. Moreover, there was fear that the very stringency of the test might provoke the courts into introducing a "rule of reason" type of interpretation. Although both of the other two standards remained, we are now asked to believe that the tendency-toward-monopoly test is a redundancy—that it can

[9]In the tobacco case the Circuit Court spelled out in explicit terms its preoccupation with this one question of the elimination of competition between formerly competing firms:

> What benefits may have come from this combination ... it is not material to inquire, nor need subsequent business methods be considered. ... The record in this case does not indicate that there has been any increase in the price of tobacco products to the consumer. There is an absence of persuasive evidence that by unfair competition or improper practices independent dealers have been dragooned into giving up their individual enterprises and selling out to the principal defendant. During the existence of the American Tobacco Company new enterprises have been started, some with small capital, in competition with it and have thrived. *But all this is immaterial.* Each one of these purchases of existing concerns, complained of in the petition was a contract and combination in restraint of a *competition existing when it was entered into*, and that is sufficient to bring it within the ban of this drastic statute. (164 Fed. 700, pp. 702–703, emphasis added.)

[10]221 U.S. 22.

reach no merger which cannot be shown also to have "anticompetitive effects." It would thus suffer the same fate as has largely befallen Section 2 of the Sherman Act—a fate against which the Attorney General warned in his argument to the Court in the old *Standard Oil* case. Why, he asked, had Congress passed Section 2 of the Sherman Act at all if it had not intended to prohibit those "attempts to monopolize" which did *not* involve any restraint of trade? Presumably all attempts which did involve restraints would be caught by Section 1. As he put it, "The two sections of the Act were manifestly not intended to cover the same thing; otherwise the several sections would be useless."[11] With the same logic we can say that the injury-to-competition and the tendency-toward-monopoly tests of the amended Section 7 were manifestly not intended to cover the same thing; otherwise the latter would be useless.

Congress was fully aware that it was incorporating two distinct and separate tests into the law, as is clear from the legislative history. The accompanying report of the Senate Judiciary Committee states,

> Thus, the phrase "in many sections of the country" was made applicable to both the lessening of competition and the tendency to create a monopoly. As the bill originally stood it applied only to the former. . . .
> Similarly the phrase "in any line of commerce" was made applicable to *both* as above. As the bill originally stood, the phrase applied only to the tendency to create a monopoly.[12]

Why would Congress want to proscribe mergers which were without a demonstrable adverse effect on competition? For the same reason that Congress had included the identical test in the 1914 law—to prevent the concentration of power ". . . which could be exercised by reason of stock ownership and control. . . ."

The trusts of those rough and troubled times, it should be remembered, were not the smoothly conforming oligopolists of today. Periods of observance to mutually agreed upon prices were periodically interspersed with outbreaks of competitive warfare, involving the most vicious and predatory practices. Congress thus tended to take a baleful view of the trusts, regardless of whether they were conspiring to gouge the public or attacking each other—and anyone else who happened to be in the way.

[11]*Ibid.*, p. 24.
[12]S.Rept #1775, 81st Cong., 2d Sess. (1950), emphasis added.

By retaining the test in the 1950 amendment, Congress was continuing to give expression to its dislike of concentration per se. Although this dislike, as will be shown later, stemmed partly from socio-political considerations, it rested also on economic grounds. Any reading of the legislative history reveals a strong congressional preference for an economy of many rather than few sellers. The view was widely shared that societies in which opportunity was unrestricted were apt to be more responsive to new ideas, more flexible in their adjustments, and better able to make the best use of the talents, skills, and creativeness of its citizens.

The conclusion is thus inescapable that by including it in the 1914 law and again in the 1950 amendment Congress intended to prohibit mergers which transgressed the tendency-toward-monopoly test, regardless of whatever other consequences they might have, anticompetitive or otherwise. How then can this test be applied to conglomerate mergers? One approach would be to focus on post-merger activity. An ideal case is presented by the rise in General Motors' market shares after its entrance, through merger, into the locomotive and bus industries. According to a report of the Senate Antitrust and Monopoly Subcommittee:

> An examination of this subcommittee's hearings in 1955 shows, however, that by 1954, General Motors shipped 100 percent of all road freight and road passenger diesel locomotives sold in the United States. The physical volume, of course, had greatly lessened by 1954 since almost complete dieselization of the railroad industry had been accomplished by 1952. In 1950—the peak year in its history—there were 4,174 switchers ordered in this country, and General Motors' share was 48 percent of switchers and 57 percent of road switchers. By 1954, total orders had been reduced to 983, but General Motors' portion of the business had risen to 60 percent and 74 percent, respectively.
>
> An increase likewise occurred in the company's share of the motorbus market. In 1950 its sales amounted to 46 percent of the total market; a steady climb resulted in a 78 percent share by 1954, and by 1955 the company manufactured approximately 85 percent of the new buses delivered in the United States.[13]

13*Administered Prices: Automobiles.* Report of the Subcommittee on Antitrust and Monopoly, Senate Judiciary Committee, 85th Cong., 2d Sess. (1958), p. 33.

But post-acquisition behavior need not be the only basis for the use of this test. It could also be used to prevent a progressive accumulation of monopoly power. The handiest instrument for such a process is the extensive use of advertising, particularly television advertising. Evidence has been developing in recent years indicating a close and direct relationship between this factor and increases in industry concentration.[14] The nature of the industry appears to make little difference: where TV advertising is widely employed sharp increases in concentration have taken place in industries having little else in common: in foods and in automobiles, in greeting cards and in refrigerators, in toiletries and in razor blades, in girdles and brassieres and in soaps and detergents, in beer but not, interestingly enough, in distilled liquors, which are not advertised on television.

The cost of TV advertising and the shortage of "prime time" effectively limit the use of the media to large companies; its relatively high degree of success makes it a heaven-sent instrument for the expanding conglomerate. Through TV advertising a conglomerate can secure substantial monopoly power in one industry, the monopoly profits from which will enable it by the same means to obtain substantial monopoly power in a second industry, which in turn will enable it to do likewise in a third industry, and so on *ad infinitum.* Common observation suggests that this is exactly what has been taking place in differentiated-product, heavily promoted consumer goods industries. In the majority of such industries the leading firms are themselves conglomerates.

This does not mean that the entrance into a new field by *any* multi-industry firm will necessarily result in an increase in the industry's concentration. First, the conglomerate must be able to finance the costs of this extraordinarily expensive form of promotion; the most convenient source of funds would be monopoly profits earned in other industries. Second, these costs, plus the costs of

[14]Cf. "Concentration and Divisional Reporting," Hearings on Economic Concentration, Part 5, Subcommittee on Antitrust and Monopoly, Senate Judiciary Committee, 89th Cong., 2d Sess. (1965), pp. 1902–1910; Charles Yneu Yang, "Industrial Concentration and Advertising," Annual Conference of *American Academy of Advertising* (reprinted in *ibid.*, pp. 2153–2163) ; H. M. Mann, J. A. Henning, and J. W. Meehan, Jr., "Advertising and Concentration: An Empirical Investigation," *Journal of Industrial Economics* XV, (Nov. 1967), pp. 34–45; William S. Comanor and Thomas A. Wilson, "Advertising, Market Structure and Performance," *Review of Economics and Statistics,* XLIX (Nov. 1967), pp. 423–440.

producing and marketing a product which is dissimilar from its existing line and with which it has had no experience, must not be inordinately high.[15] Although the willingness of consumers to pay a premium for a nationally advertised trade-marked brand has long been established, there is a limit to how much additional he will pay; in gasoline, for example, it has historically been about 2 cents a gallon. Assuming, however, a solid base of substantial monopoly power in its older industries and an ability to handle the new product without incurring excessive costs, the entrance by a heavy TV advertiser into a new industry may, on the basis of what has been learned about the relationship of advertising outlays to changes in concentration, be expected to result in an increase in concentration.

Under such circumstances a logical basis exists for attempting to halt this process of monopoly power accumulation on the grounds that the acquisition "may tend to create a monopoly." In view of what Procter & Gamble had already accomplished through TV advertising in soaps and detergents, its acquisition of Clorox could have been objected to on this basis alone; the same would be true of its more recent acquisition of the Folger coffee company, against which the FTC has inexplicably taken no action.

EXPECTATIONS OF REACTIONS

Theories of "monopolistic" and "imperfect" competition are based upon an expectation of a reaction—the expectation by each oligopolist that his rival oligopolists would react to a price reduction by immediately matching it. By the same reasoning, why would

---

[15]Since the objective is the securing of substantial monopoly power, which would provide a certain discretionary latitude for price-making above costs, efficiency is not of the same critical importance as in a competitive industry. In a conglomerate merger the opportunities for cost savings which are at least theoretically present in horizontal mergers (e.g., the centralizing of production in the more efficient plants) and vertical acquisitions (e.g., establishing a more orderly arrangement of facilities) are simply not present. Dr. Turner has attempted to dismiss these self-evident propositions on the grounds that many conglomerate acquisitions (i.e., other than horizontal and vertical) involve "significant horizontal elements" (op. cit., p. 1329). Refuting a proposition on the grounds that in the real world the phenomenon is not exactly the same as the conceptual model to which the proposition applies obviously makes theoretical analysis impossible.

not the expectation of small single-line producers as to a large conglomerate's reaction to a price cut on their part also influence their pricing behavior? The entrance of a conglomerate into an industry consisting formerly of single-line producers introduces a profound change in their price-making calculus:

> Before initiating a price reduction (or comparable competitive move) the smaller producers may be expected to take into account the new entrant's probable reaction. The smaller firm cannot be expected to be unaware of the new entrant's monopoly power in other industries and of the obvious uses to which that power could be put against any price-cutting rival. Nor can the small concern be expected to be unaware of the fact that whereas its economic life largely depends on success in its particular industry, operations in that industry represent to the conglomerate only a minor share of its total activity. The small firm may be expected to be well aware of its consequent vulnerability to the "leverage" which can be applied by the conglomerate with only a slight effect on the latter's over-all earnings. And the small firm can be expected to be very well aware, indeed, of the difficulties which it would encounter in trying to secure the financial wherewithal needed to support a prolonged period of price rivalry against any firm of great size and resources. Thus, just as in the case of oligopoly, it is a subjective attitude which is the important element. . . .[16]

This line of reasoning has been advanced in just one Section 7 case —the action by the FTC against the acquisition of Clorox by Procter & Gamble. The Court accepted the FTC's findings on this point, showing no inability to grasp the conceptual issues involved. In the words of the Court:

> The Commission found that the substitution of Procter with its huge assets and advertising advantages for the already dominant Clorox would dissuade new entrants and *discourage active competition from the firms already in the industry due to fear of retaliation by Procter.* . . .
> The interjection of Procter into the market considerably changed the situation. There is every reason to assume that *the smaller firms would become more cautious in competing due to their fear of retaliation by Procter.* It is probable that

[16]John M. Blair, "The Conglomerate Merger in Economics and Law," *Georgetown Law Journal,* 46 (Summer 1958), 689–90.

Procter would become the price leader and that oligopoly would become more rigid.[17]

It is not necessary to establish that retaliation had in fact taken place. The important consideration is the expectation in the minds of the smaller producers "... that Procter might underprice Clorox in order to drive out competition and subsidize the underpricing with revenues from other products."[18]

When the producers in the industry into which a large conglomerate enters are not small single-line companies, as in the bleach industry, but are large conglomerates themselves, the reasons for abstaining from competitive moves are different, though the results will be much the same. Assuming that the existing producers possess substantial monopoly power in one or more of the industries in which they are engaged, they can certainly defend themselves against a competitive attack by the new conglomerate. Hence, fear of reprisals *in the industry* in which they make a competitive move should not be a serious deterrent. But though they do not labor under the same restraint that inhibits the small single-line company, a restraint of a somewhat different character would logically be at work.

Such an inhibition against competitive moves would logically be present when two or more conglomerates confront each other, as competitors, in a number of different industries. Owing to differences in cost, market shares, and product acceptance, it is only to be expected that the importance of these industries as sources of profits will vary considerably among the different conglomerates. The industry which is a principal source of profits to one conglomerate is only a minor source to another, with the reverse being true of a second industry, and so on. Therefore, if one conglomerate launches a competitive attack in an industry which is an important source of profits to a rival conglomerate, it can logically expect a retaliatory attack in an industry which is an important source of profits to it. Realizing this, it will abstain from initiating a competitive move in the first industry. And the greater is the number of industries in which given conglomerates confront each other, the stronger is the reason for mutual forbearance in each of them.

---

[17]*Federal Trade Commission* v. *The Procter & Gamble Co.*, 386 U.S. 568; emphasis added.
[18]*Ibid.*

ECONOMIES OF SCALE

Regarding economies of scale, the issue raised by mergers is whether the combining of two or more enterprises under one corporate roof results in greater economic efficiency than would have been the case had the enterprises continued to operate independently. The assumption that mergers do yield such economies[19] has led a number of legal commentators to argue that in the enforcement of Section 7 any injury to competition must be balanced against the gain of greater efficiency. Thus, Turner recommends that "... the possibility of economies, to the extent it is at all assessable, should be taken into account in deciding whether a particular class of mergers should be outlawed."[20] Two questions arise, on neither of which Turner offers any enlightenment. First, to what extent are economies of scale assessable in litigated cases? Second, how are they to be balanced against an injury to competition?

If a given class of mergers results in *both* greater efficiency and a lessening of competition, which is to be controlling? And how are the gains in efficiency and the injury to competition to be measured in order that one may be weighed against the other? And how many "units" of increased efficiency does it take to overbalance a given number of "units" of lessened competition? The potential for mathematical game-playing should open up an entire new world of endeavor for members of the Econometrics Institute.

Fortunately, or unfortunately, the issue was resolved by Congress itself. The legislative history completely affirms the opinion of Justice Douglas in *Procter & Gamble*: "Possible economies cannot be used as a defense to illegality. Congress was aware that some mergers which lessen competition may also result in economies but it struck the balance in favor of protecting competition."

Companion bills to amend Section 7 of the Clayton Act were first introduced in February 1945 by Senator O'Mahoney and Rep.

---

[19]Thus Turner speculates, "... the merger *may* achieve economies of scale. ... A 'pure' conglomerate merger *may*, however, yield economies in management services ... or in advertising expenditures, or in capital costs ... *it is possible* with any kind of conglomerate merger that the acquired firm will subsequently be run more efficiently...." (*Op. cit.*, pp. 1322, 1330; emphasis added.)

[20]Turner, *op. cit.*, p. 1339.

Kefauver.[21] Acquisitions involving property with a value of more than a specified amount were to be prohibited unless the Federal Trade Commission found the acquisition "to be consistent with the public interest," and the FTC was not to find the acquisition to be "consistent" unless it also found, among other things, "that the acquisition will not be incompatible with greater efficiency and economy of production, distribution and management."[22]

These bills were modeled on the recommendation of the Temporary National Economic Committee, which had included a more stringent standard: the FTC had to find "that the acquisition will be promotive of greater efficiency and economy of production, distribution and management." In response to inquiries as to the reason for the change, Rep. Kefauver wrote:

> . . . there is a substantial difference between an administrative affirmative finding that a proposed merger will promote greater efficiency and economy and a finding that it will not be incompatible with that result. I can well understand why an administrative agency would hesitate to make such an affirmative finding in any but the most obvious circumstances and this would tend to block a large proportion of all mergers on that score alone. By contrast under the provisions of H.R. 2357, while mergers found to be incompatible with greater efficiency and economy could not meet the required standard, mergers found to be compatible and those found to be not incompatible with that standard could be approved, provided all the other requirements were met.[23]

21S. 615 and H. R. 2357, 79th Cong., 1st Sess.

22The other points on which an affirmative finding had to be made by the FTC were as follows:

1. The acquisition will not substantially lessen competition, restrain trade, or tend to create a monopoly (either in a single section of the country or in the country as a whole) in the trade, industry, or line of commerce in which the corporations are engaged.

2. The size of the acquiring corporation after acquisition will be compatible with the existence and maintenance of effective competition in the trade, industry, or line of commerce in which it is engaged.

3. The acquisition will not so reduce the number of competing companies in the trade, industry, or line of commerce affected as materially to lessen the effectiveness of competition therein.

4. The acquiring company has not indulged in unlawful methods of competition in order to induce the acquisition—or otherwise violated the FTC Act.

23Estes Kefauver, letter dated December 8, 1947 to Charles Alan Wright, *Yale Law Journal.*

Partly because of the obvious administrative difficulties inherent in any efficiency test, and partly because of the inability of the bill's opponents to produce evidence that mergers generally do result in a more efficient use of resources, the efficiency requirement was dropped. During the floor debate Rep. Boggs of Louisiana discussed the latter grounds:

> In all of the hearings before the House and Senate Judiciary Subcommittees on this bill, going back to 1945, officials of a number of large corporations have been asked specifically whether the recent mergers made by their companies had resulted in increased efficiency. It is rather interesting to note that, universally, these representatives of big business did not know whether efficiency had been increased; they were unable to present any evidence whatever showing that mergers have brought about greater efficiency; and this is not surprising when it is remembered that the Temporary National Economic Committee Monograph No. 13 found that there was no definite relationship between size and efficiency.[24]

It is interesting to note that nearly 20 years later we are still without evidence that mergers in general, to use Rep. Boggs' words, "have brought about greater efficiency." Indeed, the evidence accumulated since that time points, if anywhere, in the opposite direction. Particularly relevant is a study of the 500 largest manufacturing corporations relating merger activity to various measures of profitability. For manufacturing as a whole and for the majority of the major industry groups a relationship was found, but it was inverse in character; the profit showings were best for companies which made few, if any, acquisitions and worse for those which were most intensively involved in merger activity.[25]

SOCIAL-POLITICAL VALUES

Although many economists may be dismayed at the prospect of injecting social-political considerations into the administration of

[24]*Congressional Record*, Aug. 15, 1949, p. 11725.
[25]Subcommittee on Antitrust and Monopoly of the Senate Committee on the Judiciary, Hearings on Economic Concentration, Part 5, *Concentration and Divisional Reporting* (Testimony of Prof. Samuel R. Reid), 89th Cong., 1st Sess. (1966), pp. 1913–1940.

the antitrust laws,[26] this is just one of those realities of life in a democracy. Happily, in Section 7, unlike the case of the resale-price-maintenance laws, the social-political values and the economic objectives tend to complement and reinforce each other. Its concern with values associated with freedom of the individual, preservation of equal opportunity, and the avoidance of undue centralization of power is as old as Congress itself. There can be no question but that a principal factor behind the passage of the Celler-Kefauver amendment was the belief in Congress that the measure, by arresting the growth in concentration, would help to preserve these social-political values. Thus in its report on H.R. 2734 (the bill which was enacted), the House Judiciary Committee in the 81st Congress stated:

> The only alternative to capitalism is some form of statism—destructive alike to both big and small business. The concentration of great economic power in a few corporations necessarily leads to the formation of large Nation-wide labor unions. The development of the two necessarily leads to big bureaus in the Government to deal with them.[27]

In the 80th Congress the Judiciary Committee in its report on the predecessor measure, H.R. 3736 (which was blocked by the Rules Committee), was even more explicit:

> Nor should we forget that "man does not live by bread alone." In the choice between competition and monopoly, between real labor unions and a system of dominating, racketeering overlordship, between opportunity for youth to chart its own course as against a mere job for some far-distant master, between many thriving small towns and a few large cities, between local government and bureaucracy, between freedom and dictatorship—between these choices lie many questions involving great moral and spiritual values which cannot safely be ignored.[28]

In the 79th Congress the Judiciary Committee in its report on H.R. 4810 stated:

> The logical procedure to preserve economic democracy and legitimate private economic freedom from concentrated po-

---

[26]There are many who firmly believe that superconcentration—further concentration in the hands of large firms—is a very bad thing, even if devoid of any anticompetitive consequences. There are others who find that point of view almost sickening (Turner, *op. cit.*, p. 1394).

[27]H. Report No. 1191, 81st Cong., 1st Sess. (1949), p. 13.

[28]H. Report No. 596, 80th Cong., 1st Sess. (1947), p. 8.

litical control is to apply the restraining hand of Government at the point where undesirable concentrations of private economic control have their genesis. Today, the formation of supercorporations by the device of acquiring competitors is one of the principal means of building concentrated private controls.[29]

It is difficult to reconcile these rather clear statements of congressional intent with Turner's argument that injury to competition is the only basis for proceedings:

I do not believe Congress has given the courts and the FTC a mandate to campaign against "superconcentration" in the absence of any harm to competition. In light of the bitterly disputed issues involved, I believe that the courts should demand of Congress that it translate any further directive into something more formidable than sonorous phrases in the pages of the Congressional Record.[30]

The literary character of the Committee reports is of course irrelevant. What is germane is that the passages cited above appear in the reports of a legislative committee accompanying a bill enacted into law and therefore rank next to the actual wording of the measure itself in the determination of congressional intent.

Of less importance but still not without interpretive value are statements made on the floor in the consideration of a measure. The floor debates on Section 7 abound with statements indicating that the preservation of competition was not the only value which members of Congress saw imperiled by the rise in concentration. Citing reports to the War Department and other sources, Congressman Celler, chairman of the House Judiciary Committee and co-sponsor of H. R. 2734, was concerned over the way in which concentrated industry had facilitated the rise of fascism: "In those countries [Germany and Japan] the industrialists, because of their tremendous power as a result of constant merging, controlled the military and with the military they controlled the government."[31]

In the view of Congressman Yates of Illinois, the antitrust laws were a bulwark against the rise of the authoritarian state:

If we want totalitarianism to take the place of private enterprise in this country, we can scarcely encourage the process more effectively than by refusing to make our antimonopoly

[29]H. Report No. 1480, 79th Cong., 2d Sess. (1946), p. 5.
[30]Turner, *op. cit.*, p. 1395.
[31]*Congressional Record* (Aug. 15, 1949), p. 11717.

laws effective. The battle of freedom will be lost whenever we are forced to choose between control of economic life by private monopoly and control of it by the state.[32]

Deploring the growth of concentration because of its disruptive effect on local communities, Congressman Bryson of South Carolina listed the advantages of local ownership:

> ... there is a common knowledge and acquaintanceship between workers on the one hand and the mill owners on the other ... most of the income derived from the operation of the mills remains in the communities in which the mills are located .... there are strong social and civic ties that bind the community together.

He went on to cite findings of a study prepared by sociologist C. Wright Mills for the Smaller War Plants Corporation, to the effect that in communities in which most of the business activity was carried on by independent, locally owned enterprises there was, as contrasted to comparable "big-business" cities, "a considerably more balanced economic life" and an appreciably higher "general level of civic welfare."[33] Congressman Bryson emphasized that "It is through mergers, the problem to which this bill is directed, that some of the local southern communities have come under the domination of big business—outside, northern, big business."

To Congressman Patman of Texas freedom of the individual is dependent on his ability to establish his own small business: "Existing entrenched bigness is a threat to free enterprise in this country."[34] Contrasting the size and power of private corporations with governmental bodies, Senator O'Mahoney stated: "The purpose of the table was to show how corporations were obtaining greater economic power than that of the cities and States themselves."[35]

---

[32]*Ibid.*, p. 11724.

[33]*Ibid.*, pp. 11724–5. Among the conclusions of the report, *Small Business and Civic Welfare*, cited by Congressman Bryson, was the following:

> It was found that the chance that a baby would die within 1 year after birth waª considerably greater in big- than in small-business cities; in fact the chance was almost twice as great in one big-business city than in the comparable small-business city. Public expenditures on libraries were 10 times greater and on education (per student) were 20 times greater in one of the small-business cities studied than in the comparable big-business city. Slums were more prevalent—in one case nearly 3 times more prevalent—in big- than in small-business cities.

[34]*Ibid.*, p. 11727.

[35]*Congressional Record* (Dec. 12, 1950), p. 16609.

Senator Murray of Montana, chairman of the Senate Small Business Committee, pointed out that excessive concentration had tended to impair the nation's war effort:

> In one instance we found a high corporation getting contracts from Washington when it was already filled up with orders to such a degree that it would not be able to start filling the contracts for a couple of years. . . . Yet there were 30 small independent corporations which were willing to take the contracts. They had the ability to fulfill them.[36]

In Senator Aiken's view, the great danger was the transformation from independence and initiative to dependency and acceptance:

> It is not a crime to desire monopoly. That is an inherent human urge. However, the effective maintenance of a democratic government requires that collectively we devise a means of keeping that urge, whether on the part of a group or on the part of an individual, within bounds. If we cannot do this, if we permit economic monopolies to be formed, and permit the concentration of power in the hands of a few, with a resultant economic dependency on the part of the many, we shall have failed to maintain our example of democracy before the world.[37]

Summarizing the reasons for opposing the "tendency toward concentration of economic power," Senator Kefauver stated:

> Local economic independence cannot be preserved in the face of consolidations such as we have had during the past few years. The control of American business is steadily being transferred, I am sorry to have to say, from local communities to a few large cities in which central managers decide the policies and the fate of the far-flung enterprises they control. Millions of people depend helplessly on their judgment. Through monopolistic mergers the people are losing power to direct their own economic welfare. When they lose the power to direct their economic welfare they also lose the means to direct their political future.[38]

In this day of increasing concern over the fate of the individual—his "alienation" from society, his "depersonalization" by "faceless bureaucracies," and the increasing threat posed by organized "power

[36]*Ibid.*, p. 16605.
[37]*Ibid.* (Dec. 13, 1950) , p. 16666.
[38]*Ibid.* (Dec. 12, 1950) , pp. 16613–14.

structures" and "establishments"—who is to say that Congress was wrong in its concern with fundamental human values?

CONCLUSION

The halting and ineffective enforcement of Section 7 against conglomerate mergers is traceable in large part to certain interpretations which, whatever their substantive merits, are simply not in accord with the intent of Congress. If these interpretations were put aside, effective enforcement could be undertaken based on theories of the case which are in accord with congressional intent. The alternatives are, on the one hand, acceptance of a continuation of the current wave of conglomerate mergers with all of its dangerous implications to consumers, competition, and stockholders, or the enactment of new legislation either further strengthening Section 7 or imposing some sort of governmental control on prices and price policies.

It must be acknowledged that enforcement of Section 7 along the lines suggested here would no doubt elicit the cry that a campaign is under way against bigness as such. Yet a moment's reflection should make it quite obvious that no one is opposed to bigness per se—as no one, at least to my knowledge, is in favor of bigness per se. There are certain presumed attributes of bigness— higher efficiency, greater ability to develop and introduce new and better products and processes, a higher growth rate, easier access to capital, etc. At the same time certain liabilities have been attributed to bigness—higher and rigid prices, excessive profit rates, restricted production and employment, resistance to new technologies, etc. Those who are in favor of bigness are not in favor of it as such, but because they believe the advantages outweigh the liabilities. The Congress enacted Section 7, not because it was opposed to bigness as such, but because it felt that the liabilities outweighed the advantages. Even so, the law was not directed against bigness but only against one form of corporate expansion, external growth—and then only where there were certain probable specified results. The seriousness and complexity of the issue warrants discussion at a higher intellectual plane than is connoted by this public relations cliche.[39]

---

[39]The modest efforts undertaken thus far against conglomerate mergers have been stigmatized, even in a respectable law journal, as reflecting an attitude that "bigness is badness." (James F. Rill, *UCLA Law Review*, loc. cit) .

14

issues in national policy on growth of firms

by H. Igor Ansoff

In recent years, outside observers of business have taken two distinctive viewpoints. One of these treats the firm as one of many similar economic atoms within the total economic environment. The major difference among firms is seen in their respective size and respective share of markets. Economic competition is the subject of study in the context of pricing, substitutability of factors of production, and mutually restrictive practices. Search of maximum profit is assumed as the motive force.

The other and more recent viewpoint is concerned with the individual firm. The emphasis is on the managerial behavior and on the resource conversion process functions within the firm. Rather than one of many similar atoms, each firm is seen as a distinctive organization composed of human, monetary, and physical resources. The common features of firms are seen in their purposive behavior and their use of the resource conversion process as the means to the purpose. Profit-seeking is recognized as only one of the aims which motivate the firm; profit maximization as defined by the other view is not an operational concept. Since the firm has to face both long- and short-term goals, and since imperfect information is a major determinant of management behavior, the concept of maximum profit at a clearly discernible equilibrium point loses its meaning in terms of the objectives of the firm. A major influence on the competitive behavior of the firm is seen to lie in the attitudes and goals of the participants in the firm, particularly its management.

It is further claimed that the microeconomic theory of the firm which provides a theoretical foundation for the first viewpoint is too narrow in its scope and, therefore, not adequate for describing competitive behavior of business firms. Specifically, the theory of the firm is based on the concept of a competitive equilibrium. The mechanism of transition between points of equilibrium is not made explicit in the theory and generally is not regarded as a question of interest. Students of the complex firm observe that equilibrium is rarely maintained for any period in time, and the dynamics of change both in the productive processes and in the firm's environment, rather than static equilibria, are the central concern of practicing managements. A satisfactory explanation of the firm cannot, therefore, be handled by a "zero order" economic theory. Furthermore, it is pointed out that behavioral variables, imperfection of information, and imperfection of the firm's computational mechanism would make it impossible for managers to perceive the equilibrium conditions.

Practitioners of economic theory can easily point out similar weaknesses in the viewpoint of the students of intrafirm practices. Our reason for focusing on the shortcomings of the former stems from the fact that to date it has served as the theoretical foundation in the development and application of public policy which regulates growth of firms in the United States. Even if the theory were adequate (and the above remarks may well suggest that it is not) for determining the *inter*-firm relationships, it provides little for anticipating and explaining *intra*-firm impact of the policy.

In the days when the strength of the United States economy was characterized by a large number of small enterprises, a neglect of intrafirm dynamics was perhaps justifiable. Today, when 51 percent of the country's manufacturing output is concentrated in 7 percent of firms, such neglect is highly questionable.

Both viewpoints have been influential in the business scene. The former, represented primarily by economists and lawyers, has had its greatest impact on national economic policy and on the behavior of regulatory bodies. The latter, largely held by business journalists and management theorists, has been influential in introducing modern techniques to management of individual firms.

Both groups have observed with great interest, and sometimes with concern, two closely related trends in the American economy: the concentration of the increasing share of markets in large firms and the proliferation of a type of firm known as the *conglomerate.* While agreeing that the two trends are unmistakable, the two groups do not necessarily arrive at the same conclusions regarding their desirability. The view of the first group has been not only clearly enunciated but also translated into government action through interpretation and enforcement of the antitrust laws. The views of the second group have not produced any discernible impact on government policy. They need more elaboration, consolidation, and acceptance, if both business and government policies are to reflect them fairly. This paper seeks to make a contribution to this end.

COMPETITION AND SMALL NUMBERS

To an economist "perfect" competition is assured by a large number of small competitors in a given market. Since no firm has a decisive advantage over others, since the customer has an exogenously determined preference function, pursuit of maximum profit by individual firms will stabilize the industry at a point of maximum benefit to society. As market shares become concentrated, each reduction in the number of competitors inevitably lessens competition. The central question becomes, at what point will the action of a single competitor "substantially" reduce competition? For example, if one of the competitors is taken over by a relatively large firm from outside the industry, a strong presumption of a substantial reduction exists, because the resources of the acquiring firm will be used to dominate the market. This is socially undesirable because competition has been diminished.

To a student of intrafirm dynamics the picture is much less clear. It is not clear, for example, that when the market shares are widely distributed, the benefit to society is greater than it would be in an oligopolistic situation. The reasons are several:

1. As technology developed, in a number of industries small firms have increasingly become less efficient producers than larger ones. With many small firms competition in an industry may be "perfect" in the sense that prices and market shares are stabilized at an equilibrium point, but the costs of production and dynamics of innovation may be inferior to a condition of a smaller number of large firms. If one assumes for example, that no more than a "reasonable profit" will be allowed to such large firms by some mechanism other than the market, the consumer and the society would be better off.[1]

2. As the present "managerial revolution" advances, as computers and scientific decision-making enter the firm, management will become a capital intensive asset. This, in addition to technology, will further enhance the ability of large firms to produce goods and services more efficiently than smaller competitors.

3. Nor is it clear that, given a market of particular size, a large number of small firms will necessarily compete more vigorously. In fact, it appears that in many technologically intensive industries large firms are inherently more vigorous competitors than small ones. With increasing technological intensity, competition becomes focused on product invention, process automation, and process improvement. All three require increasingly larger investments and involve greater risks than they did in a technologically calmer era. Small firms are at a major disadvantage in this form of competition since they cannot afford to stake a major portion of their resources on a single gamble.

4. Further, in technologically intensive industries, competition is not only among firms but also increasingly against a hostile and unpredictable *nature*. For example, as one studies published accounts[2] of IBM's decision to commit its resources to the development of System 360, one is impressed with the fact that the risk involved in using advanced technology was as

[1]An outstanding example is provided by the American Telephone and Telegraph Corp., which supplies better service at a cost comparable to or lower than most (if not all) of the telephone systems in the world.

[2]T. A. Wise, "IBM 5 billion gamble," *Fortune*, 74 (Sept. 1966), 118; *idem*, "Rocky Road to the Marketplace," *Fortune*, 74 (Oct. 1966), 138.

important a factor as the risks of competitive action and counteraction.

5. In many large modern firms one observes the phenomenon of the firm "competing against itself." A search for excellence, for superior performance, is internalized by the attitudes of the management. A team spirit prevails in such organizations which is virtually independent of actions and counteractions by competition.

6. Also because of technology, many industrial activities require a *minimum critical size* below which a firm lacks the resources necessary for survival. In such activities insistence on wide distribution of market shares would deprive the consumer of *any social benefit*—i.e., his needs for goods and services would not be met at all.

When the market shares are highly concentrated, it is not clear that further reduction will necessarily lessen competition. For example, the demise of the Studebaker activities left no significant impact on the automotive industry. Nor is it clear that the present survival of American Motors is essential to continuance of the current vigorous competition in the industry. (Although its failure to survive would undoubtedly increase the likelihood of antitrust proceedings against General Motors.)[3]

The mere presence of a "significant" number of firms in an industry is no guarantee that they will compete vigorously. It is observable in mature industries and in mature firms that competitive behavior can be as much a matter of management attitudes as of economic forces.

Such firms are not weeded out by cruel forces of competition but continue for many years in a state of competitive euphoria. They can be small firms or large; their existence is protected by the imperfections of information in the market place, by loyalty of their customers, and by a general lack of attractiveness of their markets to aggressive entrepreneurs. Over the years their liquidity grows because of lack of reinvestment opportunities. Eventually they become attractive to aggressive entrepreneurs, not because of their products, markets, or management, but because of their cash. Rather

---

[3]Louis M. Kohlmeier, "Anti-trust Bombshell," *Wall Street Journal* (Dec. 31, 1967).

than invade the markets, the entrepreneurs take over the firm, rejuvenate the management, and apply its resources in an efficient manner. Thus, a takeover by a strong and vigorous outsider (and sometimes even the mere threat of the takeover) can turn a firm from a social and economic liability into a vigorous contributor to the nation's economic wealth. In the process, the firm will increase its share of the market and will become a stronger (but not necessarily dominant) competitor.

Viewed from this vantage point, it would seem that the appropriate public policy should be to encourage mergers which will rejuvenate competition *and* produce a more efficient use of the nation's resources. From the opposing viewpoint the conclusion appears to be that the nation's interest is better served if an industry is left in a state of competitive doldrums rather than subjected to infusion of vigor from an outside competitor who might "create a monopoly."[4]

The preceding remarks suggest that an assumption (which has been a cornerstone of American antitrust policy) that "the degree of competition is directly proportionate to the number of competitors and inversely proportionate to their average size"[5] is questionable when examined in the light of the historical behavior and dynamics of business firms. Perhaps more fundamentally, an assumption that "perfect" competition should be the ideal goal of U.S. public policy is also subject to challenge on two grounds: first, that the underlying model of economic behavior has never been fully adequate and is becoming progressively inadequate, and second, that the underlying goal which equates maximum competition with maximum social welfare no longer holds true.

WHAT IS A CONGLOMERATE?

In application of economic theory to antitrust policy the forms of business consolidations have been classified into *vertical, horizontal* and *conglomerate*.

A vertical consolidation builds the firm's capabilities either "forward" toward its markets or "backward" toward the sources of

---

4Trade Reg. Rep. 72, 269. *General Foods Corp.* v. *FTC*, 5 CCH (1967).
5M. Ways, "Anti-trust in the Era of Radical Change," *Fortune*, 73 (March 1966), 121.

supply. A horizontal consolidation rounds out the firm's product line by increasing the line of goods sold to its customers. A conglomerate is the complement of the above two to the complete set; it describes "all other" mergers and in popular parlance describes them as "unrelated."

Vertical and horizontal consolidations are claimed to offer a competitive advantage to a business firm. The former enables the firm to "capture" the source of supplies or a distributing network and thus deny these to competitors.[6] The latter permits economies of scale in advertising, selling, and product development denied to competitors who are not horizontally integrated.

As a result of this viewpoint, firms which contemplate vertical or horizontal integrations and which already occupy a substantial position in their respective markets are vulnerable to antitrust prosecution. The evidence of vulnerability has been substantial over the years. Therefore, firms increasingly turned toward conglomerate acquisitions as the means for growth through acquisitions.

In horizontal and vertical mergers the issue of size (and hence market dominance) as a competitive advantage is joined by a subtler one: competitive advantage through superior economic efficiency. The integrated firm can effect many economics *in overheads* and thus offer at *a given level of production* any one of its products at a cheaper price than a firm which specializes in the respective products alone. Under an objective of maximizing competition this would constitute an "unfair" competitive advantage (particularly when coupled with an oligolopistic market structure), because it creates an unstable economic situation and would drive the competitors out of the market. From the point of view of national welfare it can be argued that the public is being offered products at lower cost and lower consumption of national resources. The counterargument, of course, is that the integrated firm having driven competitors off the market, will charge unfair monopolistic prices.

The resolution of the argument is not clear and depends on individual circumstances, such as integration opportunities for other firms in the industry. What is clear, however, is that the simplistic

---

[6]This claim is made in the face of considerable history of unsuccessful vertical integrations in which the captive capability became the "tail that wagged the dog." In such cases, the capacity is too large to be fully and economically used by the parent.

assumption that the free market system of price determination must be preserved at all costs can lead to a lowering of the over-all efficiency of the economic system. Some would argue that, by forcing firms to turn toward conglomerates, the United States antitrust policy has done just that.

In the past few years, some conglomerate mergers have also received unfavorable attention from regulatory bodies charged with enforcement of the antitrust legislation. The basic contention has been that a large firm entering an industry in which the major competitors were substantially smaller in size had the financial strength to gain a dominant position in the industry.

As in the case of the horizontal and vertical mergers, a companion issue is whether the acquiring firm brings advantages beyond its sheer financial strength. If, in fact, conglomerates acquirers are by definition "unrelated" to their acquisition it would be difficult to argue that such advantages exist. The truth is, however, that the conglomerates are not a homogeneous class of firms and "some are much more unrelated than others."

In the past ten years business firms have developed a measure for the *common thread* or degree of relatedness among firms. This measure has been given the name of *synergy*, or sometimes *synergism*.[7] A quick appreciation of the differences in synergy among firms can be gained by examining a sample composed of Gulf and Western, Ling-Temco-Vought Textron, General Electric, Litton, and Lockheed, all of which on repeated occasions have been dubbed "conglomerate" in business literature. The comparison suggests that at one extreme the common thread is slim, found in common corporate management, accounting, and financing. At the other extreme units of the firm may have common research and development skills, common production technology, common marketing skills, and common management skills. This can occur without integration of either product lines or the marketing system or without common vertical suppliers. Although such firms would not be recognized as horizontally or vertically integrated, they may possess a higher degree of synergy than either of the latter. Thus, within the class of conglomerates there are firms whose units are very weakly related, as well as highly coherent firms.

The consequences of this are easy to perceive. If the present

---

[7]For a full discussion, see H. I. Ansoff, *Corporate Strategy* (New York: McGraw-Hill Book Company, 1966), Chap. 5.

trends in the antitrust policy are to continue, an increasing number of large conglomerates will be challenged not only on the issue of size but also on their ability to bring synergistic competitive advantages to their potential acquisition. This will further shift the trend of acquisition activity toward low-synergy conglomerates.

Low-synergy conglomerates do have a useful role to play in economic activity. They can provide a buffer between small firms and the capital markets through securing growth financing for units which could not obtain it on their own. They offer an opportunity to balance risks among high-growth and low-growth units in the firm. They can absorb internally temporary reversals to an individual unit, which would have meant bankruptcy for a unit outside the corporate umbrella. Finally, they can provide competitive "muscle" to small units which are pitted against larger competitors. When these potential advantages are realized by thoughtful management, a low-synergy conglomerate can thus be both a stabilizing and a dynamic influence in industrial growth. The fact remains that from the point of view of economic efficiency, the low-synergy conglomerate is the least efficient *form of growth by acquisition.*

IMPLICATIONS FOR NATIONAL POLICY

Historically national policy on growth of firms has been concerned almost exclusively with growth by acquisition. So long as the number of competitors in an industry remains the key test of policy, the effect of acquisitions on competition is significantly different from an entry into the industry by outsiders. The former diminishes competition and the latter enhances it.

When the number of competitors does not significantly affect the strength of competition, the distinction between acquisition of an existing competitor and a new entry no longer appears great enough to treat these two methods of growth as different phenomena. In both cases a vigorous competitor enters an industry. In some cases competition will be diminished and in some enhanced. The primary observable difference will be in the timing of the effect: an acquisition will produce a change more quickly than a new entry, since the latter will need time to establish itself on the market and to develop requisite competitive competences.

Thus, it seems that the historical focus of policy on growth by acquisition should be broadened to include growth of firms by internal expansion. This would be in the tradition of United States democracy to establish criteria for judging acceptability of the *results* of actions whenever possible and not to seek to violate the freedom of the actors in choosing the most effective *means*.

The broadening of the policy should be accompanied by a re-evaluation of its fundamental aims. In the early days of our country freedom of competition was a goal which served two higher purposes: preservation of freedom of a majority of individuals to act in accordance with their beliefs, and *simultaneously* the improvement of the economic and social welfare of the nation. Today a concept which asserts that competition is enhanced proportionally to the number of competitors and inversely to their size is challengeable on two grounds.

First, though it may preserve the freedom of action for a majority, it does not necessarily guarantee the most vigorous behavior by firms in search of economic efficiency. Numbers and small size of competitors are not always proportional to competitive vigor, and are sometimes inversely, rather than directly, related to it. Furthermore, other factors have a major influence on competitive vigor: management goals and attitudes, esprit de corps of the organization (firms frequently "compete" against themselves), and technological challenges of the environment (which drive firms to "compete" against nature). Thus, it is necessary to separate the concept of the freedom of the majority to act according to their inclinations from the conditions which incline them to vigorous economic action. We may still wish to retain the former as the object of policy, but we must not labor under a delusion that it will necessarily produce superior human effort.

If the object of policy is freedom for individuals to act as they see fit, it may be that the traditional criterion of small size and large number is still a fair test of its success. If the object is vigorous economic competition, then more subtle and discriminating criteria must be developed.

The second challenge is on the grounds that superior human effort does not necessarily produce maximum economic efficiency. Even if small competitors act with greater vigor, modern technology can offset this advantage by giving large firms higher economic efficiency.

In the twentieth century the industrial sector of the nation has become an essential contributor to national wealth, as well as a major instrument of national policy. If the object of policy is to maximize this contribution, then criteria of inherent economic efficiency must be developed and applied as tests of growth policies.

Thus, instead of a single objective, public policy on growth of firms would have three: preservation of individual freedoms, enhancement of vigorous competitive attitudes, and enhancement of inherent economic effectiveness. These objectives are *noncommensurate*; therefore in many test cases they will indicate contradictory actions. Resolution of the contradictions will vary from case to case and require wisdom and subtlety—a situation which is typical of decision-making in most complex social organizations.[8]

---

[8]In this paper we have oversimplified the problem somewhat by assuming that the industrial sector serves society primarily by increasing its national wealth. Since the industrial sector has come to employ a large proportion of the population, it has been suggested that it should be required to take responsibility for the development, self-realization, and happiness of individuals employed by it. Since the industrial sector represents a very large concentration of national resources and capability, it has been further suggested that it should also take responsibility for contributing to social progress through programs such as antipoverty, urban renewal, etc. If these suggestions become objectives of national policy, clearly the problem of establishing appropriate tests of growth of firms would be further complicated.

15

systems management and industry behavior

by JOHN H. RUBEL

Because of the tremendous technological advances made since World War II, projects of great complexity have been undertaken. Projects of even greater complexity are on the horizon. These projects not only represent engineering problems but also require the solution of social problems. New and important social problems have appeared: water pollution, the ghettos, the growing crime rate, traffic congestion, urban decay, the declining per capita of world food production, the need to create new cities.

Beginning with World War II, the mushrooming complexity of the problems which have had to be solved—beginning with problems related to the national defense—has outmoded traditional methods of solutions. New methods of solving these problems have had to be found.

These new methods have crystallized into what has come to be called the Systems Approach. The systems approach actually is an old procedure, but the magnitude of the problems to which it has been applied since World War II, and the success which the approach has had in solving these problems, have resulted in a whole new capability being formed in the industrial community —systems analysis.

Systems analysis has become a separate field of endeavor. A new vocation has sprung up, and our colleges and universities now graduate Systems Analysts and Systems Engineers. In fact, the systems approach is now integrated into many standard engineering courses.

The development of a new area of industrial activity naturally poses questions of its impact on competitive processes in the American economy. In order to deal with such questions, some basic background for understanding the implications of systems management must be developed. First, the nature of systems management will be explained; second, its applications will be discussed; and third, its implications for competition will be analyzed. Many of the examples are drawn from my own experience at Litton Industries because those are the ones with which I am most familiar.

THE NATURE OF SYSTEMS MANAGEMENT

The systems approach is characterized by two salient features: (1) it is a problem-solving technique, and (2) it is used to solve problems of an order of complexity that never existed before. To my mind, this second feature is the most exciting aspect of the systems approach. It enables us to do things that have never been done before.

A good definition of the systems approach was expressed by Frederick R. Kappel, former chairman of the board of American Telephone and Telegraph Company. Mr. Kappel said:

> The essence of the Systems Approach, as we see it, is to get, first, a clear view of what is both needed and potentially feasible; second, a closely reasoned determination of the best course for achieving the desired result; and third, a dependable measure of the means already available, and those we must still discover in order to make doable what we are setting out to do.[1]

[1]Speech by Mr. F. R. Kappel, "Business and Science," to the International Management Conference in New York on September 16, 1963. This speech is included in the book, F. R. Kappel, *Business Purpose and Performance: Selections from Talks and Papers* (New York: Duell, Sloan & Pearce, 1964).

The approach means that first you define the problem, that is, the goal you seek to attain. Then you analyze it in terms of all of its aspects, define all possible alternatives to solving it, develop criteria to use in choosing among the alternatives, and, finally, select the alternative that best meets all of the criteria. The criteria, for example, may be cost, speed, simplicity, performance, etc. Thus, you begin with analysis. You develop a multidisciplinary effort—utilize a variety of disciplines simultaneously—and you coordinate or orchestrate the necessary analytical and design efforts toward a common goal on a comparatively short time schedule to achieve a solution.

In one sense, the systems approach is not new. For example, the buildings of the Parthenon required systems analysis, that is, the development of alternatives and a choice among them, and the successful application of expert skills from a large number of fields. Mathematicians, transportation experts, stone carvers, painters, workers in precious metals, religious officials, historians, sailors, politicians—all of these and experts from many more fields contributed their skills. It was a focused, interdisciplinary effort of great complexity.

But the building of the Parthenon is not really a good analogy because the systems approach, as it is used today, is something new. It is a new way of solving a new order of problems—problems that never existed before. It is utilized in aerospace, in missiles, in rockets, and in satellites and will be applied to the social problems that will have to be solved.

The application of systems management in missiles has produced formidable results. An impressive example is the Minute Man missile. Solving this problem by the systems approach has enabled us to put in place a weapons system that can launch fifty missiles within the space of a few minutes aimed to hit a target over 5,000 miles away with a high likelihood of hitting within a few blocks of the target. The Polaris system is perhaps even more complex, more remarkable, and characterized by more innovation.

APPLICATION OF SYSTEMS MANAGEMENT

In discussing the application of the systems approach, several interesting questions arise. One is the organization aspect. Applying the systems approach requires the articulation of a variety of disciplines. A basic question is whether these disciplines need to be combined under a single corporate roof to be effective. There is no clear-cut answer to this because it depends entirely upon the situation. Often, there is no choice but to use outside contractors or consultants. It is difficult and often impossible or uneconomical to anticipate all peak loads and stay "manned-up" to them. So a company will use outside people, hiring other companies to perform particular aspects of the systems study—companies such as Planning Research Corporation, T.R.W., and the computer software companies throughout the country.

But there are drawbacks to farming out parts of the systems engineering. One is a psychological factor. The companies hired to perform various aspects of a systems analysis have their own pride in their work and reputation. You want them to sell you the services of a few of their people for a limited piece of work. But they are reluctant to hire out just a few people; they want the whole job. And they want to do the job their way, not necessarily your way. But their way may not coincide with your ideas or theories. The psychological drawback must be surmounted because if the outside firm is not completely in tune with your concept, they will produce nothing usable.

In addition, the management of a number of outside contractors can be difficult. Getting all of them to do designs or studies that mesh, or getting them to modify their designs or studies so they will mesh with someone else's, can be a real problem. Disputes arise over who is right and who is wrong.

Another drawback often results from a conflict of interest. You never know when an outside consultant is going to use some of your proprietary information for a competitor of yours. Then, too, you never know when an outside firm may refuse to apply his full talents in your behalf because of an obligation to someone else. The possibility of a conflict of interest often hampers your ability to use independent firms effectively.

In short, the problem with a variety of outside consultants is getting them all focused, oriented, directed, and orchestrated toward the same objective. Depending on the number of consultants and their personalities, this requires varying degrees of strength, perseverance, and patience on the part of the systems manager.

Because of these organizational aspects, it is probably not surprising that up to now the greatest application of the systems approach has been by companies containing a broad range of capabilities oriented specifically toward applying the approach to certain types of problems. The aerospace firms, for example, have assembled a broad range of capabilities directed toward airborne defense systems: planning, analysis, development, engineering, design, manufacturing, management, test, and support; all under a single corporate roof, and all organized to respond in a unified way to a project customer.

This brings up the question of whether the systems approach necessarily encompasses the production of hardware. It may be preferable in some instances to have the two under one roof, but it does not seem necessary. The systems approach is concerned with problem-solving. It is primarily the application of mental processes to a problem. It is applied to formulate the best solution to a problem and to establish the criteria and specifications for the solution. Its advantages can be awesome, indeed, resulting in new ways of doing things, new economies, and new performance criteria. But the actual performance of the solution—the construction of the hardware in accordance with the established criteria and specifications—can be contracted out. In practice, whether the systems approach encompasses only the formulation or includes the implementation of the solution depends upon the wishes of the customer.

The power industry could be an example of a situation where the systems approach does not encompass the hardware that implements the solution. In that industry, General Electric performed the theoretical work that laid the basis for all modern power systems. GE also went into the business of manufacturing lamps, generating equipment, motors, cables, transformers, and circuit breakers—all the components. But GE did not go into ownership of the system.

I think a classic example of the application of the systems approach—and the technological change it can bring about in an industry—can be seen in the shipbuilding industry today. The motivating force has been a customer—the Defense Department. The shipbuilding industry traditionally has been organized into two groups: the naval architects, who are independent engineering and design organizations, and the shipbuilders. Traditionally, when a customer has decided that he wants to buy a ship, he has hired an architectural design firm on a consulting basis. The firm would produce a design and plans for a ship, and the owner would canvass the builders for bids to build against the architect's plans.

Thus, the shipbuilding industry traditionally has seen its function as reacting to the plans, figuring out what it is going to cost to build the ship, and submitting what it hopes is the lowest bid. Neither the shipbuilding companies nor the customers, except for the Defense Department in the last few years, has been oriented toward trying to accomplish a design which in the beginning would be cheaper to manufacture. In fact, the architects have been constrained to design a ship that could be built in any of a variety of shipyards. This means that almost the lowest common denominator has determined the design so the ship could be built with anyone's method of construction.

But a couple of years ago a large ship customer—in this case the Navy (although commercial operators may be stirring themselves to follow suit)—did not ask for just the design of a new ship; it asked for a design of a ship system that would satisfy a set of requirements in the most efficient manner that a competitor could provide. This meant one thing: the ship suppliers would have to take the systems approach toward ships as other suppliers, such as the aerospace companies, have taken it toward missile and space systems. Litton participated in this approach.

The results were very dramatic. We found out, for example, that instead of just needing architects we needed systems analysts, mathematicians, psychologists, computer experts, maintenance experts, and the like. With them, we were able to design a ship which would be better matched to production techniques and better adapted to the mission it was intended to accomplish, so as to effect savings of tremendous scope in both areas.

Projects of this magnitude emphasize some very fundamental points in the application of the systems approach. One is that the only way you can utilize the systems approach is to have a market. The customer has to perceive the need to approach a problem from the systems standpoint. He may determine the appropriateness of using the systems approach himself, or he may be sold on applying the approach by a potential supplier. In either event, the extent to which the approach can be applied, or whether it will be applied at all, depends on the customer.

A second point is that in some industries, despite the wishes of the customer, there are definite barriers to the application of the systems approach. Usually these industries are the least advanced and exhibit the greatest inefficiency. Construction is a good example. Here there are institutional barriers that preclude application of the systems approach. Techniques, technologies, and methodologies are available to help accomplish tremendous efficiencies and savings in this field, but the structure of the market will not permit it.

A recent missile program illustrates the point. The program called for creating concrete silos in the ground from which the missiles could be fired. There had never been any structures like them before, and some new construction techniques were invoked, particularly with respect to the installation of esoteric electrical control and calculating apparatus. Trade unions struck the building sites because in the construction process some of this equipment had been assembled off the building site to save time and expense and to insure performance. Some workers clipped wires so they could rewire electrical panels, and some unions refused to allow delivery of preassembled items unless the work was done all over again.

A third point is that the planning stage is the essence of the systems approach. Those in charge of each discipline must work together in the planning stage to achieve optimum results. The distinguishing characteristic of the systems approach is that it is a way of solving a customer's problem, not a way of merely supplying him with an isolated piece of hardware. Once the planning is completed, the actual building and testing can be subcontracted out.

A fourth point is that the systems approach does have some inherent limitations. It is difficult to determine in advance how useful the application of the systems approach will be. In common with other innovative efforts, the results of applying new methods to new complex problems cannot be predicted with certainty.

This leads to my fifth and most important point. The successful application of the systems approach depends in greatest measure on the attitude of management. If you ask a person what his business is, you will get a response from people whose attitude is oriented toward innovation quite different from the response of people oriented toward tradition. Utilization of the systems approach requires a management with an imaginative, innovative, and enterprising attitude. It requires an imaginative attitude to recognize the areas in which the systems approach can be applied to advantage. It requires an innovative attitude because the essence of the systems approach is the pioneering of new approaches to new problems. It requires an enterprising attitude because of the uncertainty of the results and the risk therefore involved.

To illustrate the importance of these attitudes in applying the systems approach, one of our managers in Litton began studying the idea of using larger ships to haul iron ore on the Great Lakes. The inquiry grew to include the movement of the ore in all of its aspects: the loading phase, the midcourse phase, the dumping phase, and the final movement into the steel furnaces. The entire project continued to expand in scope. What began as a narrow inquiry eventually resulted in a complete set of systems designs contemplating the construction of a new kind of ore boat matched to new on-loading and off-loading equipment, in turn matched to new port facilities. The total system was designed to enable the movement of huge volumes of ore up the narrow, winding, and shallow rivers to the mills in a more economical manner. The analysis has also encompassed completely new construction methods for the ships, and the construction of a new shipyard to build the ships. The approach embraced the total problem of efficient ore movement, not just an isolated segment.

After formulating the plans and designs of the ships, we believed that utilization of our design would save enough in construction costs to pay for the investment in a new yard. This judgment led us to make the investment. In this way the systems approach has spurred new entry and innovation in a market that had experienced neither for decades.

IMPLICATIONS OF THE SYSTEMS
APPROACH FOR COMPETITION

This leads to the final point, the possible effects of the systems approach on competition. In a number of ways, systems management stimulates competition and technological advance.

Most important, the systems approach enables a firm to enter or be a potential entrant across a wide variety of industries. The traditional economic definition of industry becomes further blurred. From a systems management standpoint there are no industries, only problems to be solved and a methodology for solving them. Companies that have developed a systems capability seek profitable opportunities wherever they may be found. Backward industries or the high profits of monopoly represent particularly attractive areas for the application of the systems approach. Entry and potential entry across a wide spectrum of the American economy are invigorated.

Because its economic significance is so broad, a concrete example may increase understanding. The bidding on the three Navy ship systems cited earlier in my paper provides an excellent illustration of how application of the systems approach has spread and increased competition.

The three procurements, in the order in which they occurred, were: The FDL (Fast Deployment Logistics Ship), the LHA (Landing Helicopter Assault Ship), and the DX Destroyer. Note that with these projects the systems approach had been applied to the design and construction of ships for the first time in the United States.

Only three companies competed for the FDL award. Two of these were aerospace companies; the third was Litton. All three owned shipyards, but two of them were primarily areospace companies, and Litton, although not strictly an aerospace company, was closely related to that field. Three companies also competed for LHA, but one of the competitors was an old-line shipbuilding company which had no previous experience with the systems approach. One of the aerospace companies was back in the race, and Litton was the third competitor. When the DX program was announced, three old-line shipbuilding companies decided they also could apply the systems approach to shipbuilding and they entered the competition. Litton and one of the original two aerospace companies rounded out the competition. Thus, over the span of three contracts, four old-line shipbuilding firms decided they could apply the systems approach to shipbuilding, no doubt after seeing how Litton and the aerospace companies did it, and total competition increased from three to five companies.

Such positive advantages are not offset by anticompetitive disadvantages. First, there is no threat that the systems approach will put out of business any company that makes only hardware. The approach itself is merely a problem-solving method. It does not necessarily include the production of hardware. There will always be a need for hardware to implement the solution formulated by the systems approach. There will always be a need for companies that specialize in hardware to make the components that future systems will always require. Should hardware companies find it necessary to obtain an in-house systems capability, there is no inherent reason why they cannot, or they can team with a company that has it.

Second, no one company, or group of companies, can ever monopolize the application of the systems approach. As pointed out earlier, the systems approach is the application of mental processes to a problem. Thus, the approach is based on the knowledge in men's minds, and all that is needed to apply it is a market demand, a management with the proper attitude, and some people who know how to use it. Since our colleges and universities are training increasing numbers of people versed in the approach, the supply of persons with the requisite knowledge is increasing.

Furthermore, knowledge of the systems approach is continually spreading. A key ingredient in applying the approach is people, and people are mobile and often change jobs. They take their knowledge and experience with them. Thus, a company can acquire the systems approach by hiring people. Litton entered the systems competition for the new Navy ship systems through the efforts of one man and the proper management attitude. That single man put together the systems engineering staff that ultimately won the competition for two of the systems and is now in the final competition for the third.

Another way in which knowledge of the systems approach spreads is through subcontractors. Relatively few companies have in-house all of the capabilities required to solve complex problems. Invariably, therefore, much work is contracted out. As subcontractors learn the approach from working on systems projects, they carry that knowledge with them as they become subcontractors or prime contractors on future projects.

CONCLUSIONS

The systems approach has been shown to stimulate competition and to invigorate technological advance in a number of ways. It is potentially applicable to a wide variety of situations, but some important preconditions must be met: (1) There must be a market demand. (2) Institutional barriers such as government building codes or union rules must permit the application of the useful concepts. (3) The necessary lead time for the planning stage must be available. (4) As with other innovative efforts, the inherent uncertainties and risks of the efforts must be accepted. (5) Managements must have the imagination and entrepreneurial courage to undertake these risks.

The use of the systems approach is spreading, and its effects on increased competition and innovation are growing. The systems approach is fundamentally a problem-solving method. It does not necessarily require the production of hardware. As I indicated, there is no inherent consequence that the systems approach will put out of business any company that makes only hardware. Whether a company, after formulating a solution to a problem, attempts to enter a new market by producing the hardware to implement the solution depends on all of the regular criteria for entering new markets, primarily return on investment and prospects of success.

16

summary of discussions on conglomerate mergers

by J. Fred Weston

The discussion of conglomerate mergers contained ideas in support of recent trends and expressions of considerable concern. Each of these sets of attitudes will be summarized in turn.

SYSTEMS MANAGEMENT AND ITS IMPLICATIONS

The Nature of the Systems Approach

Considerable discussion was devoted to the role that various managerial techniques could perform in connection with improving the general efficiency of the economy and stimulating laggard industries. One of the management techniques emphasized was the use of the systems approach. The systems approach was defined by the following elements:

1. An analysis of requirements.
2. A multidisciplinary effort.
3. The simultaneous exercise of interrelated disciplines.

4. Coordination of the necessary analytical and design efforts toward a common goal.

5. Rigid adherence to a time and performance schedule.

6. Achievement of a result which would not otherwise be obtainable.

It was pointed out that one man's system is always somebody else's component. The systems approach currently employed originated in the Bell Telephone System relatively early in its history. In contrast, the systems approach was not achieved in the electrical power industry, where the manufacturing of equipment was performed by one set of firms and its utilization by another set—the operating utilities.

Examples were cited of industries in which, in recent years, stimulation was achieved by applying the systems approach. In taking the systems approach to shipbuilding, the emphasis was on systems analysts, psychologists, mathematicians, maintenance experts, etc. The aim was to design a ship which would be better matched to production techniques and better adapted to the mission it was intended to accomplish. In taking the systems approach the emphasis was on how best to fulfill a set of requirements in an optimum manner in a minimum cost.

Implications of the Systems Approach

Another general point emphasized in connection with the systems approach was that it appeared to produce increased interindustry competition. The point was made that if a company has systems competence, it apparently has the ability to apply this type of managerial competence over a wide range of industries. Thus, whenever firms in a given industry are laggard—one of the presumed characteristics of the effects of monopoly—the industry would be subject to entry by a company such as Litton with the systems approach. Thus the threat of potential new competition from a large number of firms would have an invigorating competitive effect over a wide range of industries.

Analysis of Interindustry Activity

The concern, however, was expressed that this might lead to the entry by very large firms into a large number of industries.

Two types of consequences might result. One is that industries in which small firms have traditionally performed an important role might become dominated by large firms. A second result was illustrated in the following hypothetical situation: Suppose that 90 percent of all American industry were conducted by 100 large firms and that each of these 100 firms accounted for only 1 percent of the sales in each of the industries in which it participated. Thus, concentration in the American economy in the one sense would be greatly reduced in that in no industry would four firms account for more than 4 percent of output, or eight firms account for more than 8 percent of output. This represents substantially lower concentration ratios than presently exist in a large number of industries in the United States. On the other hand, concentration would have been greatly increased in that 100 firms would account for 90 percent of American business activity.

Some members of the seminar argued that the net result would represent increased competition. Others held the view that such a concentration of economic power would inevitably lead to undue influence on government operations by such a power group. In addition, concern was expressed that if so large a portion of American business were conducted by only 100 firms, various forms of spontaneous collusion would develop. Finally, great concern was expressed that opportunities for reciprocity would be so great that they could not possibly be policed.

In connection with the concern over the widespread influence of large firms in a number of industries, the example was given of contemplating a company like du Pont having invested in U.S. Steel in the early 1920's in addition to or in place of its investment in General Motors. Again, concern was expressed that this would represent great concentration of power. The other view expressed, however, was that if the apparent stimulating influence in terms of innovation and efficiency on General Motors had been extended to U.S. Steel, the effect would have been a salutory one in terms of performance of the steel industry.

OBJECTIONS TO THE CONGLOMERATE MERGER TREND

Great concern was expressed that the developing trend toward conglomerate mergers would transform the American economy in a fundamental way. Instead of specialization of firms by industries or the participation of the firm in a limited number of standard industrial classifications, it would be virtually impossible to identify firms with industries and to analyze the flow of economic resources throughout the economy.

Great concern was felt that this transformation would not take place on the basis of rigorous economic tests. The mergers themselves result in large measure from complex and imaginative forms of financing. In many ways a conglomerate merger movement simply represents the creation of new forms of currency rather than new, well-articulated business organizations. Thus the creation of the large, conglomerate firms would meet no initial economic tests. In addition the functioning of the economy would be subject to considerable further impairment as a consequence of the resulting conglomerate enterprises.

One view expressed was that instead of having a steel senator, a copper senator, or a textile senator, a conglomerate firm could have an entire group of senators and representatives under its influence. Objecting vigorously to this point of view, a number of members of the seminar pointed out that there was no evidence in support of such an assertion.

The argument was made, however, that whether or not there was control of congressmen and senators by large business firms in the past, the increase in the size of business firms and the dominance of the American economy by large enterprise would result in increased political power in these firms. Thus a major objection to the growth of conglomerates is the implication for the distribution of power in American society.

POSSIBLE CONSEQUENCES OF CONGLOMERATE MERGERS

A number of potential abuses might result from the developing conglomerate movement. Five undesirable results were discussed: (1) inadequate reporting, (2) cross-subsidization, (3) non-price competition, (4) the raising of entry barriers, and (5) reciprocity.

Inadequate Reporting

Inadequate reporting among conglomerates has been the dominant practice to date. It is not possible to determine profitability by product line. Indeed, it is not possible to determine what a firm's sales and profits might be by broad industry classifications.

To some extent, a very difficult accounting problem of allocating fixed costs might be involved. In addition, such a breakdown might provide valuable information to competitors. On the other hand, it was argued that at least a breakdown of sales by product areas would provide a minimal necessary amount of information for government agencies in attempting to keep track of and understand economic processes. In addition, for investors to have a basis for rational allocation of investments, some such breakdown would be required.

Cross-subsidization

In the absence of adequate reporting, the inherent tendency of conglomerates to engage in cross-subsidization of activities is encouraged. Furthermore, it makes the job of policing such cross-subsidization virtually impossible. Finally, the practice of cross-subsidization encourages both direct and indirect forms of predatory price behavior. One view expressed was that a monopoly position in some lines of business enables a firm continuously to provide other divisions with undue advantages over its competitors in more highly competitive industries. This might lead to the eventual and complete demise of what otherwise would be healthy competitors, whose role in the industry was a desirable one.

Non-price Competition

Another point of view expressed was that a major source of entry barriers is product differentiation and non-price competition in general. Non-price competition was asserted to be a particular advantage of the large firm with substantial financial resources or access to substantial finance resources. This view is one variant of the deep-pocket theory, which states that large firms can incur temporary outlays or losses which smaller firms cannot bear.

Large firms can engage in such behavior as frequent style changes, frequent model changes, heavy advertising under advantageous terms. Deep-pocket resources while engaging in non-price competition gives the large firm very substantial advantages.

Entry Barriers

Both of the preceding consequences of the increased trend toward conglomerate mergers, cross-subsidization and the increase of non-price competition, are said to increase entry barriers to a very substantial degree. Thus, the stimulating influence of small-firm entry into industries is diminished. Opportunity for individual entrepreneurs is reduced. As a consequence, the processes of competition are impaired without any offsetting advantages.

Reciprocity

Finally, with the entrance of large firms across a wide variety of industries, the potentials and opportunities for reciprocity arrangements are increased. By having activities in such a wide range of industries, the opportunities for reciprocal courtesies become so numerous and easy that an increase in reciprocity arrangements becomes inevitable. An increased segment of American business activity would then be conducted not on the basis of economic tests but rather on the basis of economic power.

This summary of the discussion on various aspects of conglomerate mergers is not intended to represent a full or balanced appraisal of conglomerate mergers. The discussion reflected an increasing concern with a relatively new phenomenon affecting American industrial structure. The objective of the seminar was to provide a foundation for further future analysis of the implications of the accelerating trend toward conglomerate mergers.

BASIC ISSUES OF
ANTITRUST POLICY

17

unresolved issues and an
agenda for future research

by J. FRED WESTON AND SAM PELTZMAN

These papers and the discussions on public
policy toward mergers have by no means
resolved all important areas of fundamental
disagreement. This volume contributes to
additional empirical information relevant
to public policy issues. Some of the empirical material represents systematic, statistical studies. Other important elements of
information came from the direct personal
experience of participants reported within
the framework of a broad conceptual understanding of the issues involved.

It is therefore impossible to summarize
the results of the seminar into a compact
set of neat conclusions. Rather, some central issues have been highlighted with opposing points of view delineated. It seems
most appropriate to summarize this volume
in terms of the following outline of six
central issues and the points of view that
may be found in connection with each of
the issues.

I. EFFECTS OF CONCENTRATION ON INDUSTRY PERFORMANCE

View A

1. Concentration causes spontaneous collusion through awareness.

2. Dominant firms will discipline or coerce remainder of industry to administer prices, one form of which is price leadership.

3. Output will be limited, prices high, over-capacity and excess profits will exist.

4. Must have a *per se* rule based on structure to make antitrust administrable.

5. Entry barriers usually exist.

View B

1. Many forms of non-price competition will take place.

2. Smaller firms will be able to specialize and take advantage of any umbrella pricing by larger firms.

3. Economies of scale or lower costs will enable prices and output to be more favorable than would exist under atomistic competition. Product innovation will lead to better products at lower prices.

4. Any per se rule will fall behind the realities of dynamic markets. To define market involves all of the same range of problems as analyzing performance.

5. Entry will limit levels of prices and profits.

II. SIGNIFICANCE OF VERTICAL INTEGRATION

View A

1. Control over supply will cause monopoly power to be exercised against the nonintegrated.

View B

1. The problem is monopoly control over sources of supply, not vertical integration.

View A	*View B*
2. Will permit profit squeeze on nonintegrated by taking lower profits on some levels and high profits on other levels.	2. Assumes irrational behavior by segments of the operation and does not benefit the total operation.
3. Forward integration forecloses some outlets against nonintegrated manufacturers.	3. Independent units will suffer no disadvantages if efficient.
4. Industry instability will be shifted to outside suppliers.	4. Assumes only partial vertical integration. Such instability is also shifted in the absence of integration as well.

III. CONSEQUENCES OF LARGE, DIVERSIFIED CORPORATIONS

View A	*View B*
1. Leads to economic concentration with no offsetting benefits.	1. Large size a necessary concomitant of a large economy. New management techniques result in considerable economies from diversification.
2. Enables large firms to dominate industries that would otherwise be atomistic (deep-pocket theory).	2. Industries will not become concentrated unless there is a sound economic basis for large-scale operations.
3. Leads to monopoly practices such as reciprocity arrangements.	3. No valid economic or business basis for reciprocity. If practiced, is per se illegal behavior under Section I of Sherman Act and a violation whether resulting from diversification or not.

IV. SIGNIFICANCE OF PROFIT DATA

View A

1. High profits are associated with concentration and barriers to entry.

2. High profits are evidence of existence of monopoly power.

View B

1. Analysis of the data show no net relation.

2. High profits may be associated with desirable social behavior, not only monopoly power.

V. INNOVATION AND LARGE FIRMS OR CONCENTRATION

View A

1. Bigness and concentration represent monopoly power and remove incentives for innovation.

2. Organization weaknesses of large firms stifle creativity.

View B

1. Innovation is the main instrument of competition of the large firms.

2. Large-scale organizations are necessary for research requiring large investments. Small firms can effectively perform research in some areas.

VI. MEASUREMENT OF INDUSTRY PERFORMANCE

View A

1. High profits reflect monopoly power.

2. Monopoly power will be exercised and intent need not be examined.

View B

1. High profits may result from a number of management policies not necessarily associated with monopoly power.

2. The meaning and measurement of monopoly needs careful definition.

3. Detailed studies of performance are to be avoided since they prolong and confuse evaluation of diversification and merger activities by business firms.

3. Economic theory and quantitative methodology provide a sound basis for evaluation of performance.

4. Antitrust policies that preserve desired industry structures will automatically produce desired industry performance.

4. The consequences of antitrust policies cannot be understood without consideration of their effects on industry performance.

Our understanding of elements of these basic issues has now been more effectively focused and to some degree polarized. It is hoped that this volume will have advanced our understanding and appreciation of the issues involved. But it also has provided an agenda for additional fundamental research required to provide a firm basis for public policy toward mergers.

general index

index of authors

237

index of court decisions

This index comprises cases cited in the text plus related recent or leading court decisions. For cases or subject matter discussed, the numbers following the dates of the cases refer to page numbers in the present volume. The compilation of this index was aided by the more comprehensive "Table of Cases" found in Eugene M. Singer, *Antitrust Economics* (Englewood Cliffs, New Jersey: Prentice-Hall, Inc., 1968), pp. 270–272.

239

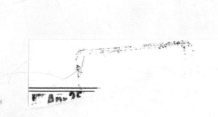